# EVERY MAN IN THIS VILLAGE IS A LIAR

# EVERY MAN IN THIS VILLAGE IS A LIAR

*An Education in War*

MEGAN K. STACK

B L O O M S B U R Y
LONDON · BERLIN · NEW YORK

First published in Great Britain 2010



Bloomsbury Publishing Plc
36 Soho Square
London W1D 3QY

www.bloomsbury.com

Bloomsbury Publishing, London, New York and Berlin
A CIP catalogue record for this book is available from the British Library

ISBN 978 1 4088 0879 5

10 9 8 7 6 5 4 3 2 1

Printed in Great Britain by Clays Ltd, St Ives plc

*To Tom*

*There is nothing farther away from Washington than the entire world.*

**—Arthur Miller**

# CONTENTS

# EVERY MAN IN THIS VILLAGE IS A LIAR

# PROLOGUE

This memory from childhood is still there: the voices of the adults bounce fretfully, eternally, in rooms that have since been sold or abandoned. Beirut, they said, never Lebanon. John was in Beirut. All meaning fit into those words. His barracks had been blown up, but he had survived.

John the drinker, the smoker, apprentice in three-card monte and hanger-out with New York street cons; his face cut by light, arms angled in salt air, his imprint lingers still in corners and amber edges. John was my father's cousin, my godfather's brother, our two Irish Catholic families braided together in city blocks, in the Bronx, by marriage and the crosshatches of godfathering. He was adrift between the generations of our family, too old to be a cousin and too young to be an uncle, but still unmistakably one of us, with us in churches and cramped living rooms and summers on the beach. In my earliest memories I waddle in his retreating shadow, arms in the air and begging, "Johnny! Uppy!" And then this skinny street hustler sweeps me into the air to swing on the rim of centrifugal force until the salty, sunny world swims.

Even then, John had endured the thing I feared most. His mother had died. He was feeling very badly, my mother said. *You shouldn't ask him about it.* John got into a little trouble, and then into some more trouble, so they sent him to live with my grandparents to get him out of New York. And when that didn't work, they signed the papers allowing him to enlist. He was only sixteen. The Marines sent him to Beirut.

Hezbollah bombed the bunkers. Thank God he's all right, the adults said. Nobody talked about Hezbollah then, not in our house. Hezbollah didn't mean anything. It was a featureless enemy in a war that was real only insofar as it touched our household.

A bomb explodes and everything goes wrong. John lived, but he wasn't all right. Three hundred and five people died around him. A few years later, he shot himself in the head. It was just before Thanksgiving. He was a father. He was young. We drove to New York for the funeral. They printed prayer cards and sewed his head back together for the open coffin. People stood around and whispered. It didn't look as bad as you might think, but it didn't look good, either.

For a long time, that was everything I knew—not just about Beirut, but about war: that it was dark and dangerous, that you could survive and not survive, both at the same time. I was twenty-five when I covered the war in Afghanistan. I wound up there by accident, rushed into foreign reporting by coincidence, because I was vacationing in Paris on September 11. Before that, I was a national correspondent in Houston. So I was a reporter who didn't really know how to write about combat, covering America from outside its borders as it crashed zealously into war and occupation. This huge change came without warning, but it felt wholly natural. It would be my generation's fate, it seemed, to be altered by September 11, so I would write about war, soldiers would fight, and Americans would rearrange the way they thought about things. Everything was negotiable; you couldn't imagine what would happen next. I got excited and felt that I was living through important times and went rushing in, and years later I came away older, different, with damage that couldn't be anticipated beforehand and can't be counted after. That's the way it goes, the way people get older and empires begin to slip. And now the fear is that it didn't mean anything. Isn't that what we all suspect about the war on terror, the long war, the war that hasn't ended? The stories repeat themselves, the same headlines, the same geography, the same mortality. We are losing interest and we fear it means nothing.

September 11 stands out now like a depot, the last train station before a vast unknown prairie, where the engine of events groaned and roared and hauled America back into the wilderness. It was the beginning of lost days, of disastrous reaction, of fumbling around in the world. We had already tamed our own hostile landscapes, the enormous stretches of the West, stamped out what came before, emptied and erased a vast run of earth so that we, the Americans, could have a tabula rasa, could invent a new nation and grow strong. And then September 11 came and infected us with the idea that we could tame all the wilderness of the world, too, and make ourselves perfectly safe.

I wanted to see, and so I went along to watch. I was younger than I realized and extremely American; sentimental but not stupid. I didn't go to Afghanistan with any strong convictions; I was a reporter, and I wanted to see. Only after covering it for years did I understand that the war on terror never really existed. It was not a real thing. Not that the war on terror was flawed, not that it was cynical or self-defeating, or likely to breed more resentment and violence. But that it was hollow, it was essentially nothing but a unifying myth for a complicated scramble of mixed impulses and social theories and night terrors and cruelty and business interests, all overhung with the unassailable memory of falling skyscrapers. There were, of course, certain wars, certain campaigns, certain speeches, all netted together under a heading. But this war we all talked about wasn't a coherent system, or a philosophy, or a strategy. Maybe it was a way for Americans to convince ourselves that we were still strong and correct. Mostly, I think, it was fear. Fear made more dangerous by gaping American estrangement from the rest of the world. Fear at a loss for an object.

As Americans we have the gift of detaching ourselves and drifting on; it has saved us over and over again from getting mired in guilt or stuck in the past. Sometimes we are too good at it. Here in the same generation, the wars happening over there, elsewhere, already have the irreality of a dream. It's the effect of time, too, and years piling up. You can't remember it all and you can't explain why you did what you did. You have a few drinks and call an old friend and say, this happened, remember? This happened and we were there. But the wars are still happening, and they have been happening all along. People died. Promises were broken. Things were destroyed. And as Americans these actions belong to us. We should remember those days, or we should admit they meant nothing, and if they meant nothing then there is the question of how much we have lost, and why.

As it turned out, the first thing I knew about war was also the truest, and maybe it's as true for nations as for individuals: You can survive and not survive, both at the same time.

## ONE

# EVERY MAN IN THIS VILLAGE IS A LIAR

Cold dawn broke on the horizon outside. The bedroom door shushed open, bringing the morning air and a warlord on predator's toes.

I lay in a nest of polyester blankets and listened to his footsteps cross the carpet. Every muscle pulled tight. *You reveal yourself in breath, in the nerves of your face. Count the breaths, in and out.* He sat on the edge of the bed. *Smooth breath, relax your eyes, don't let the lids shake.* Then his calloused old hand was stroking my hair, cupping my scalp, fingers dripping like algae onto my ears and cheeks.

The warlord lived in Jalalabad, in a swath of Afghanistan where the soil is rich with poppies and land mines, in a house awash in guns. People whispered that he was a heroin trafficker. His tribal loyalists clotted the orange groves and rose gardens outside, AK-47s in dust-caked fingers. They said he was ruthless in war, that his skin was scarred by an arrow. There was a vague whisper about a legendary ambush, the warlord killing enemies with his bare hands. And now those ropey hands were petting my hair, silent and brazen.

I clung to one thing: Brian, the photographer, was in the bathroom. Water slapped the floor. How long would his shower last, and how could I escape the warlord's lechery without offending him? The truth was, we needed him. He was an enemy of the Taliban, funded by the U.S. government, making a play for power in the vague, new order that had begun when American soldiers toppled the Taliban government. I was a stranger here, and he was my best source. He said he knew where Osama bin Laden was hiding. And now he was petting me like a puppy; nobody could sleep through it. The bed creaked. Stale breath sank in my face. Papery lips pressed my forehead. I opened my eyes and tried to look groggy.

"What are you doing?"

"Sshhh."

I struggled upright, cleared a phlegmy throat, and tried to sound dignified: "You are putting me into a very awkward position." A black-and-white-movie line, spilling out in a moment of panic.

He smiled and reached for my face.

"Please don't do that," I snapped.

Then, suddenly, silence. The water stopped, the pipes fell quiet. The warlord glanced around, stood, and slipped back out of the room.

Brian stepped out; his hair gleamed with water.

I turned my eyes to him and hissed: "We've got to get out of here."

I had met Mohammed Zaman weeks earlier, in Peshawar—a cramped kaleidoscope of a city perched on the last edge of organization and authority in Pakistan. To the west stretched the lawless tribal territories, the Khyber Pass, the Afghan frontier. Driven away by the Taliban, Zaman had been living an exile's life in Dijon, France, before September 11. Under chilly French skies he'd pined after his family's lands, the service of armed tribesmen, and, presumably, the rich, fresh fields of Afghan poppy. When U.S. jets started dropping bombs on Afghanistan, Zaman raced back to Peshawar and holed up in a rented house, waiting for the Americans to dispose of the Taliban and clear the path home—and eager to make some money while he was at it.

I sat in the shadows of a taxi late one night, my face and head draped in scarves, making my way through the jangling streets of Peshawar for an audience with Zaman. I liked it, all of it, enormously—the poetry of the place, the intrigue of war, imagining myself veiled in the back of a clopping carriage, bringing secrets to a bootlegger. The warlord's return had drawn throngs of men for endless meetings; I picked my way around the crowds on the lawn and sat waiting in a long drawing room. A door opened and out marched an American diplomat I'd seen at the embassy. His eyes skimmed mine and he hurried on, stone-faced. He didn't like being spotted there. I sat and watched him leave.

Zaman came out, tall and deliberate, face sagging from his skull. We sat with tea between us, and I asked him to take me to Afghanistan when he went.

He was solemn. "I take your life on my honor," he said from the heights of his mountainous nose. "They will have to kill me before they can harm you."

A few days later, we set off for war. The sun sank as we drove toward the Khyber Pass, storied old route of smugglers and marauders. Men pounded through a field hockey match in a haze of setting sun and rising dust. "Dead slow," ordered a traffic sign. "These areas are full of drugs," muttered the driver. In my head shimmered gilded pictures of the Grand Trunk Road, the Silk Road, *Kim*. On the edge of Afghanistan, stars crowded the sky, dull and dense. We crossed the border and plunged into the enormous uncertainty of this new American war. Forty Afghan fighters waited for us, young men and boys nestled together in pickup trucks. They shivered in the stinging night and gripped grenade launchers, chains of machine gun rounds trailing from the trucks. We drove alongside the Kabul River, past the shadowed bulk of mountains and tractors, along fields of tobacco and wheat. At the edge of Jalalabad, the deserted dinosaurs of rusted Soviet tanks reared from the ground.

In the core of the dusty night, we pulled up to his house. Zaman served a feast and stayed awake with us, lolling on the floor around the vegetables and lamb and spinning out long, fatigued stories. We blinked and yawned but Zaman pushed on toward sunrise. He was selling his case even then, from those earliest hours. Osama bin Laden had fled to the nearby White Mountains, he said, to the caves cut into stone, to Tora Bora. The terrorist and his followers still lurked nearby. If America was serious about this war on terror, the terrorists needed to be flushed out. He could do the job; he only needed guns, money, and equipment.

He talked on and on, weaving French into English, until the dawn call to prayer rang from a whitening sky. His words melted together. My chin was falling. I slept on the floor, and woke up in the new Afghanistan.

The first days with Zaman were easy. The stories fell like ripe fruit. But when he tiptoed to my bed, I knew we had to scrounge for another roof. There was nowhere to go but the Spin Ghar hotel, a crumbling Soviet relic rising from tangles of garden and derelict trees. Rank smells wafted through the cold corridors, over chipped linoleum, past cracked plaster walls. Mad jumbles of bodies crowded the lobby—foreign reporters, Afghans, hired gunmen in their robes and eye paint, all sprawled on the grass, smoking on the steps, flooding over the balconies.

The electricity died that night, and gas lanterns shivered in the dark cavern of the hotel dining room. Everybody was very quiet. There was bad news.

Some of the reporters had set off for Kabul in a convoy that day. Two hours out of town, Afghan bandits stopped the first car and shot the passengers dead: a Spaniard, an Afghan, an Australian. There was an Italian woman, too, who was raped and then killed. The rest of the reporters squealed their cars around and came back to Jalalabad. The bodies were abandoned on the road. It was the first lost gamble, and it pulled us a little farther into war. Now we in the dark dining room were rendered survivors, the ones who hadn't died. The faces swim out of darkness, painted in wisps of gaslight. They are talking about the abandoned bodies, about who fetched them. I feel empty. I have no reaction. It is a gap inside of me, like putting your tongue where a tooth used to be. I know that I should feel something; to feel something is appropriate and human. I stay silent so that the others will not realize that I am gaping like a canyon. I am not absolutely sure this is real; it's so very far from where we started. On September 11, I was in Paris, and then in Bahrain, an aircraft carrier, and Pakistan, moving slowly, unconsciously closer to here, tonight. America is at war, and we are all here too, at the edge of death, just like that, in just a few weeks. And so we are on an island, and so the roads are a place to die.

In my room the darkness is thick as tar. My fingers can't find a lock on the door. I am groping when the door cracks forward with a grunt of Pashto. I can't see the Afghan man but I push at him, throw my arms into the darkness and find flesh, drive him back. His cries are pure sound to me. I don't care. After Zaman at my bedside and reporters dead on the road, this man cannot stay. Our American and Afghan words mean nothing when they hit the other ear. We are stripped of all understanding, battling in the blackness. I shove him into the hall and force the door closed against the last pieces of him, a kicking foot, a grasping arm. Later on, I realize he was probably the sweet-faced cleaning man who shuffled like a kicked stray through the corridors at night. Later I laugh, a little embarrassed. But on this night, I have vanquished. I lean limp against the door of my stinking little cave, conqueror of misunderstood forces.

Back in Pakistan, before I crossed over into Afghanistan, somebody said to me: "Every man in this village is a liar." It was the punch line to a parable, the tale of an ancient Greek traveler who plods into a foreign village and is greeted with those words. It is a twist on the Epimenides paradox, named after the Cretan philosopher who declared, "All Cretans are liars." It's one of the world's oldest logic problems, folding in on itself like an Escher sketch. If he's telling the truth, he's lying. If he's lying, he's telling the truth.

That was Afghanistan after September 11.

You meet a man, and his story doesn't sound right. You stare at him and your brain is chewing away, and out of the corner of your eye something bizarre and fantastic trails past—a pair of mujahideen with their fingers intertwined, plastic flowers glowing in black hair, winking and fluttering with the kohl-rimmed eyes of two besotted lovers. And you can't help but look, but then all you can do is watch these strange peacocks, stunned by the magenta homoeroticism of this dry, pious land. By the time you peel your attention back and stop your thoughts from whirling, the man you were trying to weigh out is long gone. Afghanistan was meaning washed away in floods of color, in drugs, guns, sexual ambiguity, and Islam.

I met a young man who spoke Arabic and English, which was rare and fancy for provincial Afghanistan. He had worked for bin Laden, and I was certain his sympathies lay with the Taliban, with Al Qaeda. We sat together and had long interviews. Later I found out he worked for the CIA. They gave him a satellite phone, and he was calling in coordinates for bombing targets.

*Every man in this village is a liar.*

Maybe that's why nobody believed the warlords when they kept saying that Osama bin Laden was hiding in Tora Bora. A pity, because it was true: Osama bin Laden packed his bags and fled into the mountain redoubt near Jalalabad after September 11. The caves were his last stop before he lost his substance and melted into the world's most famous phantom. Catching bin Laden was the first important thing the United States set out to do after September 11. The job was bungled so thoroughly that the war never really found its compass again. Here in eastern Afghanistan, the Americans would begin to lose the plot.

Those days were deep with dimensions; conflicting things happened at the same time, on top of one another. Kabul had fallen to the Northern Alliance, but in the east, the war pounded on. The Afghans who'd opposed the Taliban were in a renaissance, and neck deep in the swirl of their ancient clan rivalries. The warlords plotted tribal revenge, scrapped for control of the heroin trade, lined their pockets and trolled for power. They tossed enemies into moldy jail cells, and sold them to the Americans who were rounding up jihadis. If you asked them why, they'd smile in chilling self-satisfaction and say, "He's a terrorist." Maybe it was true, and maybe it wasn't, but the days were slipping away too quickly for anybody to quibble.

Jalalabad had been a headquarters for Al Qaeda, home to a training camp and vast housing complexes built by the influx of Saudis, Kuwaitis, Chechens—"Arabs," resentful locals called the rich Al Qaeda members who had taken up residence in sequestered communities. Osama bin Laden, with his wives and children, called Jalalabad home years before September 11. Now he huddled a few hours' drive away in Tora Bora, the masterfully defensible cave complex built with CIA money back when America was fighting the Communists instead of the terrorists. U.S. warplanes hammered the mountains, but their intelligence was coming from Afghans who manipulated the firepower to suit their own interests.

I learned to count the fighter jets that passed overhead in my sleep. There were no other airplanes in the Afghan skies; there was only the war. When thin dawn light creaked into the room, I'd know that three warplanes had passed. I woke up knowing, and remembering nothing.

I have this memory, clear as glass: Sunset spilled all over the horizon. In the velvet grass below the hotel terrace, the drivers were bent on their prayer rugs, the guerrillas paced in the gravel, the palms and pines deepened in the dying light. Then a B-52 sliced a white gash into the sky. All of the reporters and translators and soldiers stood still, stared at the heavens, and waited to see where the bombs would fall. The planes thundered past every day, but for some reason on that day we stood there in collective awe. Maybe everybody had forgotten about the war for a minute, and then it was there again.

One day, Zaman's men brought the bodies of eight dead guerrilla soldiers down from the mountains and laid them out on the hospital floor. Then he herded in a great swarm of reporters to gape and snap photographs. He stalked over the dead, face twisted with rage, railing about the bombings. The Americans were killing peasants loyal to him, and now his mujahideen. They must be using old maps, he thundered. Who is telling them where to bomb? Do these look like Al Qaeda to you?

The dead men were skinny, all of them, muddy and ragged. One man's face had been blown off. Another lay with the back of his head gone, his brains leaking. Filtered sunlight spilled onto the floor; the smell of death was heavy. An American reporter fell on the ground and lay there crying. I looked at her, and at the corpses. Intellectually, I knew that her reaction was appropriate, but I felt disgusted by her weakness. Staring down at the bodies, I felt numb, light, as if my own body might vaporize, as if I didn't need to breathe.

The dying were worse than the dead. They came down from the hills in rattling caravans, slow as torture over bone-cracking roads of mud and rock, bleeding all over the backseats of rattletrap cars. Three hours, four hours, bright red lives seeping away.

They wound up in the dim wards of Jalalabad's filthy hospital. There weren't enough antibiotics or antiseptics. Little girls who wouldn't live through the night were stacked two to a cot, covered in blood. A baby with its head caked in scab and pus and one eye full of blood cried in the listless arms of a young, young girl. A little boy who had lost his arms, his eyesight, and his family lay motionless in the hot afternoon. The rooms smelled of sweat and infection; flies and woolen blankets. All of it coming down from those American planes.

We drifted out of the hospital. In the car I tasted metal. After a long time, Brian spoke.

"That was pretty bad." He cleared his throat.

"Yeah."

We looked out the window, and the driver turned up the music. The sunlight and the dust were gilding everything to silver. The spindly dome of trees cupped the road, bicycle spokes flickered and goats plodded in the blue fog of exhaust. Afghans were rushing home from the market, arms loaded with fresh meat and vegetables to break the Ramadan fast. The hotel room was dark and cold. I opened a pad of paper and tried to make some notes. This is what I wrote:

*I didn't mean to really see these things. I didn't know how it would be.*

Late one night, bombs fell on the village of Kama Ado, a tiny, isolated hamlet of mud houses. I interviewed people who were hauled from the wreckage. I wrote a story about it. I fell asleep.

By morning, my story wasn't the same. Instead of leading with the news of the crushed village, the top of the story had Pentagon officials denying reports of the bombing. The first voice in the article was no longer that of an Afghan victim. Instead, it was a Pentagon official who said: "This is a false story."

Defense Secretary Donald Rumsfeld said the same: "If we cannot know for certain how many people were killed in lower Manhattan, where we have full access to the site, thousands of reporters, investigators, rescue workers combing the wreckage, and no enemy propaganda to confuse the situation, one ought to be sensitive to how difficult it is to know with certainty, in real time, what may have happened in any given situation in Afghanistan, where we lack access and we're dealing with world class liars."

I read it once. I read it twice. Were we to believe the village had spontaneously collapsed while U.S. warplanes circled overhead?

*Every man in this village is a liar.*

Jalalabad slipped out of the Taliban's hold as easy as a boiled tomato loses its skin. No bloodshed, just a lot of abandoned buildings and cars, ripe for the grabbing by guerrillas who rushed down from the mountains. The mujahideen swarmed the streets, dirty children run amok in an empty house. They were old and weary, or young and wild; the middle-aged men were mostly dead. *Mujahideen* is Arabic for "strugglers," but it's understood to mean "holy warriors." In Afghanistan, they are the men with guns, the ones who sleep where they lie and fight for their tribal patriarchs in a senseless string of conflicts.

Stoned on hash and hopped up on war, draped in ragged smocks and blankets, the young mujahideen lingered on every corner, fired into the night skies to hear the guns scream in the empty streets. They imposed curfews, lit bonfires in the middle of the roads, and lorded it over the city until sunrise. They beat people to feel powerful, to watch the peasants scamper away from their clubs in the bazaar.

One day I was in an abandoned Al Qaeda compound with a French reporter. We pored through trunks of documents and the mujahideen stood around smirking at our interest in worthless paper. The sun was hot and they were fasting for Ramadan, irritable and armed to the teeth. They bickered, and then they were screaming and I heard the safeties click off and looked up. Patrice let out a roar and lunged at them just before they start shooting. "No, no, no!" he hollered. "You stop that! You will kill us!" They looked at his white hair and slowly lowered their weapons in deference to his age and gender. Like lion cubs, they responded to shows of dominance.

For a long time, it didn't matter what happened. I was high on Afghanistan. The aching beauty of rock and sky, and the thick light smearing everything like honey. The jangle of tongues, confusion of smells, every human enterprise a cheap trifle of origami against this massive, unchanging earth.

War cannot be innocent, but sometimes it is naive. At first the fight in Afghanistan felt finite and comprehensible. There had been an attack, an act of war, and America responded with conventional warfare against an objectively violent and repressive regime. You could disagree with the choice to invade, you could question the sense and bravery of bombing a country built from mud, but at least there was an internal logic, the suggestion of a moral thread, of cause and effect. And so we plunged forward, and our eyes were bound in gauze. I was acutely aware that in witnessing war I was experiencing something both timeless and particular. I expected awful sights and I accepted them when they came. The war was an adventure and an exhilaration, an ancient, human force that had found its shape for this country, in this age. Perhaps only by comparing it with all that came later can I remember it as naive. Death was everywhere, in the fields full of land mines, the villagers who hobbled without a leg, without an arm, staring from crutches. When I came to Afghanistan I had decided to look at the deaths of others, and to risk my own life. I had expected everything from war, danger and blood and hurt, and the war produced all of it.

Afghans lived on the edge of mortality, its tang hung always in the air, in their words. If death would come to us all, the Afghans couldn't be bothered to duck. I was interviewing an Afghan commander one afternoon in the mountains when somebody started shooting at us. I backed down the ridge, lowered myself out of the line of fire. "Can you please ask him to come closer so we're not getting shot at?" I asked the translator. The commander looked at me and laughed. He sauntered slowly down out of the bullets smirking all the way.

"We are dust." The mujahideen liked to say that. *We are dust.*

One day, a messenger came to the Spin Ghar hotel. Zaman was inviting me back to his house for *iftar*, the sunset meal that broke each day's fast through the holy month of Ramadan.

Zaman was about to command the ground offensive in Tora Bora and was therefore the closest voice I could find to an American representative. I wanted the story badly enough to return to his turf, but I couldn't go alone. I needed a foreign man, somebody Zaman would feel tribally compelled to respect. So I invited the AP reporter Chris Tomlinson. "Whatever happens," I told him, "don't leave me alone with him."

A flicker crossed Zaman's face when he saw Chris. We settled onto velvet cushions, and Zaman's servants heaped the floor with steaming flatbread, biryani, crisp vegetables, a shank of mutton. Chris and I had our notebooks at our sides, and we jotted away while Zaman held forth on the ground assault.

Suddenly Zaman looked at Chris. "Would you excuse us, please?" he said icily. "We need to talk in private."

Chris stared at me, telegraphing: *What should I do?*

I glowered back: *Don't leave.*

"Um, well," Chris stammered, eyes flying around the room. He pointed at the door to the terrace. "I'm just going to step outside and smoke a cigarette. I'll be *right outside*," he added, looking at me.

As soon as the door closed, Zaman announced, "You're going back to Pakistan."

I laughed. "No, I'm not."

"Yes. My men will take you there."

"I'm sorry, but that's a joke. I'm not leaving."

"You can't stay here anymore. Every time I see you, I forget what I'm doing. You are making me distracted."

Through the windows, I watched the lone red ember of the cigarette float up and down the terrace.

"I'm sure you can control yourself," I said slowly, trying to prolong the conversation. He was sliding my way on the cushions, his body closing the distance between us. His eyes were fixed on me, long face like a sly old goat.

"I'm in love with you," he said. "I love you."

"You're not in love with me!" I spat out. "You don't even know me."

"I *do* know you," he assured me.

I looked at him, his gray, dirty hair smashed down from his Afghan cap, lanky limbs swathed in yards of *shalwar kameez*, crouched in slippers on the floor.

"Look, I'm very flattered, but we are from completely different worlds. Where I come from, you can't just—"

He interrupted me.

"I want to see your world," he said. "I want to go there. With you. To know your family . . ."

I imagined Haji Zaman, decked in tribal dress, sipping coffee on my mother's front porch in Connecticut, faithful AK-47 casually propped against the rocking chair. Haji Zaman and I, holding hands, peering over the rim of the Grand Canyon.

"It's completely out of the question. And so's Pakistan."

With a sheepish look in my direction, Chris returned.

"Thank you very much for dinner," my words tumbled out. "We have to get going now, to write our stories."

Zaman protested, but I was already on my feet, swaying unsteadily on the pillows, tugging at the ends of my head scarf. We scrambled down the stairs and burst out into the orchards and vegetable gardens hemming the house, but the driver was nowhere to be seen.

"I can't believe he left us!"

"It's not too far back to town," Chris said. "We can make it walking."

"Do you remember the way?"

"I think so."

The black night opened its mouth and swallowed us whole. Darkness quivered before us, taut as a stretched canvas, demanding to be filled. Our feet fumbled forward. I couldn't remember the way; I hadn't been paying enough attention. I'd been letting myself get carried along in days, flooded by experience, and now I was lost. Stars glittered overhead, brilliant scattershot. Beyond the road sprawled unseen fields, and land mines festered in the dirt. Figures moved in houses. A flush of light bruised the edges of black in the distance, and we kept walking toward it. The light grew and swelled, a distant peach rising into the night. Finally we could see the road ahead, the lights of cars swimming.

On the road, we flagged down a bicycle taxi. "Spin Ghar hotel, please." We climbed into the tiny carriage, and the man pedaled off. Everything was color and light, chasing the black from my eyes. Music was playing somewhere, night rushing past. No steel car doors, no glass, no roof split us from the world. The bicycle cab trembled over ruts, plastered with diamond-shaped mirrors, gaudy with pink and blue and yellow paint. Strings of coins jangled as we careened through the electric wildness of open air. The night pressed cool hands against my hot cheeks, ruffled my hair. Wind caught in my throat and then I was laughing, laughing to think that luck can change, just like that. The night was right there, choked with mysteries, shadows sliding down rutted roads, smells of sweet and dank from cooking pots, and the vastness of countryside. For a few minutes, death fell away, and it felt like freedom.

# TWO

# CHASING GHOSTS

It had been weeks since Kabul had fallen to the Northern Alliance, and plans were already under way for a *loya jirga*, the tribal conference that would divide power in post-Taliban Afghanistan. American newspapers and television brimmed with self-congratulatory features: women taking off their burqas, fathers and sons flying kites, little girls heading back to school. But the war was not gone.

There in the east, tension still laced the faces of the triumvirate of warlords who ran the region, each man boss of his own sumptuous headquarters. Every time one of the warlords saw a reporter, he pointedly reminded us that Osama bin Laden and his band of diehards were hiding in the mountains outside of town. They wanted the message to get back to Washington—bin Laden was an American problem, after all, and the United States had just invaded and occupied the country. The warlords were waiting for U.S. money, men, and supplies to flush out Al Qaeda, or so they said. These pleas started out quietly, discreetly. Then Zaman, the most tempestuous of the three, lost his patience and began calling noisily for America to pony up guns and cash. He sent word to the hotel one morning, inviting journalists to a bombed-out military base on the outskirts of Jalalabad. His men hauled an upholstered sofa down into a bomb crater, and Zaman reclined splendidly in the wreckage. We gathered on the rim, peering down at his majesty. The point, I think, was to display the shambles of Afghanistan's virtually nonexistent military infrastructure.

"We're just like a new-bought car," Zaman said that day. "We just need a drop of gas."

I kept remembering a U.S. official I'd interviewed back in Pakistan, and his palpable distaste for these warlords. "They're parasites, this is how they make money," he said. "What they love about foreigners is they can get something and there's not a lot of likelihood they'll have to reciprocate. Be it the CIA or whomever. If the CIA gives them a satellite phone they come out [of Afghanistan] and get it, then go back inside and say, 'Oh, now I need guns.' "

The warlords talked, and then they talked some more. They sent scouts to Tora Bora to spy on "the Arabs." They muttered through midnight meetings and summoned tribal elders from obscure villages to secure promises of loyalty in the coming battle. They droned on about the victorious ground offensive they would prosecute when they finally sent the mujahideen up into the mountains to track down the terrorists.

Time trickled on. We were all waiting for the war, but it didn't come. A battle thundered slowly toward us, but it was dreamy, disarming. Like watching a race in slow motion: the leg rises, falls; the action is muddy as hallucination.

One day Hazrat Ali, another warlord making a hard play for U.S. money, wandered through the hotel lobby. A plump, bearded fighter with twinkling eyes and a dramatic flair, Ali lacked Zaman's gravitas, but he made up for it with moral authority: while Zaman had slunk off to France, Ali stayed put and fought an insurgent war against the Taliban. Now he'd been named local security chief; soon he would rise to power within Hamid Karzai's government. Reporters clustered around him. The conversation went like this:

Reporter: Where are the Taliban?
Ali: What do you mean? They're in their offices.
Reporter: You mean your offices?
Ali: Yes. We're going to work with everybody in the new government.

Reporter: So let me get this straight. The men working for you are former Taliban?
Ali [impatiently]: Of course.

"The Taliban was 95 percent of our country," an Afghan friend told me. "Look around you. We didn't kill everybody."

Whenever the translator, Naseer, took me to his house, I could feel the knowledge of Taliban lurking among the women. We'd drop by in the afternoon, and I'd sit for a time with these spectacular women, their cheeks and eyes full of light. They fussed over me, flounced around, touched my hands and my face, giggled and cooed. I was a piece of the world, delivered to them in their cloisters, and although we could not trade a word, they lavished me with emotion. Their husbands were doctors and merchants and engineers, but none of these women had the equivalent of a middle-school education.

In the middle of fruitless pantomime, Naseer's niece turned on him one day. "You know English, and you never taught us!" she lashed out, eyes narrow in her face. Her name was Rina. She was fifteen years old, already promised in marriage to a cousin. "You should have taught us English!"

These women had been waiting in these dim rooms for years, waiting so long that they had turned anticipation into a state of grace. They had waited for the neighborhood schools to reopen, for permission to show their faces in public, and for the right to walk out the front gate to the mud road. Waited for decades of war to pass out of these valleys and farms, for one government after the next to swell and crumble, for untested men to rush forward to unleash new laws. They learned from the BBC's scratchy Pashto-language service that the Taliban was gone, but so what? Still they waited for their world to change. The women in Naseer's house were not liberated beings. They couldn't remember the last time they shopped in the bazaar, or ate a picnic, or strolled in a park. They couldn't even buy their own vegetables. They had learned their lesson swiftly when the Taliban took over.

"We knew they hated women, and we were afraid," Naseer's wife,

Sediqa, told me. "They said we had to wear our burqas, so we wore them. But they beat us anyway. We knew it wasn't safe to go out into the streets."

Everybody remembered keenly the day in 1996 when the seventy-five-year-old matriarch next door set out across town to visit her daughter. She had no money for a taxi, so she walked. The Taliban hadn't been in power long, and Afghans were still discovering restrictions by trial and error. The old woman didn't wear a burqa, because she was frail and nearsighted and the netted face covering was uncomfortable. She was halted by the religious police, who hollered that her robes and head scarf were immodest, that she was violating the laws of Islam. They beat her with lead rods and bamboo canes, dragged her home bruised and bloodied, and scolded the family for letting the woman wander the streets without proper dress. After that, by their own will or by mandate of their husbands, all the women on Naseer's street were locked away.

"I knew then that I hated the Taliban, and they were different. Other times, things had been bad. But nobody had beaten an old woman before," the woman's daughter told me. She had slipped into Naseer's house, curious to visit with the American.

Sitting on mattresses on the floor with these women, I felt that I had tunneled deep down into the middle of the earth. Their tiny universe—tight rooms with dirt floors strung around a muddy courtyard—felt sealed off from Jalalabad. This was only the first layer of withdrawal: Jalalabad was far removed from Kabul, and Kabul from the rest of the world. Still, because of September 11, Americans were aware of the women who dwelled in this forgotten place. Worse, popular imagination back home already considered them liberated by U.S. benevolence. As if the freedom of these women, caught in the strings of their marriages, family honor, tribal code, and morality police, could come so cheap. I got Naseer to translate our conversations, and I learned that the women themselves knew better; knew enough not to get excited. They stayed put in the world they'd hollowed out for their families. When they heard that Americans thought they'd been freed, they frowned in befuddlement.

In the yard, they split firewood and hoisted water. Inside, they sweetened the air with drugstore perfume. They rolled their words out quietly, petted one another's arms, stroked the children's hair. They had pierced noses, brilliant eyes, and dark hair woven into complicated braids creeping from embroidered scarves. Gold vines crawled up sleeves, a wink of bead, a glimmer of thread, lace shawls. The world never saw any of it. I watched Sediqa, Naseer's wife, rip off her burqa one afternoon and throw it on the bed.

A few days before the battle of Tora Bora, Sediqa went into labor. They brought her baby girl home from the hospital and carried her out of the darkness and over the dirt yard. Naseer had invited Brian and me to celebrate with the family. "The baby is here!" the women called from the yard, and the men spilled out to regard the tiny creature in buttery light from the sitting room window. "Come and see her, she's here!"

One of Naseer's brothers shook his head and whispered: "This is not so good for Naseer, because it's his firstborn. Everybody wants his firstborn to be a boy."

"For me, they're both good," Naseer argued, overhearing. "A boy is okay, a girl is okay. This is a democratic house."

The men withdrew to talk politics. The women grabbed my hand and pulled me into a back bedroom. Sediqa lay with blankets to her chin, pale and silent. The other women dribbled tea into the baby's mouth. Somebody slipped a cassette into a dusty tape player, and Indian music wailed from the speakers. There was music here all along, even when the Taliban banned song and the men of the family had to stuff cassettes into their pockets and smuggle them from Pakistan.

And then, in that cramped little room, we were all dancing. The women were stomping and arching, shaking their hips, describing small pictures with their fingertips. It was sexy, sultry, joyful. They were dancing for a new life, another soul indoctrinated into their private sorority. Even the smallest girls, the ones who were babies when the Taliban came, knew how to dance. They had learned from their mothers and aunts, even when it was illegal, even when the women were weary from chores, even when the government told them it was frivolous and wanton and sinful. The women didn't care. Maybe there would be more years of Taliban, maybe the American occupation would replace the

Soviet occupation, maybe anything would happen. But they believed in their bones that Afghans would dance again one day.

And when the dancing came, they wanted their daughters to be ready.

The money finally came through, and the warlords got their war. Workers scrambled out to Jalalabad's shattered airport to patch up the runways. Soon we began to see the traces of U.S. Special Forces, who moved into the region but stayed hidden from view. They left empty bottles of Poland Spring scattered at abandoned campsites. On December 4, America's proxy troops began a ground assault into the Tora Bora cave complex, hoping to capture Osama bin Laden. Zaman, Ali, and Abdul Qadir, the third powerful anti-Taliban warlord, split responsibility for the Afghan troops, arguing and elbowing each other every step of the way.

As the battle began, the mujahideen prowled the mountains underfed and shivering, clad in tattered tennis shoes and old sweaters. Many of them were young, and had spent their adolescence in a seamless stream of war. They didn't know how to read. They didn't know how old they were. When the tanks bellowed they leaped around and shouted and clapped hands. Their commanders spent their time arguing cartoonishly over who controlled which chunk of hillside, whose men should do what. The mujahideen mooned around, stroking one another lovingly and dreaming of their next meal.

Watching the mujahideen, I tried to imagine how this war looked to them. Afghanistan was a sandbox for generations of men who wanted to play at war, one conflict bleeding into the next. The twentieth century was an ordeal of civil wars, unrest, and coups, culminating in the Soviet invasion. The U.S.- and Saudi-funded jihad against the Soviets had wedged the notion of holy war firmly into the contemporary Afghan consciousness, and armed and funded the men who would emerge as the Taliban in the chaos of civil war. The Taliban had sheltered Al Qaeda, which in turn plotted September 11 and drew the wrath of the Americans. This was the war God had brought them now, God and the Americans. And so they fought.

I asked a twenty-two-year-old soldier when he had learned to fire a rocket launcher. He let out a huff of laughter. "What do you mean? I always knew how. I learned when I was a baby." He dropped his head and bounced his gun, testing its weight.

"I never went to school, and I don't know how to do anything. Just fighting."

The ground assault played out like a pantomime of war. The mujahideen hadn't captured a single prisoner, and had no idea how many men they'd killed. The same patch of ground was gained and lost, over and over again. At night they lay on the earth under thin wool blankets, bitter wind coursing through the hills. They knotted rags around their wounds because they had no bandages. Sometimes, the television crews paid them to fire their tanks into the canyons, and happily the fighters obliged. The mujahideen got so hungry one night they broke into a television news trailer and stole all the food. These were the foot soldiers of the U.S. war on terror.

One of the mujahideen thought he was twenty-two, but he wasn't sure. His skin was drawn tight over pinched features. "We have no food or blankets. Our lives belong to God," he said resentfully. "The Americans should come. They should be in the front line, and we will get behind them."

I learned more from the mujahideen than I did from the smooth-talking warlords. The mujahideen predicted that they would never take Tora Bora. The Soviets had pounded away at the honeycombed network of caves for years and never managed to get inside, they pointed out. The older mujahideen had fought from within the caves back when they had battled on the side of bin Laden and the Americans. In those days, Tora Bora was the epicenter of their jihad against the godless Russians. They thought this latest mission was a lost cause, even when the United States dropped the 15,000-pound "daisy cutter" bombs. The mujahideen talked every day about the Pakistani border, the ease with which the Taliban and Al Qaeda fighters could escape. Even knowing the futility, the fighters didn't flinch. They shouldered their Kalashnikovs and rocket launchers and trudged dutifully into the hills to fight the war set before them. They sat around camp and told folk stories about Osama bin Laden. He was spotted astride a red pony. He was seen playing with his small son. Somebody saw him crossing a stream late one night. He was melting into myth.

After a week of fighting, the Afghan troops were still scrapping at the fringes of Tora Bora. Zaman was petulant, griping about his American backers. Thirty-one days had passed, he told me pointedly, since Osama bin Laden had fled Jalalabad under the protection of a Pakistani tribal elder. "I've been telling America all along," he said. "If America wants to capture bin Laden, why aren't they trying?"

I was in the mountains one day. The sky was white and gray and empty overhead. Bitter cold swept down from the north. I was close to the front line, but not quite there. Deep below, a river cut through the cliffs. There were land mines and gun skirmishes on these twisting trails. Sharp mountainsides plunged into deep valleys. It was hard to keep your bearings, hard to understand who was shooting at whom, and why. It was utterly confusing.

Then a commotion of voices echoed through the valleys, and the Afghans began to race up the mountain. All of the reporters charged instinctively after them, choking for oxygen in the thin mountain air. At my side ran another woman, a reporter.

"Where are we running to?" she gasped.

"I don't know," I panted. "But it must be something."

She screwed up her face. "I think it's really disturbing that we're all running up the mountain and we don't know where we're going," she yelled.

She was right, of course. It was disturbing, random, and emblematic. But at the time, each of us squinted at the other as if she were dim-witted.

She stopped running. I kept going, chasing my curiosity up the hill. But when I got to the top, there was nothing to see. We were charging after ghosts.

When the end came, it came quickly. It was another bitterly cold afternoon in the mountains, and I sat listlessly on a rock, listening while the warlords squabbled. Zaman was in the middle of it all, nested in some boulders a short walk up the mountain, juggling two conversations.

Languidly, he negotiated by radio with a representative from bin Laden's encampment. In between, he argued with an enraged Hazrat Ali, who was listening in on the talks, convinced that Zaman was bungling negotiations. I watched Hazrat Ali pace in a grove of thorn trees, barking at Zaman by walkie-talkie.

Zaman had wrangled a promise out of the shadowy Al Qaeda negotiator. The fighters would crawl out of their caves and surrender at eight the next morning. Zaman kept telling Hazrat Ali that this was a fair plan, a good compromise. "That gives them time to talk," he urged a skeptical, irritable Ali.

"Don't give them time!" Ali exploded. "The Arabs are disagreeing! Three Arabs have three ideas!"

Zaman and Ali hated each other. After battling for supremacy for years, they were now grudging allies, forced together by mutual dependence on American money. As far as I could tell, each was more interested in outmaneuvering the other than in fulfilling any duties on behalf of America. It all comes down to this, I thought. This is the tip of the spear. These slippery, wild-eyed figures are the men fighting on behalf of my country.

Blackened tree stumps and bullet-torn car doors, detritus of war, lay strewn on the ashen hillside. Ali's soldiers rooted busily under the trunk of a bombed-out pickup in search of salvageable parts and combed shattered bunkers looking for spare bullets. Soldiers giggled over the bodies of three dead Arabs. They had been shot to shreds by machine guns. The mujahideen thought it was hilarious.

"We want to have safe passage out of your province," the voice of the Al Qaeda spokesman scratched through the radio.

"Your blood is our blood, your children our children, your wives our sisters. But under the present circumstances, you must leave my area or surrender." Zaman never passed up an opening for flowery tribal flourishes.

Ali was screaming at Zaman. He thought the whole thing was a trick. "Don't give them so much time," he urged the other warlord. "And don't pull out of your positions overnight."

But Zaman's soldiers were shivering and ravenous. "Come up and hold the line yourself," he snapped. As daylight thinned, Zaman swept triumphantly down the rocky mountain trail. His mujahideen thronged behind him, kicking up storms of dust. Gleefully they waved at the journalists, chins high as conquering heroes.

"Don't worry!" they shouted, skidding down on their heels. "Al Qaeda is over!"

At sunrise the next morning, Tora Bora was quiet. A warplane circled in the sky overhead, spewing white rings against a vibrant blue. Silence swallowed the mountains like some foreign fog. For the first time in days, no bombs were falling. And for the first time, we reporters couldn't get close enough to see anything. Afghan guards had closed the roads and trails leading up the mountain. I took this to mean that the Americans were up there. The Afghans would take us anywhere, straight into the line of fire, but the Americans didn't want to be seen. When we spoke to them, they'd pull their tribal blankets tighter around themselves and pretend they didn't speak English.

It was still five minutes before the eight o'clock deadline when Haji Zaman's pickup bumped its way down the mountain. I ran to the roadside and flagged him down. He rolled down the window. Tears stood in his eyes.

"What happened? Why aren't you at the surrender?" I asked.

He shook his head. He didn't say a word.

"Are the Americans there?" I asked.

"Yes," he said.

"Did they tell you to leave?"

"I can't talk about it."

"Did they take over the surrender?"

"I have to go," he said. He rolled up the window, and drove on.

A few minutes later, a crash echoed across the mountains, and the ground quaked. Warplanes pounded the hills with bombs. It kept up for hours, all day long. If the surrender had ever started, it was certainly over now.

That afternoon, I found Zaman sulking in a bombed-out building in the abandoned village he sometimes used as a base. We paced up and down a chicken yard. The sky was huge overhead. He was quiet. Sometimes he said, "How do I know I can trust you?"

"You can," I said. I think we both knew the dynamic: he could trust me, but I couldn't trust him. At least he was no longer hitting on me. That was all gone, replaced by this wary willingness to accord me more information than the others could get. But then, what good is information when everybody around you is lying? That day, he never explained anything.

He made me wait until the next day before he told his story. By then, fresh fighting had erupted. Negotiations were more than dead; they were now viewed as an embarrassing faux pas on the part of the Afghans. Sitting in his pickup truck in Tora Bora, Zaman told me the story:

"I told the Americans, take these men and question them, get intelligence from them. Let them surrender. And they said no. No negotiations, no negotiations, no negotiations. Americans wouldn't accept the surrender. They wanted the Al Qaeda soldiers dead. I suggested we question them. I said, if you want them dead, we can put them in a farmhouse somewhere when we're through questioning them, and bomb the house. Nobody will know. But the Americans said no, we want them dead immediately."

This may or may not have been one piece of truth, but Zaman was surely playing more hands than he'd admit. Other Afghans have since accused all three U.S.-backed warlords of helping the Al Qaeda fighters escape into Pakistan—for a fee, of course.

It is possible, of course, that every one of those stories is true—that Zaman wanted to capture bin Laden, tried to broker surrender, and eventually helped him slip out the back door, stuffing his pockets at every turn. These things are not mutually exclusive. Very little in Afghanistan is mutually exclusive. It is also possible that none of it was true at all, that the real story of Tora Bora is something else that we'd never imagined.

News writers depend upon the world to organize itself into some kind of tale, a story that can be told in short, recognizable form. People rise and fall; murder and redeem; cheat and reconcile. In Afghanistan, I kept waiting for a narrative to assert itself. A battle had begun, and so there must be a climax, there must be a resolution. I expected something to happen, in the end. The Afghans and the Americans would keep pushing forward, and sooner or later they would clash with the Al Qaeda fighters. Osama bin Laden would be captured, or he would be killed, or something else would happen. But whatever it was, we would see it and we would be able to recognize it.

Instead, events flickered, split, and rolled away like mercury. To write about the battle in an organized way, to shuffle the pieces, tap the sides, and square it into paragraphs and quotations was a fabrication. The mujahideen pushed forward until they became ghosts, thinning out into the mountain air. The battle never reached a climax. The other side was never seen, it melted away. Osama bin Laden flickered into a hologram, elusive as a lick of light, hidden somewhere behind the maddening maze of liars and heroes and hidden agendas. American officials talked about "the enemy" and "the evildoers" and it sounded odd, empty, like a legend. Even in the heights of Tora Bora, on the front lines of this vague new war, the enemy was nowhere to be seen. He was just a rumor, secreted in shadows, and sometimes a few bullets rained down from his heights.

I woke up in an old Pakistani sleeping bag one morning, stretched on a fetid mattress in the Spin Ghar hotel, and found that, for the first time in months, I was too worn out and sad to get out of bed. The adrenaline had dried up in my sleep, and there was no other force left. I stared at the ceiling, craving Steve Earle, a Shiner Bock, a long drive on a Texas road with the windows rolled down. I thought about a half-forgotten day deep in the Rio Grande borderlands, an ancient bar with a broken jukebox, shooting pool with the door hanging open on the limpid afternoon until a big purple thunderstorm rolled in off stretches of mesquite. Impossible that those things still existed somewhere, that I was still carrying around the key to an apartment I hadn't seen since early September.

I left Afghanistan—the light that falls like powder on the poppy fields, the mortars stacked like firewood in broken-down sheds at the abandoned terror compounds, the throaty green of the mineral rivers. In the back of the car, I stared into a scrubbed sky as empty plains slipped past. It was Eid al-Fitr; Ramadan was over, and a hungry land sat down to eat. Along the road women split pomegranates, and the red juice stained their fingers. Men roasted lamb shanks over open fires, and children turned from the blaze to watch us pass with eyes like globes. The road was cloaked in the amnesia of holidays. We drew close to the Khyber Pass. The mountain route would drop us down into Pakistan.

Then everything slipped: A tire snagged on a roadside rock and the car spun out and swung in sickening loops. The grill of a cargo truck reared up before us, and I was certain I was about to die, so I closed my eyes. I remembered that drunks survive accidents because they don't stiffen, and told myself to go limp. The car, this seat, was a fixed point in a slipping-away landscape. I was the axis now; the country, the mountains, the war, and the wide yards of dirt stretching back to Tora Bora revolved around me.

That was illusion, of course. I was the one careening. I was the one out of control. These old hills, what did they care? This smuggler's path, the road to Pakistan and India and China—these things stood where they'd always been. I was the element that did not belong; we were the ones who had come plunging in. I remembered what Naseer, the translator, had said. "I am not afraid of killing. This is a country of killing. Only I am afraid for my family." His eyes were calm and knowing.

There was a great, grating crash and everything, everybody slammed. The car stopped, shuddering and smoking, wrinkled as a steel leaf. I sat and breathed. Alive should have been impossible. I scrambled from the car and took the air, cold and sweet with gasoline. I was running then, pounding over the empty land. The adolescent guard laughed so hard his Kalashnikov clattered onto the rocks. I stopped and shook. The men looked politely away.

•

# THREE

# AS LONG AS YOU CAN PAY FOR IT

Coming home from war is a strange and isolating experience. This shouldn't come as a surprise, given all the books and movies detailing the strange and lonesome journey home from war. But after Afghanistan, I didn't expect it. After all, it was only a few months. I knew I had been scrambled a bit by the things I'd seen, but I didn't understand that I was returning to a country transformed. I couldn't anticipate the changes in the atmosphere, and in the people I knew. There was still raw trauma in the air, and the remnants of a fear I had been too far away to feel in full force. I was carrying my own fear around, but I kept it quiet, turned my ribs into prison bars to trap it inside. This seemed to me proper, to carry it there, unseen.

And then I was at my mother's house in Connecticut, walking known floorboards, the same naked trees in the windows, blocked by familiar walls. The silence of the house screamed in my ears, and my bones and skin hung like shed snakeskin that wouldn't fall away. A plane lumbered overhead, slicing white blood from a bright winter sky. My eyes darted around, looking for cover, until I remembered with a start: planes in America don't drop bombs.

I'd walk into a room and somebody would say, " . . . and Megan just came home from Afghanistan!" and all the faces would turn and exclaim, "What was it *like*?" And I would look for words in a mouthful of air.

I drifted down to New York to see an old friend, Lisa. I was trying to stop feeling like a piece of wood, to shake the suspicion that I had one life and everybody around me had a different life, a different rhythm, bound together by implicit, inscrutable codes. I was still trying to get home.

Lisa had been a near-socialist, free-wheeling, hard-drinking international relations student when we were in college together, a smoker of cigarettes, an ingratiator of professors, a waster of hours and days. Then she'd gone off to a village in Burkina Faso for the Peace Corps and come back different, hardened, talking about God and MBAs and the bloody diamond trade. "There is nothing we can do. We might as well get rich." She was alone for the holidays, and I wouldn't have to explain anything to her. We drank wine, played with her cat, listened to songs from college, swooned on sofas. We cooked fish and drank more and finally we slept. I awoke in gray light on a futon, staring at pictures of Africa tacked to white walls. I tiptoed into Lisa's room. "Coffee," I told her.

"You remind me of the cat," she muttered through her hair.

We drank too much coffee. Then we put on sweaters and trudged down 11th Street, crossed the West Side Highway to the Hudson River, and turned south toward the financial district and the remains of the World Trade Center.

"Do you really want to go?" Lisa said. "There are tourists."

I did, but slowly. The Hudson was a sheet of steel. We sat on a bench by the river. Joggers bobbed past, heads swallowed in wool, legs in spandex. I was trying to explain how it seemed like a lot of dead people, dead Americans and dead Afghans and me stretched thin between them. The conversation was disjointed. We stood up and walked. The buildings reared up around us, swallowed the sky and the horizons. We were the only people in the entire city, walking between gray cliffs of downtown. In my memory, it is like that: a city hollow as a stage set, a place where we trespassed. "I used to run down there but now it's all closed." Lisa kicked a crumpled Coke can. The tin skittered ahead over the pavement. We followed its clunky dance down the street. I saw a poster, faded already and peeling from the side of a building: "These colors don't run."

"What does that mean?"

"Oh, yeah," she said. "America is like that now."

"But what does it mean?"

"You know, like red, white, and blue," she said.

I looked at her.

"You know how colors run? They fade, they run?"

"Oh!" I said. "Oh."

"Yeah," said Lisa. "So, the colors don't run, but also, Americans don't run. Like that."

"Okay," I said, and laughed nervously.

"Yeah," said Lisa.

We were drawing closer and I was feeling sick to my stomach. Cold was seeping through my jeans and the coffee buzz was fading.

"Forget it," I said. "We don't have to go all the way down."

"We're almost there."

"I don't want to anymore."

Walking back we came across a group of tourists. They wore red, white, and blue sweatshirts and stared somberly at the buildings. Their cheeks were ruddy and chapped.

I met another friend during the gray afternoon, and the two of us stole into a bar. We sat in the flat winter light, the bar deserted around us. I was into my second glass of wine when it came to me that I had to get out. Immediately. Out of New York. Away from the big buildings, the tourists, and the somber, awkward mood. It was more than I wanted: September long gone, and the clump of people who fussed nervously over the leftovers of violence, looking for grief and meaning in a hole in the ground. "I'm going straight home," I told her. "What do you think?"

"You should," she agreed boozily.

On the curb I flagged a cab to Penn Station and bought a ticket on the next train to Hartford. If you have cash in your pocket you can change scenery just like that, leave and forget. Everything in America is easily gotten, I remembered—as long as you can pay for it.

I have a friend, a Russian man. He told me about his mandatory stint in the Soviet army. He said, "Every single day was absolute shit. I was beaten and abused. I froze my feet, my ears, my balls off. And yet when

I remember it now, it was the best time of my life. Because I was young and I was overcoming obstacles. When you are young and you live through an unbelievably hard time, you remember it later as the best time of your life."

And that was part of it, too. I dreamed about dead children and bullets on mountain passes. But then I was already nostalgic, for Afghanistan and for myself in Afghanistan, for the rush of sights and feelings, the crystal cut of every moment, sun so sharp it sliced newer, flatter surfaces. Now I was shipwrecked in the trappings of home, car, job, and country.

It was a strange time to come home. From television screens and podiums, politicians urged America to be frightened, and the people nodded and agreed to be afraid. Mortality predictors glittered on the television networks, meters striped in the colors of the rainbow—red for severe, orange for high; angry, flashing hues. Never blue for guarded or green for low. Terrorism had become the most important question—everybody thought so, all at once. I read that terrorism had inspired Americans to appreciate their families; to report suspicious behavior; to eat macaroni and cheese for comfort. People had begun to imagine the country as a place waiting to get hit, defined by impending violence. And yet there was the war. We were warriors abroad and victims at home, and it didn't add up to anything coherent.

It was January when I unlocked the door and cracked into the museum vault of my Houston duplex. I could barely shove the door open against the landslide of mail, months' worth of defaulted bills and defunct magazines and slick department store circulars, all the yellowing *Houston Chronicle*s and *New York Times*es that had come until the subscriptions petered out, shoved through the slot and drifted against the door like blown snow. The answering machine was littered with September 11 messages, the voices still wet with emotion that had since dried out, like fossils from another time. I wanted to tell you we're all right. I wanted to tell you I love you. Where are you?

The country moved forward around me. The Enron story was breaking in Houston and I couldn't muster any interest. This is a great story, reporter friends said, you've got to get a piece of it. I shrugged.

My neighbor, Duc, had moved to Houston from Brooklyn. Until September 11 we had never had a serious conversation. We cut up, watched *The Simpsons*, drove down to Galveston with raw chicken and string to catch crabs.

Then it was January and we were sitting in a cluttered bar and Duc had just come back from visiting New York. We were talking about the war and how Osama bin Laden was nowhere to be found, and then everything got tense. Nobody wants to talk about civilian casualties in Afghanistan, I said. That's because who really cares, Duc said. You don't mean that. Yes I do. They can't kill that many of our people and get no reaction. But a lot of the people getting killed in this war didn't kill our people; there's a difference between Afghan civilians and Al Qaeda, don't you understand that? I don't care, he said. And his eyes flicked and I thought I saw tears buried down behind them. I went to New York. *I saw the firehouses.* Whatever happens to those people, they deserve it. And I sat there thinking that the country was in bad shape, really, if sardonic Duc had turned so dead serious. We sat there, each cradling our own ugly memories and resenting the other's, suddenly nothing to say. I swallowed at my beer, resentment growing in my throat, the jukebox wailing. But this was America now, America at this moment, altered. The emotions were not the same. You behaved one way if you were attacked, and a different way altogether if you had invaded. Here at home, people still felt assaulted, they believed they had the moral high ground. But I had seen U.S. warplanes drop bombs on villages of mud brick, and children killed and bin Laden vanish and the future of a broken land becoming the moral responsibility of my own country. September 11 already seemed very far away, buried under the war it had called down.

*I am losing America*, I thought as I lay in bed that night. *I got caught out on the other side, stayed out there too long, and now I can't get home.*

I would put on a dress and sit in a restaurant that shone and clinked, but I was sure that everybody could see the filth in my face, and hear it in my voice. I was just a web of skin and underneath were dirty hospitals, naked rocks, cold wind, the bullets and shit and desperation.

Everybody wants to hear war stories. They expect the stories to be funny and brave.

It must have been incredible, people said.

Weren't you scared?

What did your poor mother say?

You are so lucky, they said.

I am lucky, I would repeat, yes I am so lucky. Yes Afghanistan. The people were friendly with us. Really. Even the food was good. Yes, really. There's something in the light there, a magical quality. An amazing country. Really. No, I haven't read that, but I should. I know. I don't know. I am just really lucky.

I was a puppet jabbering in my own hand, filling dead space with words.

I went to see my grandfather in Virginia. He had sounded old on the phone. "A new world order." He kept saying that. He took me out for dinner and as we sat there drinking whiskey, he started to talk about World War II. He'd joked about it before, about athlete's foot and drunkenly throwing a Russian soldier down the stairs of an officers' club. But now he was describing his march across Germany.

The bombs left so few houses intact, he said. When we got tired, we just walked into any standing house we could find and evicted its inhabitants. We sprayed bug killer on the beds, unrolled our sleeping bags, and slept.

I tried to imagine my grandfather, this old man in a tailored suit, peeled of half a century and trudging across Europe, young and uncomfortable. Tried to imagine a war like that, and all the people who had come home to have families and jobs and forget.

"How did the families react to you? Were they scared?"

My grandfather gave me a pointed look. "We had just conquered their country."

But what was their attitude as they left?

"Sullen."

Later that night, we sat in the thick quiet of his condominium. The lights of the city quivered in the Potomac far below, marble monuments scattered across its banks like dropped toys. My grandfather scratched at the *Washington Post* crossword, murmuring to himself. I stared at him, wondering how long years of war had faded inside of him. He was bringing up these stories, I thought, to signal to me that I would survive, that we would all survive unless we didn't, that war was a condition and part of the continuum. It was something I had touched, and something the country would pass through, and other things would come later. What was the secret to putting war aside, I wanted to ask him. Was it three Scotch whiskeys, taken religiously with dinner? Was it church every Sunday? Was it years? I was too embarrassed to ask, and so I asked him about bigger things.

"How many Americans died in World War II?"

"I don't know," he said. "I imagine a lot."

"More or less."

"Four hundred, five hundred thousand," he suggested.

"So the World Trade Center was minor, then, after all."

"Well, yes," he said. "Except."

His reading glasses came off.

"America hasn't known war since Sherman marched through Georgia and left devastation in his wake. That was a war," he said. "Those of us who went to Europe, we knew, because we saw it. You know now, too. We have that in common.

"But America didn't know. So that was the worst thing to happen to America in 150 years. And in that context, it is important."

His enormous grandfather clock clicked and ticked, an hour turned over. He turned his head and frowned at its face.

"How does that clock know when it's night and when it's day? It's a twelve-hour clock, but it never chimes at night."

He looked at me. His thoughts were pooled behind pursed lips, behind the stitches they laced into his cheek when they cut off the tumor.

"There must be a little man in there. But," he looked at me hard, "what does he eat?"

He sighed.

"I can't think of these complicated questions," he said.

He tugged at his earlobe, smiled like the Sphinx, and padded off to bed.

Before you get somewhere, it's hard to take seriously the idea that it will change you.

It's the oldest story going: you head off to make a mark on the world, but in the end the world marks you, instead. It happened to me, and it happened to the people I knew, and I believe it happened to the country, too.

It doesn't take long. Once you go a little bit into the business of being a witness, once you have been cut by what you've seen, it takes a lot of strength to stop. It doesn't matter anymore why you went at first; now you are bound to stay. The importance of it gets inside of you, and then nothing else feels important at all, you are pale and flaccid in your days. You sense that you have already lost something in the war, so you stick around waiting for the missing parts to come back, to restore themselves, or at least to lose enough so you don't notice the gap anymore.

By accident I wound up nowhere, neither here nor there. Listless in Houston. Jagged in New Orleans. Confused in Austin. When the editors asked me to go for a temporary stint in Jerusalem, I told them I'd stay as long as they needed. Then I begged and pleaded and cajoled until they let me move there for good. I would have to go farther, go so far there was no other place to go except home again. I left Texas and moved to Jerusalem, trying to get back home, taking the long way around.

## FOUR

# TERRORISM AND OTHER STORIES

Armageddon is a place in Israel. I drove there on a golden morning in apricot season. In Hebrew, the name for Armageddon is Megiddo, and Megiddo is an ancient crossroads watered by centuries of blood. The warriors and zealots who prowl the Holy Land have paused for centuries there to decide which direction to take. The roads stretch west to Tel Aviv and the Mediterranean Sea; east to the Galilee; north toward Lebanon; or south toward what is now known as the West Bank. At Megiddo Junction stand a military prison, an old kibbutz, and a bus stop.

The number 830 commuter bus was hit on the dawn run from Tel Aviv to Tiberias, crowded with dozing, daydreaming soldiers, men and women in their late teens and early twenties, on their way to military bases that pepper the mostly Arab-populated Israeli farmlands. A seventeen-year-old boy from Jenin had stolen a car and packed it full of homemade explosives, pulled up alongside the bus's gas tank, and blown himself up. The boy, Hamza Samudi, had been sent by Islamic Jihad. The Palestinian prisoners in their cells heard the explosion and cheered.

On that June morning, clean breezes and honeyed light fell on the watermelon fields of Armageddon. Sunlight sprayed the yellow grasses and fresh pine trees shaded the road. Pieces of people had gotten blasted onto the roadsides. Sheets of bus siding lay tangled in barbed wire at the prison's edge. Men in long beards and rubber gloves, Orthodox Jewish volunteers, combed quietly through the grassy slopes, hunting for pieces of human flesh, gathering every last bit of dead body for proper burial. Later that day I found the bus driver in a hospital cot, and he talked about the soldiers in their smart khakis. He knew their faces and their schedules, where they climbed aboard and where they hopped down. They reminded him of his sons, of his own younger days fighting in the 1967 Middle East War. "They were wonderful," he said.

That was the first suicide bombing I covered, and it sticks there in my memory, the brightness and the death of it. A morning in June; a morning in apricot season. Night had dragged itself out of morning's way, but no freshness broke through a swelter that warped the windows and stuck to the skin, even at dawn.

Israeli news wires are trails of gasoline; the bombs are matches. News races, burns, and gallops. Seventeen people died at Megiddo, most of them burned alive. Eighteen, if you count the teenaged bomber, and I think we should. Islamic Jihad bragged that it had carried out the bombing on the "Zionist bus." The group's leader, Sheikh Abdullah Shami, said the attack marked the thirty-fifth anniversary of the Middle East War, when Israel seized the West Bank, Gaza Strip, Golan Heights, and East Jerusalem, wresting the land from Arabs. "We say to the enemy, we will continue to destroy the protective shield Sharon talks about," the sheikh said. "They will never enjoy security as long as occupation exists in our land."

In that spring of 2002, the second Palestinian intifada was nearing two years old. Suicide bombers came by day, and at night Israeli tanks seized Palestinian turf in the West Bank. Things had gotten out of control. Violence fed violence. Blood washed blood. The Israelis launched Operation Defensive Shield, which later morphed into Operation Determined Path. Behind the names, it meant that Israel was reoccupying the West Bank. It meant that the Oslo Accords, the exhaustively argued framework for peace and a Palestinian state, were lost.

It was late afternoon when I drove back into Jerusalem from Megiddo. By then everybody had seen the pictures of the burned bus and the dead soldiers. Israeli tanks had already groaned into Jenin, the bomber's hometown. I sat in the car, waiting for a light to change at the edge of East Jerusalem. The heat hummed and buzzed. Hasidic boys in their brimmed hats tripped along toward the walls of the Old City, carrying bottles of soda pop, sweating into long-sleeved oxfords.

An older Palestinian man crossed their path and they surrounded him, jeering and taunting. They crunched their features in disgust and threw their shoulders back, unscrewed a bottle of Sprite and splashed the older man's face and shirt. These are our streets and our city, their stances said. They were poking the Arab and spitting on him. A taxi squealed to the curb; the Arab driver pushed up his sleeves as he ran, shoes slapping clumsily over the pavement. Another Arab man leapt out of another car. They pulled the old worker away with pats on the back, threw glowers and threats over their shoulders. The Orthodox boys shuffled off. Jerusalem rearranged itself. The light changed and I drove away. It was over, except that it was never over.

After midnight, tanks and bulldozers arrived at Palestinian Authority president Yasir Arafat's Ramallah headquarters, the Palestinian government center just over the line from Jerusalem. By first light, the compound had been demolished and Arafat, the crooked president of a country that still doesn't exist, waddled through the remaining rooms. The walls were blasted off the soldiers' sleeping quarters, the floors toppled like a fallen layer cake, clothes and wires dripping from the squashed rooms. A skinny soldier shimmied like a child on a jungle gym, sweating and grunting in sock feet, to rummage in the wreckage. Finally he tugged his shoes free of the rubble and held them aloft like trophies; his comrades cheered from the ground below. The summer light came thick and naked, laying it all bare, and Palestinian families walked aghast through the wreckage, silent and stunned, entire clans come together as if on picnic to inspect the broken structure of their national dreams.

Twenty-four hours in Jerusalem spread like a road map to misery.

I knew a Palestinian woman who lived in Jerusalem. She was pretty and slim from living on cigarettes and Nescafé, but her eyes were old and sad. Sometimes she drank iced vodka until she was drunk, leaning over with curses falling out of her mouth, stabbing the night with a cigarette, roaring in broken laughter.

She was still a teenager when Israeli soldiers arrested her for membership in an underground Palestinian political movement. That was back in the bad old days of the first intifada. *Break their bones.*

That's what Defense Minister Yitzhak Rabin told the Israeli soldiers, or so the story goes. Some Israelis insist this was a command to be soft with the Palestinians. *Break their bones but don't kill them, beat them but don't shoot them.* But an American reporter who covered that intifada told me he saw Israeli soldiers systematically break the arms of little boys, one by one, working their way through a village, so they couldn't throw rocks. Israel is merciful; Israel is brutal. The two deathless story lines of the Jewish state, crowding the streets and minds of Jerusalem. Most people believe one or the other, and believe it fervently. It is hard to find anybody who acknowledges that both might be true, and then some.

The Palestinian woman told me her own story one night. We were both drinking and I didn't take notes, but I never forgot it: When they arrested her and brought her to jail she made the soldiers angry because she yelled at them, *Fucking Jews, I wish I were Hitler*. She was embarrassed about yelling those things. *I was so crazy*, she said. *I was just crazy.* She told me that she was tortured for days, beaten, abused, threatened with rape. One day a particularly brutal Israeli interrogator wounded her breast with a nail, left it bleeding. She pulled her blouse aside and showed me the scar, deep and permanent. Then she told me about the young Israeli guard. This stranger, this anonymous Israeli man, sat with her hour after dark hour, fanning her raw wound with a magazine. And all the while, he cried.

I saw her scar, I listened to her words. I don't know if the story is true, in that I don't know if it actually occurred. It may have been apocryphal. These are my memories of her memories. And this is Jerusalem, world capital of dubious stories, centuries of stories half forgotten and passed on, stories of saints and prophets and torturers, everybody fighting for the best story, the one that gives you a religion, a claim, a right. But I never doubted the emotional truth behind this one story, and I have kept it because it encapsulated the things I could sense but not say: that after their awful history, locked in a death match for survival, Israelis and Palestinians had become what they never wished to be—one people after all, each one half of a whole, locked together in a union you could not touch or understand from the outside, torturing one another, tarnishing their own souls with each other's blood, speaking hidden words in voices pitched so only the other could listen, maybe even loving one another in some secret and sublimated way. Each capable of a cruelty that is deeper because it understands exactly what it does, because it is not blind. It is a story not only about pain inflicted, a strong torturer and a helpless victim. It is that story, yes, but it's also a story of a weeping teenager confronting the underbelly of his own country, fighting his conscience with nothing but a magazine to flap in the dark. It's about the pain that turns back to gnaw on the tormenter, about the damage we do to others because we want to protect ourselves, and how that damage echoes back into our own souls. This is not, perhaps, a productive way to think about foreign affairs, least of all in the Middle East, where power is currency and weakness must be hidden at all costs. In this part of the world, statesmen survive because of what they smash, not because of what they say. And yet there was truth and humanity in this story, and so I kept it. Maybe I needed the story, and need it still, to organize my thinking. Maybe I clung to it because it helps, when people are killing their neighbors, to believe they cry over it in the dark. Years later, I do not track down the woman who told me the story. I don't want to double-check. Maybe I am afraid she will take it away again. I have lived with it too long to give it back now; it has become mine, and that is how the stories of Jerusalem have worked for centuries.

I meditated on the story when I jogged along the clean rock walkways of the Sherover Promenade, through the clumps of sweet lavender and sage, past the strolling settlers who gave me silent approbatory looks and the skinny Arab boys who scrambled after me, bawling *yahud, yahud*—Jew, Jew. The path scooped around the hillside, over the ancient Old City walls, and the church bells and the call to prayer quavered from below. The last rays of light glinted off the gold Dome of the Rock and the sweet smell of herbs came up as the dirt grew cold at the roots. Palestinians trailed through the hills, prodding their goats. I ran through the olive trees and up, ancient rocks beneath me, the wonder of the Old City of Jerusalem. The physical beauty of Jerusalem, the transcendent power of a place packed with prayer and reverence, is not a myth. I felt it every day I lived there; it was the consolation for the politics and oppression and misery, and that wonder never faded. Everybody wanted that city for themselves, but in the quiet hours of twilight they just walked and looked down at it, Arabs passing Jews, war suspended for no reason but that it cannot always, every minute, exist. Everybody has a Sabbath in Jerusalem and sometimes the war does, too, although it doesn't come regular or announced.

I thought about the story, too, when I walked the glistening aisles of the Israeli shopping malls and supermarkets, among bent Holocaust survivors and olive-clad soldiers and settlers with small arsenals strapped to their backs. One of these anonymous men once sat in secret and wept with a Palestinian girl because she had been tortured. All Israelis had served in the army. What had they done, and who had they been, and what did they bring back home with them?

There was a problem with the corpses of the suicide bombers. They were piling up in the steel refrigerators of Israel's morgue, and nobody could figure out what to do. The force of the blast eviscerates the middle part of the bomber's body, sending the head and feet sailing off into the air. Now all those salvaged heads and feet were jamming up the morgue, crowding out the dead Israelis. Palestinians couldn't get into Israel to pick up their dead; they wouldn't dare come, anyway, as the widow or mother of a bomber. Under both Muslim and Jewish law, the bodies should have gone into the ground by first sundown after death, but many Jews were squeamish about burying a suicide bomber in the dirt of Israel. It came up on the floor of the Knesset, the Israeli parliament, and the attorney general's office struggled to invent a policy. But they came to no resolution, and the pile of heads and feet kept growing. I visited the morgue, met the director, and wrote a feature. Nothing long or fancy, just a surreal little glimpse of war warping the most ordinary corners of the country.

The story ran. And then the hate mail began.

They called me stupid. They called me an anti-Semite. They lashed me with language so bilious I felt uncomfortable reading the letters, as if a stranger had suddenly pulled down his pants to show me something private and deranged. One of them went on at ranting length about how the Palestinians were pigs who deserved to have their bodies soaked in pigs' blood and burned. Hundreds and hundreds of e-mail messages clogged my inbox. A right-wing, pro-Israel website called "Boycott the Los Angeles Times" posted: "Megan Stack, another PLO propagandist, takes anti-Semitism to a level reminiscent of the 1930s."

Everybody knows about the Jerusalem hate mail. All the reporters get it. You think you are ready to read mail like that. You're not. Not at first. The smears are too personal. Suddenly friends from home were saying, "My mom saw this stuff about you on the Internet . . ." It's meant to be like that: personal and awkward. Until you're so badgered that you catch yourself reading through the stories—not for truth or good writing, but weighing phrases, wondering how much hateful e-mail they're going to incur.

I hadn't expected it, not for a story so innocuous, even marginal. Just a policy debate in Israel over a pile of old body parts. None of the Israeli staff in our bureau had been fazed or offended or even particularly interested. None of the facts were wrong. What was the big deal?

"You humanized them," a reporter friend said. "You're writing about suicide bombers as people who have corpses and families. They can't stand to see them written about like that."

"It's not like I said suicide bombers were noble or good," I said.

"It doesn't matter. You *humanized* them."

By 2003 I'd settled in Jerusalem, and everybody was talking about a war in Iraq. By then I was used to accepting vitriol and character attacks as another part of the war, and they had oxidized me. This was an old battle of narratives, all the stories fighting to be the most true, and as a writer of stories you couldn't help getting dragged into it. I printed one of the e-mails and tacked it to my office wall:

"You and the LA Times should go FUCK yourselves."

It was part of the crusting you develop in Jerusalem. When the phone rang at four in the morning, I fumbled for instant coffee in a dark kitchen and hacked out a story about some fresh assault on Gaza, knowing even half asleep that nobody would read it—that many Americans don't fully understand what Gaza is or how it was created, or what the presence of Israeli tanks there denotes, and that the people most likely to slog through twenty column inches of wire-style reportage are the ones scanning for a hint of bias, a misplaced adjective, a mistaken fact. But I got up and wrote through the dawn all the same, because it was the job I had pined after and now it was mine, in all its dubious glory. Work was becoming work.

Arab children could be trained to think better. Miri really thought so. She was an Israeli photographer with a rusty scrape of a voice and big dark eyes under torrents of wild curls. Miri was liberal. She believed in peace past the point when most Israelis had thrown up their hands and decided to build a wall. She maintained what I imagined to be careful, fraught friendships with Israeli Arabs, as the Palestinians who live inside Israel proper are called. (On my first trip, I annoyed the Jerusalem bureau chief by asking, "But aren't there also Jewish Arabs? Like Israelis from Morocco and Yemen?" "Yes," she snapped, "but you don't *call* them that!")

I was sitting around a Tel Aviv television studio with Miri. Midnight was coming and we were eating sushi and talking about animals. Miri had been teaching Arab kids about animal rights.

"It's terrible what you see," she said. "They tie a cat or a dog to a stick and torture it. But you can explain to them. They don't know any better."

I was skeptical. "I would think that either kids have compassion, or not," I said, soaking a tuna roll in soy sauce. "How can you put compassion where it wasn't before?"

"Oh, you can," Miri said. "They don't know. So you say, 'I have a cat at home and he's very smart, he does this and that, his name is Frank.' So they start to think of the cat like a person with feelings."

"Do they respond?" I asked.

"Yes," she said firmly. "They are very interested."

Israeli news was running; it was late in the newscast, in the features. There was a talent show in an Israeli prison. The prison looked jolly and clean. An inmate chatted with a voice coach. The two men joked back and forth, chuckling and nodding their heads.

"That's not where they put the Palestinians," I said. I had driven past the tents out in the desert, tried to get permission to pay a reporting visit and been denied.

"No," Miri said. "That's for regular prisoners. Criminals. Not the Palestinians."

I watched for another minute. Men were prancing onstage.

"It looks very nice," I said.

"They try to be humane," she agreed.

On the map, Nablus was right up the road. It seemed all you had to do was drive to the Israeli town of Kfar Saba, hang a right, and cruise to Nablus. The trouble with the geography of the occupied Palestinian territories, however, is that maps are misleading. Space yawns and vanishes. Checkpoints and closures crop up and disappear again. There are some roads for settlers and other roads for Arabs, and woe unto the unlucky driver who confuses his way. But on this day, I wasn't thinking about any of that. I wanted to visit a family in Nablus, and I was going by the map.

I'd met this family back in 2002, when Nablus was under Israeli closure and we'd had to drive a twisting, dusty path through the olive groves, hiding from the Israeli tanks, to reach their house. I hadn't seen the family since then, and I had no particular errand with them now. But I wanted to visit this town, whose name Palestinians spoke with soft smiles, asking if you'd tried the honey-dripping *kanafeh*, if you'd visited the olive oil soap factories.

And now I found myself in Kfar Saba, spinning around grassy traffic circles and trolling the back streets, sense of direction scrambled, in the absurd position of looking for the West Bank in Israel. Understand: Kfar Saba is right next to the West Bank. Imagine driving around El Paso discovering that nobody knows where Mexico is. It seems logically impossible, except you keep slamming into it, this blank unknowing. I pulled over and asked some kids on bikes. Empty stares. Suspicious frowns. An old man at the roadside shook his head. The mechanics at the gas station weren't really certain, either. If you lived in Israel and weren't a settler, you could block the West Bank out of your mind. You'd have no business going there, and so you could simply remove it from consideration. Looking for the crossing in this sleepy Israeli community was like hunting for a gap in time and space, the gateway to another dimension. In the end, somehow, I found the checkpoint that marked the line between Israel and the West Bank.

The soldiers let the armored car through. Except the road didn't go the way the map suggested. And soon I hit another checkpoint.

By now I was in the middle of nowhere, surrounded by fields of dead grass. I let the car shudder to a stop and took in the scene before me. About twenty Palestinians stood listlessly in a neat line, waiting their turn to be searched and interrogated so that they could continue along the country road. They stood on a line to nowhere, all spiffed up because they had someplace to be. They were mostly old men, their patched polyester blazers and stiff shoes coated in dust from walking the dirt trails out of their villages and scrambling over sand berms. They stood there like something out of an absurdist painting, as if they were queued up at a turnstile or ticket office. As if they'd been cut out of a city block and pasted over these golden fields.

A small cluster of Israeli soldiers in olive fatigues administered the checkpoint. They were in their teens or just out of them; they sneered at the Palestinians and horsed around among themselves. One of them sauntered over to the car, gun in hand. I shoved open the heavy, armored door; the shatterproof windows didn't roll down. The soldier looked like a child to me.

"What are you doing here?" he demanded.

"I'm a journalist. I'm trying to get to Nablus."

"You can't go down this road."

"Why not?"

"You can't go."

"Is it a closed military zone? Because if it's not a closed military zone, I *can* go."

He just stood there and smirked.

I felt like informing him that I was an American taxpayer, that my family and I had been compelled to pay for his guns and tanks and jeeps, for his salary, to the detriment of schools and homeless shelters and other miscellaneous things for our own country. That his country would surely have been overrun by hostile Arabs long ago without the billions of U.S. tax dollars pumped into the Israeli military. That I understood that's what we'd collectively chosen to do with our money and I didn't expect him to thank me. But that he could at least wipe the smirk off his teenaged face. Because every time I went to Gaza or the

West Bank and saw his colleagues harassing old, sickly Palestinians with the same youthful vigor with which old, sickly Jews had been tormented in Europe, I wanted to burn my notebooks and join a Buddhist monastery someplace. That I didn't want to be staring at him and thinking these acutely uncomfortable thoughts. All I wanted was a small and theoretically simple experience: to drive down the miserable road and pay a visit to a miserable family a few miserable miles away.

But I didn't say any of that. I just glared, feeling anger boil in my face.

The soldier did not let me through. I had to turn around and drive back the other way, plunge off into the West Bank and lose myself in the maze of roads. By the time I reached Adeeb's* house, a cold dusk was gathering in the streets. I'd have to drive back after dark. I was tired, my bones ached from jouncing over the broken roads, dust matted my hair and streaked my face. I drank the tea his wife brought, struggling for small talk. They hadn't been out of Nablus in months. They smiled strained smiles and had almost nothing to say. Had I heard that the Israelis destroyed some of the famous soap factories? Yes, I'd heard. Well then. Well. My family is fine, thank you. It was like a prison visit. Less than an hour later, I was headed back to Jerusalem. I got on a settler highway back, and the ride was smooth and fast.

It was dark, late, and cold when I got back to my little stone apartment in the old Israeli artist colony. Lying in bed, I felt the heaviness of melancholy inside my chest like a small spot of deadness, a Palestinian cancer. The entire West Bank was withering away, choked off by occupation. It was nothing but roads you couldn't take, checkpoints you couldn't pass, the spots of troubled Arab turf laced into the network of settler roads and settler towns like flies tangled in a spider's web. Who was everybody kidding—where was a Palestinian state going to come from? There was no solid piece of land.

The maps around here didn't mean a thing.

I loved living in Israel. That was the hardest part. I loved it every time I climbed the dry heights of Masada and felt the desert wind and saw the Dead Sea gleam below like spilled ink. I remember restaurants in

* "Adeeb" is a pseudonym.

Tel Aviv; the cliffs of Jaffa; a few sticky summer mornings when I woke up with the sun and drove to the shore to swim, watching the old white men splash their flabby forearms, opening themselves to the Mediterranean like wary bears come out from winter hiding. I loved the music that dripped from the clubs on gritty summer nights in Tel Aviv, the darkened streets and young bodies and the sexiness of it all, the intensity of youth and desire against a backdrop of war.

But you went to the West Bank or Gaza and saw the way the Palestinians lived, and it ruined everything. You realized it was rotten underneath; it was impossible. I could be in Herzliya, eating buttery sea bream and drinking mojitos on a terrace over the beach, watching the sun set the Mediterranean skies on fire and the children kick at the edge of blackening waters, hearing the voices of mothers, the shush of waves, the pulse of music playing somewhere. But inside of me was the corruption of memory, knowing the underbelly of the state, thinking about what all of the people around me were determined to ignore. It made everything filthy.

The bombings were huge and awful, but the suffering of the Palestinians was chronic, dripping through the days like acid. All the small horrors that get washed away from a distance, that never make the news but are the grains of earth in that place—the Palestinian cancer patients who are not allowed to leave the Gaza Strip for treatment; the Palestinian mothers who gave birth at checkpoints; the people who hadn't seen their families for years; the shepherds who led their flocks accidentally into the wrong spot and got blown away; the Palestinian-American woman who came to visit her family one summer and got stuck because the Israelis wouldn't give her a permit to drive back to the airport, because even Palestinians with American passports are treated like plain old Palestinians once they set foot inside Israel; the settlers who ransacked the olive groves; the market stalls and greenhouses torn down. The occupation was a cloud of punishment that raged in times of suicide bombings and in times of quiet, a few miles away, invisible.

At the time the Palestinians drew my attention most of all, because their culture was the most foreign; because they were killed far more often and yet their slaughter was treated more casually, packing lower news value; because they were trapped both by Israel and by their own leaders, their own killers.

But I am haunted now by Israelis. By the overlay of realities, the way they knew, and didn't know. Like the people in Kfar Saba, they lived right next door, there and not there. They ignored it, or they told themselves stories that made it all right, horrible stories, and worst of all the stories were true—the injustice and blood of Jewish history.

And yes, Israel has a reason for everything, and there is a national myth that theirs is the most humane army in the world. But in Jerusalem I learned that good intentions and lofty ideals are among the most dangerous tools of all in a war, because they blind people to what they are doing, to the blood on their hands.

One morning I got to work early, and found nobody there except Abby, the office manager. Abby was hyperactive and giggly and screechy. She wore crazy socks and wild clothes in orange, purple, and lime green, and she bought us little treats like chocolate chip cookies and peanut butter. She had three kids at home but she never seemed tired or down. At least, she hadn't until today.

Abby had seen a documentary on Israeli television the night before. It was about impoverished Palestinian children who picked a living out of a garbage dump near Hebron, waiting for trucks to haul in the trash of Israeli settlers. The kids combed the settlers' garbage, looking for scraps of edible food, foraging for clothes, hunting for a living. The settler garbage was the best, the kids said, because the Palestinians don't have much to throw away. Abby had tears in her eyes. Abby had never been in the territories, and she seldom talked about politics, but now she wanted to know if what she had seen was true.

"It was just like the ghetto," she said quietly. "Is this true? Is this what we've come to? Our families left Poland because of these things, and now we are doing the same to other people?"

"Well," I said uncomfortably. "I've never seen that place, but I've heard about it. The situation is not good there."

"I know, I know," she said, swiping at her eyes. "Oh my God. What's going to happen to us?"

After September 11, many Israelis said to the Americans, now you know what terror means. And soon the United States, too, had an occupation of its own, and then a second occupation. We lived even farther away from our wars. Israel built a fence; we had an ocean. But the comparison was there. Some Israelis wanted badly to believe they could be all right one day in spite of the anguish in their backyard, others were hardened beyond caring. They ignored it as best they could, sealed themselves into Israel, but it was always there. As the intifada grew more violent, the use of sedatives rose and more Israeli husbands battered and killed their wives. Soon a spike of suicide and rapes among American soldiers would tell the statistical story of our own trauma. You can overcome the things that are done to you, but you cannot escape the things that you have done.

Here is the truth: It matters, what you do at war. It matters more than you ever want to know. Because countries, like people, have collective consciences and memories and souls, and the violence we deliver in the name of our nation is pooled like sickly tar at the bottom of who we are. The soldiers who don't die for us come home again. They bring with them the killers they became on our national behalf, and sit with their polluted memories and broken emotions in our homes and schools and temples. We may wish it were not so, but action amounts to identity. We become what we do. You can tell yourself all the stories you want, but you can't leave your actions over there. You can't build a wall and expect to live on the other side of memory. All of that poison seeps back into our soil.

And it makes us lie to ourselves, precisely because we want to believe that we are good, we do not want to interrupt a noble national narrative. But there are things we try to obscure by talking about terrorism: things we do to others, and to ourselves. Only the most hawkish Israelis say that they are oppressing people in order to take away their land. There are other stories to tell; other ways to frame and explain military campaigns. Israelis are looking for security; they are fighting terror; it is ugly but they have no choice. Every nation needs its stories, never more so than in times of war. And so the Israelis tell themselves they are making the desert bloom, that they are the only democracy in the Middle East, a humane land that is sometimes forced to behave inhumanely, and we Americans tell ourselves that we are fighting tyranny and toppling dictators. And we say this word, *terrorism*, because it has become the best excuse of all. We push into other lands, we chase the ghosts of a concept, because it is too hard to admit that evil is already in our own hearts and blood is on our hands.

# FIVE

# FORGIVE US OUR TRESPASSES

*Quite a few things happen only because we've written them up first. This is what modern journalism is all about. I know you don't want to stand in the way of our being modern.*

—**Orhan Pamuk**

And then the war came that would tangle America in time and blood, and make us forget, for a time, the other wars, Afghanistan and Israel. In the corpus of the Arab world, Iraq is a nerve center and a soul. Baghdad was magnificent at a time when Arabs were glorious and powerful, and so it is a place that still matters; its history and legends are cherished by millions. The ancient Babylonians developed mathematics and split the day into twenty-four hours centuries before Christ; the Abbasids built their round city in the eighth century; the Shiite scholars at Najaf still interpret Islam for millions of followers. If you invaded Iraq, you invaded all of the history and meaning, too—you plunged into the heart of how a people sees itself, its complexes of defeat and dictatorship, the whiff of dissipated, dusted-over greatness. The United States was determined to take Baghdad, and they did it fast. Just twenty days after the war began, American tanks had churned into Baghdad, Saddam Hussein's statue was off the pedestal, and the dictator himself had fled.

I would leave Amman in the middle of the night to reach Iraq at first light. The hotel phone screeched and the driver announced in broken English that he had come to take me to Baghdad. Night was coming unspooled in the lobby. Wilting wedding guests dragged themselves over the floors, old men muttered into cigarettes, and late-night playboys in dark suits chased their own laughter into the darkness. I walked into the cold night and climbed into the backseat of an SUV. The bellhops in their monkey suits slid the door shut behind me. I was being escorted off to war.

"Okay?" the driver asked.

"Okay."

The hours flew past like billboards on the black, dull road east. The driver slurped at a thermos of hot tea. A truck stop, the sharp smell of diesel, the drone of cassette-tape Koran. More darkness then, drawing close to the border. A hand takes my passport and melts into night. We inch along, from one administrative building to the next, out of Jordan and into Iraq. The border offices loom frozen in the dimness, painted against the velvet screen of a coming dawn. A figure materializes from the night and swings himself into the passenger seat.

"My cousin," the driver says.

"Okay." This wasn't part of the deal.

"Hello," says the cousin, twisting around. Street lamps on their stalks waver in his pupils.

"Hello." He is a young man and suddenly I want him there. He looks too healthy to get hurt.

Darkness thinned and faded as we rolled through the desert of western Iraq, desperately awake. Delivered into something we could not control, we hurtled along in a machine; wheels ate the highway, and I was comfortable knowing that I was just a passenger, I was not responsible for what might come. I closed my eyes and watched waking dreams like movies. The road disappeared behind us. We spat it out and hurtled forward.

A hot dawn came, the air in the car tight and edged with body smells. The dust storm smelled, too, stirring in the yellow sky. In the desert you learn that dust has a smell, a little like washed cotton sheets or baking bread with the texture of scratchy silk in the back of the throat. Arab springs always bring winds and the smell of dust. We were almost to Baghdad now. I played with the name like a small charm, jingling it in my palm like a jack. A mystical, shadowy city. Babylon, the House of Wisdom, *One Thousand and One Nights*. As we drew closer through the desert, little shards of wonder spiked through the slur of my thoughts. I sat up and looked out the window. Everything was mustard and ocher, weary and wilted. A landscape so unremarkable you forgot it before you stopped looking; stretches of sand and dust without the startling scale of a great desert. This was a petty desert, mean and brown, spotted with rotting structures, the listless monuments of disinterested men.

Cars packed the roads on the edge of town, inching along. Nobody bothered with the confines of lanes, and every bit of pavement was packed tight with humans and their machines. The cars lurched, staggering elephants lashed with marauded booty—embroidered sofas, farm animals, paintings. Looters hauled their stashes. Families fled toward the city and away from it. The cars braided the intersections like pick-up sticks; nobody gave the right of way and so they were all locked into place, paralyzed by the mute jam of collective stubbornness. A man with a swinging potbelly hopped from his car to holler at another driver. The faces of women were framed in the glass, sour and small. Horns squalled. There was no power in Iraq. No electricity and nobody in charge. All the traffic lights were dead. Without the commands from the dangling lights, the Iraqi drivers got themselves stuck in deadlocks and quarrels.

I imagined people treated like animals for years—ignored when they kept their heads down, kicked when they straggled out of formation, expected to wag their tails for a pat on the head. And now every last system was gone, and smothered humanity exploded, unbound, over a grid of cracked infrastructure teeming with testy American soldiers. I rubbed the grit from my eyes and watched. Men and women boiled raw, hitting against each other, free to react in dangerous compounds.

I rolled down the window, got a lungful of dust, and sank back, coughing.

The lobby of the Palestine Hotel swelled with life, a dim womb packed with bodies and drained of electricity. The elevators were dead, and so were the phones that called up to the rooms. I was supposed to find

John, the *Los Angeles Times* correspondent who'd been there through the war. He'd arranged accommodations for us. I found his room number on a hand-scrawled registration log and climbed up the dark stairs, along hot caverns of corridors. I knocked on the door, and nobody came. So I decided to take a walk, to write down some notes. Dust still blotted out the world, biblical and sobering, scattering locusts, foretelling the plague.

Marines had surrounded the hotel and sealed off the side roads. Beyond the checkpoints and razor wire, masses of Iraqis swarmed. They had come for help, sniffing around for jobs, or to stand and glower at foreigners. Everything had collapsed, and there were Americans inside the hotel, so they clumped as close as they could get and stared, looking for clues to the new Iraq. The Iraqi army had melted away like wax brushed against a flame. Saddam was on the run. They had been left to their own devices.

I waded into that crowd with a notebook, looking for an English speaker to hire as a temporary translator. I couldn't get a question out of my mouth before they pounced on me and closed in, ranting.

"All the world was putting its hands on its eyes when Saddam killed us. Why now? Where is the food? Where is the medicine?"

"They've been fifty years in London, drinking and eating. They don't represent the Iraqi people. We want somebody from here, who suffered with us."

"Bush wanted to make this a civil war. They make no safety. They intend to. They know everything."

"Iraqi people, we know nothing about democracy. Until now we've had a knife over our head by Saddam Hussein."

It was all there: the tortures of the past; the irritable chaos of the invasion; every woe that was about to crash down. At the time, these rough men in their sweat-stained clothes sounded paranoid. I would soon interview professors and merchants who were less aggrieved and more reasonable, who sounded more correct, predicting that security would soon return, that early spasms of violence were just a mob reaction to sudden, total change. These were comforting things to hear; they matched what U.S. officials seemed to expect. Many of those merchants and professors are gone now, dead or fled. The vision of the mayhem to come was in the collective howl of the street, among people who'd learned to expect nothing. The poor people were the ones who got stuck there, and they were the ones who saw it coming. Strung out on sleeplessness and adrenaline, I was clobbered by the first wave of a feeling that kept coming back for days: that it was all a mistake, that none of us should be there, the soldiers or aid workers or me. It was all a misunderstanding, and now we were lost abroad and the Iraqis were lost at home, and from this chaos absolutely anything could be born.

I stayed out too late that night. I got stuck on the streets after dark, and had to find my way back to the little hotel where I was to sleep. I barely remembered where it was by daylight, and now there didn't seem to be a lightbulb burning in the entire city. The sandstorm had thrown a gritty blindfold over the stars. My stomach began to twist.

"There's a curfew," a marine warned me as I moved past a checkpoint, an American voice in the dark. "You shouldn't be out on the streets."

"I don't have any choice," I told him. "I have to get back to my hotel. It's right up the road."

"Be careful out there."

I waded into night, and the lights buried themselves behind me. In this absolute darkness, the human enterprise of pharmacies, pavement, and mosques seemed like folly, cardboard things thrown together in denial of their flimsiness. A darkness like that overpowers everything. War comes studded with darkness, power outages and shadows and dark roads. But I never saw anything as black as that first night in Baghdad.

I smelled bodies passing unseen: the rotten tang of sweat; the heavy sag of flesh. Over the roar of blood that rushed and crashed through my veins, I imagined I could hear the thoughts of criminals snake past. When a person had crazy eyes, my mother would say, "If he were a horse, they would shoot him." The streets of Baghdad were like that, except instead of seeing a glimmer of madness, you could taste and breathe and brush against it. Crazy pressed in on all sides, jabbered in gunfire, chafed every sense. The whisper of sleeves, pants, stitch on stitch, weave on weave. The glance of skin against fiber, hairs pricked up and throbbing, and even the stir of air, pushed in currents by breath and bodies and fear. The sandstorm churned the sky overhead. Danger gelled in the streets like floodwater; I swam through it, breaststroking through mud, and all the time my heart was throbbing.

*If I disappear in this dark, they will never find me.*

I don't know how I got back that night. One foot before the other. I groped my way to the corner, and remembered to turn left. Even now, writing about it, I am nervous. My heart picks up and my pupils grow wide. The notebooks look ancient to me. The writing is forgotten. After I turn the pages, I drop the books and wash my hands with soap, as if I have touched an infection, and watch the water slip off down the drain.

We stayed in a little dive called the Swan Lake, its lobby plastered with whimsical pictures of gondolas and swans. There was no security, only an old man with an AK-47 who slept like a street bum, sprawled across the doorway. I stepped over his old bones without rousing him. My eyes felt wild in the stab of light.

Gunfire popped in the street all night. Brushing my teeth, I imagined them shooting their way into the hotel. There was nothing to stop them. Every ill-intentioned man in Baghdad ran wild in the streets below. I slept anyway on the hard bed. Fell silently into black and dreamless slumber, quick and melting, a sugar cube dropped into hot tea.

We drove away from a burned-out museum on a heavy, dank afternoon, and as we slipped toward the Rasheed Bridge, I glanced idly over. "Stop here, stop!"

They were digging fresh bodies from the dirt of a scabby little park. Nurses in paper masks clambered in and out of trenches, bringing up the dead. The park stretched parallel to the Tigris, tapering off at the gates of Saddam's palace. Some diehard Iraqi soldiers had dug trenches and made a last stand here, firing their guns against the American tanks.

"I talked to them," one of the neighbors told me. "I said, 'Run away, because nobody should kill himself for Saddam Hussein.' But they refused. They said, 'We will fight the Americans here.' "

When the battle was over, the neighbors said, U.S. soldiers had wrapped the dead in body bags, dumped them down into the soldiers' trenches, and bulldozed the earth back over them. But the graves were shallow, and after a few days the stink of decaying flesh rose from the ground, winding around the houses like lace.

It's hard to misunderstand the stink of death. If it gets into your nose, you know what it is. The body knows; the nerves know. Something like rotting vegetables or spoiled meat, except there is an awful note of metal. Now the smell poured out of the earth as if they had drilled a hole into the rotten heart of the war itself. The volunteers wiped at their eyes, hoisting the heavy flesh from hand to hand, laying the bodies onto orange stretchers. The smell drew young boys; they pulled their T-shirts over their noses and squatted at the rims of the trenches, as close as they could get, staring down. The old men stood a little farther off, muttering. The nearness to death fixed their faces in masks. Even the little boys were silent beneath widened eyes. Everybody stood and watched as the earth relinquished its bodies. American tanks groaned past on the road toward town, sightless beasts with bigger troubles to attend to. The wind changed; the neighbors clutched rags to their faces and gagged.

A quiet spring afternoon spread itself over the riverbanks, exploding in brassy sunlight. Shadows stretched themselves long under the palms, and purple flowers burst over a bullet-pocked fence. War stained the landscape like streaks of rust. Bomb-singed buildings rose. Birds wheeled in the sky overhead. Stone women posed with their upturned jugs, frozen, pouring air perpetually into the green waters of a decrepit fountain. Teenagers cruised by in an antique car they'd stolen from Saddam's palace. A stray dog trotted to the edge of the park and sniffed the air, caught the reek of death and turned tail. Rocket launchers lay in the grass like forgotten toys. The neighbors were afraid to touch them.

"What else could they have done, eh? At least they had the decency," one of the neighbors told me. He was a forty-year-old Iraqi-British banker, come home at this most unpropitious time to take care of his father, who'd had a stroke. His name was Haytham; he'd been trapped in Baghdad through the weeks of war.

"There's a few hand grenades lying around. My nephew picked one up the other day. These kids haven't got a clue, they just think it's an amusement park."

A baby camel hoofed the earth nervously in a penned garden outside Haytham's house, blinking at us. He had escaped from the presidential palace up the road, presumably from the menagerie kept by the cruel and capricious Uday Hussein. Nobody knew what to do with him.

"It's a lovely camel, isn't it?" Haytham said, and grinned. At our backs, the workers went on, digging the dead from the dirt and piling the bodies into trucks.

Down at the children's hospital, the staff had dug up the rose gardens to make room for the nameless dead, and tacked a list of identified corpses to the door. Families crowded forth, looking for missing sons, for young army recruits who'd gone off to do their duty in the twilight hours of a cracked and collapsing regime. Some had been killed. Some were taken prisoner. There were no cell phones, no landlines—no way to know anything. The Iraqis could only drag themselves around the city, find one person after the next, and ask. We were all stripped of technology, reduced to our ancient selves, to faces found and words spoken in person.

A man stopped me at the gate. He had driven with his brothers all the way from the southern city of Karbala. His eyes were rimmed with red, his mustache sagged. They were looking for their twenty-nine-year-old brother, who had deserted the army in southern Iraq and caught a ride to Baghdad with a buddy. His brother talked to me slowly, carefully, staring into my face as if I might conjure the truth if only he got all the details straight.

"My brother was seen somewhere around Baghdad on the fifth or seventh, but he never returned home," he said quietly. "If he was a prisoner, where would he be?"

"I don't know," I said.

"God willing he's a prisoner of war, rather than a dead body," the man muttered. His eyes skimmed on, probing the hospital yard. The three brothers spread out, moved slowly around the fresh mounds, stepped around the empty holes, squatted to read the descriptions tacked up on stakes. If this were still a garden, the hand-scrawled placards would list a variety of rose or thyme. Instead, the cards announced the kind of body that had been planted:

"Republican Guard," one of them read. "Tattoos on hand: 'Ahmed, you are my brother,' 'You're my life, Haidar.' "

"Unknown soldier. White trousers and brown checked shirt."

"Girl, 2–3 years. Wearing yellow and red dress, white vest."

The bodies came and went fast. At first the staff had segregated the Muslims from the Christians; the Iraqis from the other Arabs. But it had gotten too complicated; by now, the dead were jumbled.

A group of men hoisted a body into a crude wooden crate and headed for the road with the makeshift coffin on their shoulders. "There is no God but God," they chanted. Their blank eyes betrayed only fatigue.

"We try to reduce the fear and shock out of them, to ease the shock when they find the bodies," one of the volunteers, a slight young man in a white coat, told me. "We don't break bad news to them right away. We remind them to have some faith, he might be alive. Even if we know he's dead, we don't tell them straight off."

"That sounds cruel," I blurted.

"We are dealing with thousands of families," he bit off the words. "We couldn't even walk into the freezers, they were so packed with bodies."

The desire to get out of Iraq broke over me like hunger. I felt revolted. The story line of the news reports—a dictator toppled; the hunt for weapons of mass destruction; the officials in Washington wearing suits and uniforms and congratulating themselves on Operation Enduring Freedom—what did any of that have to do with the waste of these families, trawling in the chaos for one particular person? The invasion was a nasty, impersonal force, and people had been walloped. And me, pretending I could encapsulate it all in a few paragraphs, grabbing a quote from this victim or that, scribbling scraps of description.

The families were still coming, pushing for a better look at the handwritten inventory:

"Man wearing khaki trousers and shirt."

"Age 50–60. Balding."

"Wristwatch in reception for identification."

The driver swerved through the clots of Baghdad traffic, pressing toward the Catholic church. Sunday is a working day in Muslim countries, and the streets clanged with heat, dust, and machines. But this was Easter Sunday, and I was going to Mass. I stepped into the shadows of the church, crossed myself, and headed up the aisle. Among primped and perfumed Iraqis, I was self-conscious in dusty jeans and a stained cotton shirt. On my knees, I rattled off a silent Act of Contrition. When I was a child, I was instructed to say this prayer on my deathbed, told that the admission of sin and regret would cleanse my soul and usher me straight into heaven. And so I had learned to say it faster than how-much-wood-would-a-woodchuck-chuck, convinced the words would deliver me from purgatory, but only if I could push them out in time.

*Oh-my-God-I-am-sorry-for-my-sins-in-choosing-to-sin-and-failing-to-do-good-I-have-sinned-against-you-and-your-church-I-firmly-intend-with-the-help-of-your-son-to-make-up-for-my-sins-and-love-as-I-should-Amen.*

I said it a few more times. Then I sat and tried to imagine my family. They would still be sleeping. My mother would go to church in a few hours, and she would sit scared, praying for me. She had been alone since my father died four years earlier. I had waited until the last minute to tell her I was going to Iraq. I had called her from the hotel in Amman, just a few hours before I drove over the border. She had said, "Oh my God," and her voice broke. I remembered being at church with my mother on a Sunday morning. One of her friends said, "Well, every time I feel sorry for myself because my kids are in another state, I think of *your* poor mother."

I had come to church because I wanted to sit someplace that felt like home. Like St. Paul's, with its enormous stained-glass saints and the one pane darker than the others since the long-gone day when a boy threw a snowball through it after catechism class. We had stood with frozen feet and gaped at the awesomeness of his transgression.

We dyed eggs every year on Easter Sunday, punched a hole at the fat end of the egg, pricked the thin end with a needle, and blew them hollow. My father whipped all those raw eggs, chopped potatoes, and cooked Spanish tortillas. He knew how to drop a little oil into the dye so that the colors came out swirled, churning, like the sky over the sea. The firehouse on Main Street sold spring plants to raise money for the firemen: lilies, grape hyacinths, tulips. The spice of the bright blooms, the cool press of earth, the wet greenery packed in the cement depths of the firehouse. You breathed it and knew the long winter was over. I remembered the smell as Mass droned on in Arabic.

The hymns had the same swooning wail as Muslim muezzins. Rendered in Arabic, the prayers were unrecognizable, the sermon a glaze of language. I tried to feel some holiness seeping off the worshippers, but I couldn't feel anything. Only the press of madness outside, in the streets and the country beyond. In my head I chanted the rosary, clinging dumbly to the words.

*As it was in the beginning is now and ever shall be.*

*Forgive us our trespasses as we forgive those who trespass against us.*

# SIX

# THE LIVING MARTYR

The Shiite pilgrims walked south into the first sun. They had been marching for days, from the south and from the north, past the palm groves and abandoned battlefields and farms. They came in cars and trucks and buses, too, the women squeezed into flatbeds, veiled heads bent together. They clotted the road, choked our path, and we eased the car into the space they left. We had driven out of Baghdad in the dark, glided south as blackness melted into dawn and villages shook themselves from slumber. When traffic tangled the car, we climbed out and walked with the pilgrims.

"This is incredible," I kept saying to Raheem, the translator.

"Yes," he beamed. "It is."

A thirteen-year-old boy doggedly pushed his crippled brother in a wheelchair. Old men crawled along the road until their knees bled. Villagers sprayed water over the pilgrims' heads to cool them; stirred cauldrons of tea and vats of rice; offered spigots to rinse their feet. Holy men clambered onto cars and serenaded passing crowds with passages from the Koran. When time came for prayer, men spread their rugs in the road and bent their heads to the earth.

We were tracing the path of the American invasion in reverse, and war still littered our way: stray cluster bombs, blasted craters, and burned-out cars framed the road. Nobody cared. They were going to Karbala, not slinking or sneaking, but proclaiming themselves all down the country's main highway. After the U.S. invasion, this was the first move Iraq's Shiites made: they marched en masse to Karbala, to the tomb of Imam Hussein, the martyred grandson of the Prophet Muhammad. They marched because the time had come in their religious calendar, because tradition and faith demanded it. They also marched because, for the first time in recent memory, they could. They had woken up to find themselves the unfettered majority. Saddam Hussein, tormentor of the Shiites, was gone. Now every Shiite wanted a taste of a pilgrimage that had been outlawed under Saddam, and so they walked those country roads, roaring out all that had been suppressed. Not just marching, but announcing themselves, showing the Sunnis, showing the Americans, showing the world—*we are here.* In its free-wheeling ecstasy, the outsized worship of a saintly man, the pilgrimage was closer to a Catholic procession in Mexico than anything I'd seen the Sunnis do in Afghanistan or Gaza. The saucer-eyed portrait of Imam Hussein hung everywhere, pasted on car windshields and hoisted in thick frames. His face against a flaming sky; his body punched by infidels' arrows, burning eyes on a field of green. Hussein died on the plains of Karbala in AD 680, and Shiites have punished themselves ever since for abandoning him to his enemies. Every year, his martyrdom is mourned for forty days; afterward, Shiites march to his tomb and deliver themselves back to life through torments of the flesh.

In the churn of pilgrims we poured into town, blasting past the warrens of shabby shops and through the maze of the market. The crowd pushed and skipped and tripped, the smack of fists on chests rang like the stomp of soldiers' boots. Caked with sweat and blood from cutting themselves, the pilgrims pushed forward. One million souls jammed the hot, bright streets and more were coming all the while, as if the river of bodies would never be dammed, as if all of Iraq were suddenly Shiite and taking to the roads.

"Where is the reckless Saddam? The oppressor of the pilgrims to Karbala?" taunted the crowds. "There is only Hussein now."

In the shadow of the shrine the crowd drew into itself. A moon-faced old woman jabbered angrily and poked at my forehead with a dirty finger—a strand of hair had slipped from my scarf.

Everywhere there was a face, and every face was packed with some enormous emotion: the dumb, slack-jawed visage of sleepwalking worship; the knowledge of bloody secrets; pride tangled with rage.

Men had whipped their own backs with chains and slashed themselves with swords, and blood mixed with their sweat. Wild sunlight painted everything a crazy yellow, and the ghostly eyes of Hussein burned the crowds. His story had been whispered for years, until the secrecy under Saddam became a parable of martyrdom in its own right. Now all those layers of righteousness and death spilled into naked light.

The pilgrims stumbled down the steps to the shrine, weeping and shouting and kissing the tiled walls. The women touched the doors as if they were talismans, and as their fingers found wood, their bodies swooned toward the dirt. A dense sea of worshippers swirled and seethed in a courtyard under an open sky. The walls rang with prayer and with the clapping of hands on hundreds of breasts. One by one, as the pilgrims set foot on the holy ground, they surrendered themselves to worship and disappeared into the crowd.

The shrine's lush gardens smelled of sweat and rosewater; slumbering pilgrims smothered the grass. Peddlers hawked chunks of dirt because, just maybe, the earth of Karbala might contain a trace of the martyr's blood. "They are telling the story of Hussein's death," Raheem murmured. The women wailed and wept and beat their faces as if the message had just arrived, as if this were news and not history.

A small, older woman squatted on the hot earth, staring wearily up at the pilgrims and clutching a black-and-white photograph in her fingers. The tomb of Hussein hulked to the sky at her back, an exquisite mountain of turquoise tile and yellow brick. The woman in the picture was young, maybe a university student.

"Who is that?" I asked.

"It's the martyr," she said, and stared hard into my eyes. It was her daughter.

The woman was only sixty, but her face was withered by tears and sun, scratched by wrinkles. Her daughter, Amina Abbas, had been twenty-two years old when she died.

"She was executed by Saddam's government officials in 1982." The woman spoke quietly. "She was visiting me here when they took her away. I never knew the reason." Finally, the government had ordered her to claim the corpse of her daughter. She picked up the body and buried it herself, in secret. She never told a soul. She had lived through twenty years of silence.

"I am here to prove to people that my daughter has been executed," she said, and tears cracked down her face. "People are saying she's in prison. I want to prove she was executed."

She was talking into a roaring crowd; nobody was listening. There were too many dark stories for hers to catch anybody's attention. Every family had scars, secret graves, people who got erased from the world. In this communal frenzy, there was only room for the tale of Imam Hussein. Beneath his overarching martyrdom, all the other martyrs took their place. It was a straight line of Shiite souls, stretching from 680 down to this moment.

Other pilgrims hesitated before they answered questions. When I asked their names, they cringed. Agents of the former government lurked in their midst, they whispered, and bore their eyes into mine. When I said "Saddam" to an elderly woman, she shook her head wildly from side to side and clapped a hand over her mouth in elaborate pantomime. They were struggling, still, to shake the shades of the past.

Yesterday I had been in Baghdad; now I had crossed into another plane of reality, but this, too, was Iraq. There was no strongman now to force the Shiites, Sunnis, and Kurds into their former roles. And in those earliest days, each community was living through its own particular reinvention. The Shiites gloried in newfound power, the Sunnis realized they had lost their grip on government and would languish in regions empty of oil. The Kurds set about rebuilding their private corner of the country. The notion of Iraq was yesterday's invention, a place carved out by European meddlers in the twentieth century. Now it had been dropped and smashed, and each shard was an island. The tides rose in between and swelled into seas: waters of oblivion and loathing, time and tears.

Raheem and I spent weeks traveling southern Iraq together. He was a short, tidy man nearly old enough to be my father, a moderately religious Shiite from the southern town of Amara. Raheem never looked mussed, tired, or cranky. He tucked his button-down shirts into work slacks, cropped his silver hair so it sprang from his scalp like bristles of a steel brush, and kept his feelings to himself. He was discreet, perceptive, skilled at getting information out of people without letting them realize they'd given it. They say in dangerous places it's best to be the "gray man"—the person who does not stand out. Raheem was a gray man.

At the time, I knew only that Raheem was a Shiite teacher who seemed secretly pleased by the U.S. invasion. I didn't know that he hated Saddam Hussein and his Baathist party or that, in his quiet way, he had resisted them fiercely. When he was a young man, good government jobs went to members of the Baath, but Raheem refused to join. His truculence got him stuck in the army for ten years, eight slogging through the war with Iran. He saw other teachers, Baathists, get rushed through the army in a few months. It was a compromise his conscience would not let him make. He was out of the army and driving a taxi when he heard that Yemen needed teachers. He sent an application and wound up overseas for nine years, languishing in financial exile, teaching first in Yemen and later in Libya. He couldn't afford to bring his wife and children along. He couldn't even afford a house in Baghdad at first, so his family slept in a room at his brother-in-law's place. He could only afford to see them every eleven months or so, but he couldn't find another way to support them. Like most Iraqis, he did what he had to do.

We traveled those first weeks with an American photographer I'll call John. If Raheem was the East, John was the West. On long rides between southern towns, Raheem talked about the pilgrimage to Karbala, the martyrdom of Imam Hussein, the repressions under Saddam. John squinted at passing Iraqi women, shrouded from head to toe in black *abayas* and *hijab*, and said, "Look at those ninjas! That's a lot of ninjas."

John had been embedded with the Marines during the invasion, and he made it known to us, day after day, that life with the soldiers had been infinitely preferable to the privations he was suffering in provincial Iraq. He also intimated that he'd never seen a land so devoid of redeeming value. One day he went on a tear in front of Raheem: "This country is so shitty. Everything is shitty. And everything is broken. And the people are just sitting around, doing nothing. Don't they want to work? It just seems like they're lazy. I think in the U.S., if we were in this situation, people would be working, trying to make things better. All they do here is sit around and complain."

Another time he claimed, also in front of Raheem, that Iraq had not produced a single attractive woman. "Show me one! You point out the next pretty woman you see. They all wear those head scarves. It makes them look like hawks. It looks terrible."

He griped about the dingy hotels. He complained about the food. He didn't wander the marketplaces or explore the riverside villages. Unless we needed a photograph, he stayed in his room. He badgered us to find American soldiers to hit up for an MRE or "meal ready to eat," the processed, dehydrated American food packets he preferred to the fresh-baked bread and spit-roasted chicken from Iraqi cafés. I wondered how Raheem was taking it all. He never said a word when the photographer complained. One day, when John had skulked off to his room, I looked at Raheem.

"Well," I ventured, "John doesn't seem very happy."

"Mmm," Raheem said in his ponderous way. "I think he is miserable."

He started to giggle. I did too. Then we both laughed so hard that I leaned against the wall and Raheem took off his glasses and pressed his fingers into his eyelids. After that, it became a joke.

"Where's John?"

"We-ell," Raheem drew it out, as if it were a dilemma of the ages, "I think, you know, he is in his room." Snicker.

In Baghdad I had felt a heaviness hanging on me, seen every scene painted in the obscenity and confusion of a nightmare. It was a bad feeling, deep and dark, the collapse of a capital. But in the south with Raheem, it was almost beautiful, sometimes. Quiet came up from the marshes when the light went down in Nasiriyah, soft ticks and screeches echoed from the swamp, and bats and white owls stirred the thick soup of spring sky. At night the heat let up and little boys crept out like crabs to play soccer in the street, skittering barefoot after the ball, their voices ringing down warm alleys. The ice-cream parlor served soft strawberry and vanilla in stale cones and we stood on the sidewalk, slurping at sweetness and watching the night settle. Raheem smiled quietly, saying nothing. It was in those moments, seeing scraps of Iraq the way Raheem saw them, that I felt the first traces of affection for the place, even that way, even broken.

As we drove deeper into the southern heartland, Raheem began to walk like the earth was soft beneath his feet. He had an air of quiet buoyancy, as if this war were a brave experiment that might just work. And I understood that he, for one, was willing to take the great mad gamble, because he'd concluded that any risk was better than Saddam Hussein. Why not try, said his posture and his quick, sharp glances. When we met American soldiers he drew back and let me do the talking. But he studied them, stood perfectly still and stared with wide, respectful eyes behind his glasses. And later, when we got back in the car, he'd tell me excitedly about the American soldiers, what they'd said and done, repeating their names as if I had not been there with him, watching too. Raheem never sold the Americans out, not even years later, when the war slithered into his house and broke his heart for good. He felt he had no right to complain about what had come, because he had been in favor of the war from the start.

Raheem woke up before sunrise and spent the early morning hours chatting with the people in the hotel lobby or out in the market. I'd find him when I stumbled down, deep in conversation, twirling prayer beads from his fingers in a stream of morning sunlight. He'd already sauntered down to the souk, bought a sack of fresh-baked bread and processed cheese. "Coffee," I'd croak to the man behind the desk. "You want some, Raheem?"

"No, thank you," he would say crisply. "I have had my breakfast."

As soon as we were alone, he'd tell me the pieces of gossip he'd gathered, the scraps of ideas for stories, the leads we could investigate. He brought them out confidentially, proudly, and spread them out between us like seashells he'd stuffed in his pocket.

One day, during a long, bleak desert drive, we pulled up behind a truck crammed with sheep. "Look at all those sheep!" I said.

Raheem laughed, raised his arm in the air, and wiggled it around, making a scooping motion with a thumb. The skinny shepherd signaled back, scarf flapping wild around his head. "He is going to sell the sheep in Saudi Arabia, because the price is better there," Raheem announced.

"What? How do you know?"

"He has just told me."

"But, how?"

"You know, we have these signals . . ." Raheem seemed muddled now, as if I'd asked him to explain something as instinctive as breathing. "I said with my hand, 'Are you going to take them over there?' And 'over there' means Saudi Arabia. He said, 'Yes, it's better.' And he means the price."

He turned his face back to the desert.

American and British soldiers roamed the roads, but the Iranian-backed Shiite clerics were in charge. They had posted orders on the door of Imam Ali's shrine in the holy city of Najaf. "A Declaration to Keep Peace," the announcement said.

*Do not receive or sell any looted goods.*
*Protect government buildings from looters.*
*Maintain unity among the Shiites.*
*Kill any members of the Baath.*
*Don't spy on people.*
*Unite all Shiite Muslims of all types and origins to allow American forces to settle in this part of Iraq.*
*Support the creation of an Islamic government.*

A body drifted past, borne on bony shoulders. There was no coffin, only a wooden crate, and the lid bounced as the men marched, wafting the death smell into the afternoon. The massive Shiite cemetery on the outskirts of town had halted burials during the war. Now, I saw, the Shiites were back in business.

When I set off to drive through southern Iraq, I expected to find plain stories of liberation and jubilation, open torture chambers and religious pilgrimages. There was an expectation among U.S. officials that Shiites would emerge as the natural allies of the Americans, who had stormed in and freed them from Saddam. But the days among the Shiites were strange from the start. Families draped black banners over their gates to announce the death of people who'd been gone for years. Men crept to the bombed shells of intelligence offices where they'd been tortured to paw in the dirt for documents, kick the rubble in rage, revisit the site of a torment they'd been forced to keep silent about—and to see that site broken and defunct. Gangs hung handwritten lists of suspected Baathist collaborators in town squares, vigilante death sentences. The marshes and farms convulsed with catharsis.

Underneath the top layer of joy, there welled a pool of disappointment, abandonment and disillusionment too deep to dry. Something dark, strong, and tortured had been uncorked. As far as the Shiites were concerned, America had shown up a dozen years too late. Nobody had forgotten what had happened in 1991: The first Bush administration urged Iraqis to rise up against their government. The Kurds and the Shiites heeded the call and launched a grassroots insurrection against Saddam, expecting the Americans to back them up militarily.

But nobody came. Saddam's government slammed down, slaughtering thousands, razing fields, tossing men and women into torture chambers. They filled mass graves, sacked shrines, and drained the storied marshlands. An Iraqi friend who worked for the Baathist regime told me that when Saddam sent the army to slaughter rebels hidden in the shrine at Karbala he told his advisers, "We're both named Hussein. Let's see who's stronger."

The collective punishment dragged on for years. The graves were secret; some families still held out hope that the disappeared would yet return. "We have been killed not by Saddam," a Shiite man in Najaf told me, "but by America." He did not say it with venom. It was, for him, a matter of fact.

I did not come to Iraq expecting to hear about 1991; the stories at first rang strange in my ears. And then stranger still to understand that those days still stirred around us. In my mind, that earlier Iraq war belonged to another time. We are Americans, after all, living on our island, and it has always been easy for us to detach from history, even fast like that, in the same generation. We are struck by the distant echoes of events, and the arrival of refugees who are urged to dream forward, not back. We live isolated not only by stretches of ocean and space, but also by kinks and voids in time. We keep our history in a museum case and consider it; but we don't have much of it, and we don't regard it as alive. We are here, we push forward, we manifest destiny. Iraq does not live like that. Nobody in the Middle East lives like that. In Iraq, there is no past or present, there is only everything, and it weaves together, shimmering and seamless. Ghosts move among the crowd, fed on stories, fattened by prayer. Hussein dies, year after year, on the plains of Karbala. When looters raged in the streets of Baghdad, the Mongols had come pounding back across the sands. Saddam is still with us. And the Americans come, lofty and unscathed, cloaked in the power to spin dreams of freedom and break hearts.

The Shiites would crow, "Thank you, George Bush!" and poke up their thumbs, but if you scratched off just a tiny flake of gilt, if you stopped and asked a simple question—What do you think of U.S. troops occupying Iraq? Who do you want to run the country? Do you want a democracy? What does democracy mean to you?—you gazed into an abyss. It was Iran who'd reached out to help the Shiites through sanctions and collective punishment, given them shelter, medicine, and guns, absorbed the refugees. It was Iranians who were now in a position to influence the Iraqi clerics. And, in turn, the clerics were the only figures trusted by the Shiite masses, many of whom pined for an Iranian-style Islamic republic. Maybe the Shiites would never be America's friends, and it was hard to blame them. They owed the Americans nothing, as far as they could see, except payback for years of suffering. By toppling Saddam, perhaps the Americans had broken even—or perhaps not.

The hotel in Najaf was a desolate tower on the edge of town. Out back, the poorest merchants pushed flimsy Chinese toys and rotten vegetables from stalls of calcified wood and cardboard. When they closed down the market and faded homeward for the night, garbage blew on desert winds and packs of wild dogs snarled through the maze of locked stalls.

The hotel manager was a small, balding man. He covered the dining-room walls with mirror shards and sat daydreaming in his crazy den of infinite, broken reflections. He drank little cups of what he said was tea, the stink of liquor steaming out with each breath. He called himself Abu Adi; he was fifty-three years old, the father of five children. He was one of those people who populate Iraqi towns, a living library who kept local history stored in his mind. We discussed documents. We had been driving to bombed-out, abandoned intelligence headquarters around the south, picking through the rubble, collecting paper that painted a picture of the old regime. Abu Adi said that looted documents were now going for a price. People pored over them, discovering their neighbors had been spying on them, learning who had collaborated with the regime.

Then, suddenly: "Could you please write down the following statement: 'What I have seen in courts and prisons, if you hear, you'll quit your job. If I told you what happened in prison, you would quit journalism.'"

Like so many other southern Shiites, Abu Adi was a little twisted by torture. He'd been arrested for trying to escape to Syria in the 1980s, and spent three years and four months under torture in prison. Three years and four months, he told us, the number seared into memory, and when it was over they sent him to the killing fields of the Iran–Iraq front.

"As soon as the government is established, I'll make a court case against the manager of public security," he said.

"What's his name?" I asked.

"I don't know his name," he said too quickly.

It was a lie. I knew it was a lie, Raheem knew it was a lie, and he knew we knew. He was still too afraid to say the name out loud.

"I have to chase him," he filled an awkward silence. "I'd like to see whether this man is a beast or a human being. It bothers me."

"And now," I asked, "do you feel safer?"

"We're still afraid," he said. "They are talking about liberty, but Saddam's followers are still here among us and we don't know what's going to happen."

His nerves seemed to sway back and forth, blaring into bravery, then shrinking back into themselves. He grew bold and cursed the old regime stridently, or gave us a crumb of a story. Then fear would slip over him like a hood, and he'd fold back into himself.

"Saddam's people are devils and shades of human beings," he spat out.

But then he leaned forward and said softly, "I'm afraid. Please, if Saddam Hussein comes back, come back here and take me out."

Then, slurping down one last glass of spiked tea, he told us how we could find a local hero: the man who survived the mass grave.

---

His name was Hussein Safar, and around Najaf they called him the "living martyr." We found his cousin selling Islamic cloaks in the market, and he sent little boys scampering to find Hussein. While we waited, the cousin led us under the awning of his shop and served bottles of sticky-sweet juice. He smoked cigarettes from a gold plastic holder, stroked his graying goatee, and then he, too, told us calmly about the day he was arrested, along with his mother and three brothers, on suspicion of conspiring against the regime. They had tortured his mother and made him watch. He begged for a piece of paper to sign, eager to confess to anything. They pulled out his fingernails, hung him from the ceiling, electrified him, and set dogs upon him. He confessed to links to Iranian and Kurdish groups, hoping a false admission would make the torture stop. It didn't. He didn't get out until his family gave $5,000 to a well-connected neighbor.

As he spoke, his hands trembled. He grew silent. And then, shyly, he said: "Really, it is a shame upon us that we have such things."

*A shame upon us.* I shivered in the heat. Yes, that was it, somebody had finally said it out loud. These people were embarrassed about what they had endured, about the parts they had been forced to play—victims or tormentors, it was all unendurably shameful. They had been co-opted, tortured, spied upon, and had spied themselves. They had sunk deeper and deeper into collective guilt until the moment of their final humiliation: they had been invaded by the Americans. They felt inferior, as if something must be wrong with themselves, in their culture or their souls. Was it liberating for this small-time merchant, admitting these torments to a young American woman with pity written all over her face? My country had just conquered his country, and he was giving me juice, offering me shade, telling me about things I had no capacity to imagine.

Then Hussein arrived. He stood at the edge of the stall and stared defiantly at us. "*Salaam aleikum,*" I murmured. Raheem spoke softly, rolling out more elaborate blessings, letting the man see that he too was Shiite, that he, too, was from the south. Hussein's shoulders fell slack.

"Look at this." He turned his back and yanked up his shirt. The crater of a bullet yawned on his left shoulder, deep pink, the size of a crabapple.

"This," said his cousin, dragging on his cigarette holder, "is why he thought he was dead."

"So you want to know about the grave?" Hussein's eyes sized us up.

Raheem assured him that we did. A pause. And then:

"Do you have a car? I'll show you."

We slipped into the desert, wrapped in air-conditioning, blinded by sun. As we drove along, Hussein's story spilled in broken sentences, fits and starts:

It was 1991, the year of the first American invasion and the failed Shiite uprising. Iraqi troops swarmed Najaf to crush the insurrection. Shiite blood ran in the streets. They stopped Hussein at one of the checkpoints choking the city, heard his name and tribe, and arrested him. He and scores of others were carted to the Salaam Hotel, the Peace Hotel, and herded into the garden, where they stood crammed together so tightly nobody could sit down. Lorries came rumbling to take them away with hearts shaking and hands bound. They drove out into the desert, the same road we bounced over now. Finally, deep in the stretches of dunes, they stopped. The soldiers hadn't bothered with blindfolds. Hussein saw everything.

He saw trenches. He saw four security officers, each one holding a rifle. He understood that it was a firing squad. He understood that there were bodies in the trenches.

Four by four, the prisoners were forced to stand at the edge of a trench. Four by four, the blasts echoed over the desert, and the bodies dropped down into the graves. Hussein stood and watched while they killed four of his cousins and one of his uncles. The sun was slipping low. Hussein would be among the last killed.

He took his place on the lip of the grave. He looked down and saw men still squirming in the pit. Then the guns crashed. The bullet bore into his shoulder, sliced up through his neck and tore out through his cheek. He toppled down into the pit, cushioned by dying men.

"I lost my sense in the beginning, but then I heard something, I felt something," he said. "They were checking if anybody was still alive, looking at people, shooting." He heard voices at the edge of the trench. Somebody said, "Just leave them, we have other things to do."

Hussein listened to the silence. He wondered whether he was alive or dead. Finally he crawled out and stumbled into the desert darkness.

He stayed with the Bedouins at first. They patched him up, but begged him to move along. He moved from house to house, called on the aid of fellow Shiites. When he was well enough to move, he sneaked over the border into Iran and hid there for months. He finally came back with a counterfeit identity card.

Now Hussein murmured directions into the driver's ear. We turned up a dirt road, bumped along, and stopped. We would have to walk from here. Our shoes sank in hot sand. The desert was blank as forgetting.

"I never came back to this place," Hussein said suddenly. "I was afraid."

We came to a ridge. "It was here," Hussein said, his face twisted. "Here." It was almost a bark. He bent down, hands scooping around in the sand, throwing fists of dirt, sliding over slick dunes. His fingers pored over the grains. I glanced at Raheem, but Raheem's eyes were fixed on Hussein. Now Hussein had turned up something in the sand. He held a bullet aloft, eyes gleaming: "See? You see?

"When I got better I went to see a man whose father was killed with me," he said, fingering the bullet. "I said to him, 'Your father died with me.' I thought he should know."

Your father died with me. As if Hussein had died that night, too.

Villagers from a nearby outpost had drifted over the sand to see what we were doing. They stood at a respectful distance and nodded as Hussein spoke. They had seen the graves. Everybody knew, but nobody dared to talk about it. One year the desert flooded and the bones came to light. The men from the government showed up with shovels and forced the villagers to dig fresh sand over the old remains.

"The families ought to know that people have been killed here," Hussein said. "They have to come to see the graves, because this has to be part of history."

The villagers nodded as if he were an oracle.

Hussein never got his day of justice. Two years later, in 2005, he was called to testify about the mass grave before the supreme court committee investigating the crimes of Saddam's regime. He traveled to Baghdad and gave his testimony. As he drove back down to Najaf, a taxi pulled abruptly in front of his car, forcing the driver to jam on the brakes. Gunmen leapt from the taxi, hauled Hussein from the car, and shot him dead. They dumped his corpse at the side of the road, and drove on. They didn't bother with the other passengers. They only wanted Hussein, to silence a voice that had spoken out.

He had survived Saddam by a miracle, but the U.S. invasion and resulting civil war swallowed his life down. Iraq gets you in the end, one way or the other. One after another, people we met during that ominous and heady voyage through the south have since been killed.

When Raheem told me about Hussein's death, I remembered the last thing he said to us as we pulled back into the market to drop him off.

"Yesterday a car passed in front of me and I saw two police officers. I know them very well. They were torturers. We are thankful to the American government because they got rid of Saddam. But the Americans have left those who tortured and those who wrote accusations. The power of Saddam was the public security officers and intelligence people. They are still here. We're afraid they are going to join the new government. We don't even—we don't prefer people to be killed, but we think the government should kill them."

Those words held the presage of Hussein's death and the seeds of civil war. At the time, I wrote them mutely, hurriedly, the letters smearing together. I'll sort it out later, I thought. For now, just write it down.

## SEVEN

# THE LEADER

*When countries make difficult strategic choices, the United States responds. And of course, I hope that others will see that lesson and learn from it. It's why it's important to reach out to Libya.*

**—Condoleezza Rice**

*I support my darling black African woman. I admire and am very proud of the way she leans back and gives orders to the Arab leaders . . . Leezza, Leezza, Leezza . . . I love her very much.*

**—Colonel Moammar Qaddafi**

The war rolled right over President Bush's announcement that major combat operations in Iraq had ended and raged down into the oven blasts of summer as soldiers combed the sands for weapons of mass destruction. In Washington, questions started to surface—political, procedural inquiries about who knew the intelligence was bad, and when did they know and who did they tell. Meanwhile, there was a bigger demand. The war had been sold to the American public as a bold response to the threat of unimaginable attack, and now a costly occupation had to be justified anew. The bloodier Baghdad grew, the more the question gaped—insurgents bombed the Jordanian embassy and truck-bombed the UN headquarters. Bodies poured into Iraqi morgues. And why had we gone?

To answer the great and growing question, U.S. officials launched into a rhetorical crusade against the dictatorship of Saddam Hussein. We stopped hearing so much about preemptive strikes and U.S. security. Instead, we heard that the war had been necessary because of our rigorous American ideology and morals. Saddam was an oppressor and a tyrant and so we had deposed him. But other Arab dictators still sat among their riches and their torture chambers. If the United States was in the business of clashing with tyrants, how bad was too bad?

I landed in Libya nearly six months after the war began. It was still illegal for Americans to travel to Libya, and the withered man at the passport counter summoned his friends to watch the stamp come down with a gleeful smack on my U.S. passport. Libya was still under American sanctions, and only recently freed from UN sanctions. Yellowing countryside slipped past the taxi windows on the road to Tripoli. It was the crisp end of a burned African summer, all the lives driven indoors, in hiding from a punishing sun.

Rearing grandly in steel and glass over Tripoli's fading downtown, the hotel had recently claimed distinction as the only establishment in town to accept credit cards. The clerks hovered over the card, whispered instructions to one another, and bustled nervously before, finally and proudly, presenting me with something to sign.

The bellhop sweated unabashedly, pounding at the elevator buttons. He was a round man, hair gone to drab gray. When the doors clamped shut, he eyed me.

"You are a journalist?"

"Yes." I hadn't told him that.

"The things journalists say about Libya, all lies," he recited sternly. "Libya is great country. Good country."

"It's my first time here."

"They are lying always about Libya," he repeated. This was the full elasticity of his English.

The room was opulent, tiny, and overstuffed. The phone was scratchy and probably bugged. Maybe it was the weird little bellhop, or the general air of lassitude, but I couldn't shake the sense that I was being watched. I wandered around the bed, glaring at the vents, staring into the light fixtures. I remembered stories about Saddam's intelligence officers videotaping reporters' hotel rooms. I stood against the window, pressed my forehead to the pane, and looked down at the sea.

Saddam Hussein and Moammar Qaddafi of Libya were a matched set, the two leaders known in the West as madmen. They belonged to the same generation of Arab potentates: the ones who had used their wits to grab power, who had been molded by the pan-Arab philosophies of Nasser, by global Cold War chess games and the Arabs' morale-shattering military losses to Israel. Qaddafi and Saddam had dominated their lands because they were cruel, ruthless men, wily manipulators who kept their power no matter how many of their own people had to be killed, tortured, or terrified. There is no Arab leader who has not done these things, done them a lot or dabbled in them. But these two were dictators who wouldn't be dictated to, not even by a global superpower. They had stood up to the Americans and taken sanctions for their rebelliousness. Now Saddam had been driven from his palaces by American tanks. Qaddafi was the biggest scofflaw still standing.

In Iraq, I had seen the lid snatched away and dark secrets freed. People had told me what they had suffered, and they had told me what they would have said if we had met when Saddam was still around. Now I was in Libya with those memories clanking in my thoughts. From the rogue dictatorship smashed, I had moved backward in time, into the rogue dictatorship preserved under glass.

After pacing for a while, I called a man. Somebody had given me his name as a potential translator. He picked me up and drove me through the salt-gnawed streets to meet his wife, who wore *hijab* and glasses and smiled sweetly. They pressed tea upon me and spun a web of flowery greetings until, through a thick mustache of sweat, he finally choked out the news that he was afraid to work with a Western journalist. That information came camouflaged in a forest of Arab hospitalities and salutations, and by the time I got it I had realized that the man didn't really speak English, anyway. So I went back to the hotel and called the official in charge of foreign press to announce myself. He hadn't been expecting me, and wasn't entirely glad to hear of my arrival. I'd been granted a visa earlier in the month to cover the thirty-fourth anniversary of Qaddafi's power grab, but had skipped the celebration and saved the visa for an unscheduled visit. It was preferable, I reasoned, to bump around alone than to be herded along with the other reporters, crammed into buses and ferried from one staged event to the next, frustrated and scrapping for stories. I was gambling that I could appear flustered and harmless enough to avoid getting kicked out, and it worked. The foreign press official brought me down to his office for tea, and assigned a minder to keep an eye on me. I was in Libya, and in the system.

Nobody in the world drives like Libyans. They slam the doors, turn the key in the ignition, and press the gas pedal all the way down to the floor. They shred the highways, scream through backstreets, hurtle like mad fish chased by some unseen shark. There is no middle speed. Never mind that the economy was almost dead, that nobody I met ever had anything to do. They were going nowhere at breakneck speed.

In the heat of afternoon, men lined the waterfront and stared off over the Mediterranean, clothes flapping like loose rags in the wind. Sub-Saharan immigrants crouched on roadsides, dark faces cut from bone. Behind them stretched dull, sagging market stalls, and dusk drew the fading light back out to sea. Yet the streets were gaudy with strings of light, and shop windows twinkled with sparkling party dresses. A mask of whimsy sweetened the anguish of isolation and sanctions, but there was something unsettling about it, like the beach-front high-rises somebody had erected without plumbing or electricity. The party dresses looked as if they had been copied from some other place, a land that worked, as if people had been left on their own so long, cut off from the world, that they'd started to imitate their imaginations and memories of other realities.

Nobody in Libya talks about Moammar Qaddafi. There is only the Leader, and when Libyans talk about the Leader, you hear the invisible capital letter. The Leader is a man of mysterious motives and sweeping decrees. The Leader rose to power in 1969 through a small, quiet military coup that, like all small, quiet military coups in the Arab world, is officially referred to as a "revolution." Since then, he has luxuriated at the core of a personality cult that would make Stalin blush while his regime squashed all political back-talk with a campaign of imprisonments, torture, and disappearances.

When Qaddafi wanted to play tough, he liquidated enemies and slaughtered political prisoners. His relatives and top officials put state-sponsored terrorism to use, bombing passenger planes in midair. When he grew cranky with his "Arab brothers" and decided Libya would focus on being an African country instead, he offered a cash payout to any Libyan who would marry a black African. In a flourish of empire, he sliced his nation with a vast waterworks project, the Great Man-Made River. The Leader woke up feeling whimsical one day, and changed the names of the months. February is "flowers," and April "bird." September, the month in which the Leader grabbed the throne, is *fatah*, or "conquest." When the United States invaded Iraq, he suggested Libyans dig trenches in their yards.

The Leader's favorite color is green, and so Libya is resplendent with green. Even the Leader's political manifesto is entitled the Green Book. The Leader also invented a name for his country: the Jamahariyah. The word is a mash of Arabic loosely translated to "ruled by the masses"; it was born in the crackle of synapses and free associations in the Leader's mysterious mind. In truth, it means only Libya.

One fine morning in that sagging seaside city, the woman I'd come to regard as my head minder marched into the hotel. She had smooth, black hair and a youthful face, and she never allowed herself to smile at me. She shuffled me from one appointment to the next in the diligent, pained manner of a governess with a bad hangover. This morning, she announced, she was taking me to the World Center for Studies and Researches of the Green Book. This is Libya's version of a think tank, a sun-dappled library dedicated to studying the fickle philosophies of the man who invents the country as he goes along. Every table, chair, door, and shelf glows with fresh green paint. Tucked into the shelves are copies of the Green Book translated into twenty-five languages, and scholars huddle at verdant tables to pore over every speech and proclamation Qaddafi has made, divining the direction of the country from the muddle of his words. Bars sealed the windows, and only the turning of pages broke the silence of cold, quiet rooms. Students looked up with wary frowns.

When I sat in a green den with a pair of government analysts, I was prepared for almost anything except what I heard.

"We learned how vulnerable a country like Libya can be. Everything had to be thought afresh," one of them said. "We have a defunct system here. It is not working."

The men went on: Libya has made mistakes. Libya is flawed. Libya has decided to reinvent itself. Libya did not understand how the world worked. Libya had been a little naive—even stupid. I was shocked. *He just called the Leader stupid.*

These men were the first to tell me unequivocally that the Bush administration would soon lift sanctions against Libya. Negotiations had been going on for months, they said, and although Libya refused to acknowledge its guilt, it had agreed to pay cash to the families of victims killed on the bombed airplanes. U.S. oil firms were drooling to get back into Libyan fields, and had promised to convince Congress to vote in Libya's favor. The Libyans were confident that the Bush administration would get its way at home. "The Americans do what they don't say, and they don't say what they do," one of the men said.

"The war in Iraq?" I asked Miloud Mehadbi, the center's director of foreign relations. "What was the lesson there?"

He didn't miss a beat.

"It showed there is no democracy, no international law, no human rights. It's your own selfish interests you should pursue. You should not give a damn about anything else."

His eyes were hard.

"No one is in the position of being apologetic to the regime of Saddam Hussein. They see what's taking place and the picture is very gloomy. Unless you give in to the United States and its interests, then consider Iraq. The Leader was clear that we're paying money to buy our safety, to avoid a confrontation with mad, runaway U.S. power."

He wasn't talking only about money for the victims, but about purchasing a place in this new, post–September 11 world. Libya had realized there was no more patience for a country like Libya. The Cold War was over. Two Palestinian intifadas had failed. And then September 11 fixed American attention on terrorism. As I talked to people in Tripoli, I began to understand that Qaddafi had embarked on his second revolution, an image rehabilitation on a grand scale. The UN had lifted sanctions after those first payouts to the terror victims, leaving only American sanctions to dispel.

Anybody who believes Qaddafi is addled by madness should consider his clever maneuvers after the invasion of Iraq. The fate of Saddam Hussein was a morality play writ large across Arabian skies. If Saddam had been the tyrant, Qaddafi would be the model pupil. He would bring Libya back into the world, and bring the world back to Libya. And Qaddafi, arguably the most terror-friendly ruler in all the Arab lands, would use the war on terror to get it done. It was cynical and hard-bitten. It was brilliant.

Over and over in Libya, I heard a repudiation of the past, and the cocky brag that the country would buy its way back into good standing. This was the conclusion dawning on many Arab despots: that Saddam had been forced into hiding because he refused to play along, not because of democracy, human rights, political prisoners, or press repression. The reasons Saddam Hussein no longer deserved to rule—the torment of his own people; the cruelty of his prisons; the midnight disappearances; the megalomaniacal grip on power—also existed under Qaddafi. But in Libya, not only were such offenses not casus belli, they were forgivable traits to be brushed aside while patching up bad relations with an oil-rich state.

"They think we're a purist country. No, we were practical. We had to buy peace," Prime Minister Shukri Ghanim told me.

"By some of our estimates, we lost more than $30 billion because of sanctions. For us, it's an economic venture. We're sick and tired of this. If it's only money at the end of the day, we have to pay money. The United States has the means and the power and they will not hesitate to use them. What can we do?"

He looked at me, the visiting American.

"You can change the rules in the middle of the game," he said, "so what can we do?"

"Do you like my ass?" The girl in the tight white pants had her face up to my ear; she was hollering.

We'd been watching her dance for the past half hour, shaking her hips alone and half drunk in a circle of men. She and I were the only women. I laughed. We were drinking illegal red wine.

"Your ass is *fantastic*!" I yelled into the dark cave of her blow-dried mane. "Just like Jennifer Lopez!"

She cooed, touched my cheek, and staggered back to dance some more.

"She does look like Jennifer Lopez," Nabil* mused. The party had been thrown by his cousins in the sprawling family estate on the outskirts of Tripoli. The ceiling beams had been imported from Italy. Albino peacocks roamed sandy gardens. Muhammad Ali's autograph was still visible on the bar, the ghost of a long-gone day when Tripoli glittered fashionably.

Nabil had dropped into my life fortuitously, introduced by a mutual friend as I headed into Libya. When I finished the official interviews and bid good-night to my stern minders, Nabil and his cousin picked me up and we plunged into Tripoli. We watched a soccer game at sunset, ate ice cream and smoked sheeshas in the old Italian plaza, and trolled the beachside shantytowns to buy black-market booze. The government knew, of course. They knew everything. One of the minders sat in a stuffed chair in the hotel lobby, watching me come and go. Nobody ever discussed it, but he sat there and slid his eyes after me.

"I like house music, *crazy*," a skinny young guy was yelling now. He wiggled his head and rolled his glassy eyes. He kept slipping off into the darkness and stumbling back more stoned. We were sitting out under the stars.

"We're not terrorists here, you know," the guy said.

"I know."

The music pounded, and he bounced in place. There were only a handful of guests, and they clustered around; it seemed significant to them that I was there. Sanctions had turned this ancient Mediterranean capital, roved for centuries by Romans and Africans and Greeks, into a shadowland. At least now commercial flights could land at the airport again. For years, Libyans got out of the country by hopping a ferry to Malta, or crossing the excruciating deserts of North

* Name has been changed to protect the family.

Africa by bus, driving all day and all night to reach Cairo. Still they were eager to tell me of the countries they had visited, to display their urbanity, their hunger for the world. They wanted to tell me about Rome and Paris and London, about everything under the sun except for the one thing I had come to write about—their lives at home, under Qaddafi.

Here is the mental rearrangement: People who live in a dictatorship will tell you the most with awkward silences, the fear that flashes on their faces, and the implausible exclamations of rote enthusiasm. It's what they don't say that counts. You have to consider the negative space, to trace the air that surrounds the form to get an idea of its shape, because nobody will dare to articulate the thing itself. If you accumulate everything that is unmentionable, feared, stamped out, then you have an idea of just how much terror people have swallowed over the years. You begin to grade the repression on a spectrum. Egyptian politics have been languishing in a torture cell for decades, for example, but people on the street still gripe about the government and roll their eyes at the president.

Not in Libya. The people I met in Libya were locked in the basement of an asylum. Social interaction was all nervous smiles, evasive answers, and cups of tea. Nobody wanted to talk about the Leader. When I tried to interview fans in the soccer stadium, they stared in mute panic and skittered away. A Libyan oil worker agreed to talk, but only in his car. We spun down empty streets on a blazing afternoon and he delivered a long monologue, filled my ears with stories of mass executions, corruption among Qaddafi's children, and torture, and I wrote it all down, knowing that I could never quote him. When I met a young Libyan official for coffee, he glanced over both shoulders before confessing his hope that Libya could become a "normal country"—in spite of the Leader. I was filling my notebooks with scraps and bits, and it all added up to fear.

"I'm sorry," one of the men said gently. He leaned closer and murmured: "I have already been twice to jail."

The hotel telephone shrilled at midnight.

"We want to talk to you," the man ordered in broken English. "Come downstairs now, please."

"It's very late," I said. "I'm just going to bed."

"Now, please." And the line went dead.

I stood up and struggled into my clothes, disoriented. I must be in trouble. They're angry because I've been hanging around with Nabil and his family. I pulled on my jeans.

The men waited in the lobby. "Dr. Giuma wants to see you." This was the official who had issued my visa. They marched me out and drove me wordlessly through the darkened streets. Dark waves tumbled onto the shore and sizzled to flatness on the sands.

Lights blazed in the information ministry. Dr. Giuma was all toothy smiles. He served me a little glass of tea. He wanted to know if I was happy, was there anything I needed? I began to relax, to chat.

Then he got very cold, very fast. It had come to his attention, he said, that I'd been complaining about his staff, saying that they were not sufficiently helpful.

"On the contrary," I told him. "I've been very pleased." It was true. I wondered if this was a meeting he held out of habit.

"We have reports," he said.

"I don't know where you are getting your information," I said, flushing but trying to speak slowly, clearly. "But it's wrong. I haven't complained to anybody. So your information is wrong." Even to my own ears, I sounded guilty. *Guilty of what*, I wondered.

"You know, we were not expecting you to come now," Dr. Giuma pressed on. "We had a program for the journalists. It was before. You were not here. We are trying to do our best for you although we did not expect you now."

"I know," I told him. "And really, I am most grateful for your trouble."

Then, the sugar-crusted bottom of the tea glass, and a sudden standing up, a thank you, a tacit invitation to leave. There was no explanation or apology. No acknowledgment that it was strange, hauling me down here in the middle of the night to make me squirm. They were through with me. We had talked about nothing.

Back within the dry, bright walls of my hotel room, I sat very still and listened to the blood rage through my ears. I was wide awake.

---

The doctor swept into the lobby clutching a little bouquet of tea roses from his garden. "On behalf of the Libyan-American Friendship Association, welcome to Libya," he said officiously, dipping into a little bow as he handed over the flowers. He was most delighted to make my acquaintance, and his wife sent her very best regards.

"Do we have time for a cup of coffee?" I asked.

"Of course!" he said grandly. "We have plenty of time."

The Libyan-American Friendship Association had caught me by surprise. I'd called the doctor because I'd heard the hospitals were falling apart under sanctions, that medicine and sheets were in short supply, that the entire medical infrastructure was on the edge of collapse.

The condition of the hospitals was relevant because of the Bulgarian nurses. Six foreign nurses and two doctors had been languishing in jail, reportedly under torture, for four years already, accused of injecting hundreds of Libyan children with HIV-tainted blood. The children were sick; that much was undeniable. But the government's insistence that it was an Israeli conspiracy, that the hapless nurses were in fact Mossad agents, sounded insane. I suspected it was easier to blame Israel than to own up to the truth: that the Leader's great revolution was a bust, that the Jamahiriya was a land where incompetent and cash-strapped hospitals pumped people full of bad blood.

The doctor had concocted a plan: He'd pick me up on my last day in town, take me for a tour of the hospital where he worked, and then drop me at the airport. If we got caught together, we'd say he had offered me a lift to the airport. The idea that we'd elude the notice of the government was quixotic, even semi-delusional, but it was all we had.

"So what is this friendship association exactly?" I asked him, studying his calling card. It was red, white, blue, and, of course, green. We were sitting over cappuccino in the café off the hotel lobby.

"Some of the American wives here, like my wife," he said. "They just like to get together. We celebrate, like, the Fourth of July."

"So your wife is American?" I was intrigued. "How does she get along here?"

"Well, to tell you the truth, she is very happy," he said. "It's better here than where she comes from."

"How so?"

His wife, he explained, had been a local teenager from a hardscrabble background in West Virginia, where he'd been sent for medical training.

"I met her when she was nineteen. We got married when she was twenty-one," he said. "We live in a farm outside Tripoli. She has freedom here. She has whatever she needs. We have two daughters and a son.

"She's happy here," he said again. "She'd be very interested to meet you, if you ever come back to Libya."

We had finished our coffee. Shall we? We shall.

The car was an aging sedan, rusted and streaked, sagging wearily down on its wheels. With a grunt, the doctor gallantly hoisted my suitcase into the trunk. The car bounced and settled, taken aback by the weight. We arranged ourselves in the front seat, slammed the doors, and began to bake like a pair of hams.

"Let's see," he muttered nervously.

He turned the key in the ignition. Nothing happened. He clenched his jaw and tried again, throwing a little shoulder into it. The car sat, implacable.

"Heh, heh. I don't know why I brought this car. I have other cars at home," he said. His embarrassment was palpable. I caught it like a yawn.

"It doesn't matter," I told him lamely. "I'm just so grateful that you're trying to help me."

Finally, with a wheeze, the engine rolled reluctantly over. "There we are," my host said briskly. We eased out of the hotel parking lot, toward the coast. The entire city was frozen in a swoon of heat. Even the waves seemed exhausted, as if the water had grown heavier, straining to heave themselves onto the sands. Sun glinted evilly on the sea, tinting the Mediterranean a sickly turquoise.

The car rattled, shuddered, then found its gear again, jolting like a child's toy car sent skittering along a racetrack. The other cars screamed past, wild and fearless, swerving around our limping rattletrap. The windows opened just a crack. My cotton blouse was as wet as a used washcloth; I pushed damp tendrils of hair behind ringing ears.

"Is it far to the hospital?" I ran my eyes over the dashboard in search of a clock.

"No, no, no," he said. "We have plenty of time."

"That's good."

Then, right out in the middle of the reckless veins of Libyan traffic, the car died. Horns and squeals rang in circles around us; my host managed to force the car onto the shoulder. He hopped out and I did too, drowning for a breath of stultifying air. "I don't understand this. What's happening?" he said, and disappeared under the hood. I watched the traffic thunder past. There were cabs.

"You know what," I leaned into the hood with him. "I think I'm just going to grab a taxi to the airport. It's getting late, and I'm starting to worry about my flight. Will you be all right here?"

"Yes of course," he said. "But I'll take you to the airport! Just wait one minute while I see what's happened."

But we were out of time. A slick, black sedan with tinted windows shot onto the shoulder, and all of the doors sprang open. Out jumped the lanky man who sat in the hotel lobby, shadowed eyes following my footsteps, and other men in blazers and slacks. They had been trailing us all along, of course. My stomach clenched. The doctor looked stricken.

"What are you doing?" barked the man from the lobby.

"My friend here was just taking me to the airport," I said.

"Why did you do this? You disappeared from the hotel. We were going to take you to the airport."

"Oh, well I appreciate that very much! I had no idea." Big smile.

The doctor, stammering in Arabic, was surrounded by two of the government men. One of the men yanked open the trunk, pulled out my suitcase and, without a word, threw it into the back of the black sedan.

"Get into the car," the man from the lobby snapped.

"Actually, I need to go to the airport," I said.

"We will take you there."

"What about my friend?"

"Don't worry," he said coldly.

This sounded ominous. I walked over. Sweat was pouring down his face. "They say they're taking me to the airport," I said.

"Yes of course," he looked at me significantly. "You must go with them."

"Will you be all right?"

"I'll be just fine," he smiled a sickly smile. "It was a great pleasure to meet you."

"The pleasure was mine," I said slowly.

I left him there, in the custody of the government. They could do anything they wanted, sooner or later. The more fuss I kicked up, the worse it would be for him in the end. So I left quietly. They packed me into the backseat and slammed the door behind me with a ring. The air-conditioning was cool on my arms; my face began to dry. I settled into the plush seats, and nobody spoke. They drove fast, plunging through the afternoon, swerving around the other cars. We were driving away from the airport.

"Are we going to the airport?" I tried to keep my voice cool. "It's getting very late."

"Wait," the minder snapped.

"Well, I need to go to the airport!"

"Okay, okay!"

"I can just take a taxi," I offered.

He laughed nastily, and kept driving.

I gave up and stared out the window. Had they concluded I was a spy, or were they just teaching me another lesson? We wound up back at that same government compound, the one that vaguely reminded me of an army base. "Wait here," the minder told me, and disappeared.

The minutes dragged by. The car was running out of air. I swung the door open and listened to the heat sing under the trees. I knew I couldn't leave; the gate had clamped shut behind us. I gave up on my flight. It would take off soon, and the airport was far away. I felt desperate to get out of Libya and away from the pressure of being watched, of being suspicious to everybody, of fretting about getting others into trouble. It had been obvious the moment the black government sedan swung out of the traffic, glinting with power and inevitability: You can't do anything in a dictatorship. You construct little facades of freedom, but that's just a child's game of pretend. The eyes are on you, always, watching and judging and remembering. Sometimes the regime will let you think you are moving around freely. Sometimes the regime will remind you that you will never be free. This was the message: Don't think you are anybody important.

Don't think we can't squash you, if we feel like it. You are on our turf now. This was not a personalized message; it was just their way of being, and it came naturally to them.

They gave the message plenty of time to sink in. They let me stew in trepidation for twenty minutes.

And then the Libyans surprised me, one last time. They came to fetch me. They walked me inside. There I found my main minder, the woman, along with Dr. Giuma. My minder beamed at me. You gave us quite a scare there. We didn't know where you had gone. We just didn't want you to leave without a proper good-bye, they said with eerie smiles. Then the exclamation marks started popping. Thank you for coming to the Great Socialist People's Libyan Arab Jamahariya! We have enjoyed working with you!

"I'm sorry, I thought . . ." I trailed off. "You see, I'm very late. I'm worried I'll miss my flight."

"Miss your flight! Never!" these unrecognizably jovial figures cried. "We will take you to the airport ourselves, and make sure that you get onto the plane," Dr. Giuma told me.

They packed me into the car and the driver crushed the pedal to the floor, throwing us all against the back of the seats. My minder was still smiling, thin and stiff. At the airport, she put a hand on my back, flashed some identity cards, and marched me to the front of every line. She walked me all the way to passport control, and then shook my hand in a firm and almost fond good-bye.

I turned around after a few steps. She was still standing there, waiting for me to leave. I waved the doctor's wilting bouquet in limp farewell.

"Partners, not wage workers!" boasted a sign on the wall.

"Desire it," proclaimed an advertisement for European chocolates.

And then there was a message from the Leader: "Wine and drugs are total destruction weapons. Hash is like the bacterial and chemical weapons and the atomic bomb.—The Revolution Leader."

At the gate, I tossed the roses into the garbage. The plane lifted up into the sky, and Libya dropped to a blur of land, spread there beneath the clouds.

---

Qaddafi kept all his promises. He relinquished his weapons of mass destruction program. Though still grumbling that Libya wasn't to blame, he agreed to pay billions to compensate the victims of the two airplane bombings. Bush removed Libya from the list of state sponsors of terrorism. The United States opened an embassy in Tripoli. Tourists and oil companies poured in. Vacations in Libya are all the rage these days. In the *New York Times*'s list of fifty-three places to visit in 2008, Libya came in tenth.

This worked out very well for Qaddafi and his son and heir apparent, Seif al Islam. He didn't have to stop being a dictator. He didn't have to put up with free speech, a free press, or opposition parties. He got to keep a stranglehold on the country—and he got to make a lot of money, to boot.

I heard about Libya from Arabs around the region for months. "What is this war on terror?" they'd say incredulously. "Now America says Qaddafi is a good example! *Qaddafi!* And then they want us to believe they have come to bring us democracy."

"I know," I'd say, and shrug uneasily.

After a while, people stopped shaking their heads about the newfound Libyan–American friendship. That was even worse: it disappeared into the vague cloud of disillusionment and disgust that had thickened around the idea of America ever since the invasion of Iraq. Soon it barely rated mention.

A few years later, I slipped into a conference room at a Dead Sea resort to hear Qaddafi's son speak at the World Economic Forum. Saif al Islam was the new, Westernized face of the Libyan dictatorship. He was olive-skinned, athletic, and almost handsome. His rangy body was clothed in a well-tailored suit. The first thing I noticed was that he, too, referred to his father as "the Leader."

He had come to drum up tourism and investment, but the audience kept asking him about politics. "Libya is a very attractive market," he'd say, or "Foreign banks are applying for licenses." Come to Libya, he said, and "you will see the difference." Then he would stretch his lips and show his teeth in a massive, lopsided grin.

But questions about the dictatorship kept coming, and Saif grew snappier. He was losing his cool. His father's son, after all.

Libya was not a dictatorship, he informed the audience, slipping into incoherency. "We can't talk about an absolute dictatorship," he equivocated.

Why aren't there any opposition parties in Libya?

"Even people who call themselves opposition and whatever and are not in line with the Libyan regime and Moammar Qaddafi," he said, "I know them personally. They say, 'Saif al Islam, we don't *want* parties in Libya.' "

"All the world is visiting Libya." Suddenly affable, he slipped back to his talking points. "And Libya, which was a closed box and a representative of terrorism, this box suddenly opened and we're saying we have desert, we have oil, we have culture, we have many things."

Listening to this pampered young heir with his tailored suit and air of entitlement, my thoughts drifted back to the night of the party in Tripoli. I looked at Saif al Islam and remembered how the night had ended.

It was one in the morning, and we were driving home. I sat in the passenger seat, and an older party guest sat in the back. He had lingered quiet and staid all night, nodding his graying head as the young cubs bounced and hollered, but now he was buzzed on black-market wine. He spoke in faltering English of political chants and soccer songs. "The soccer stadium is the only place people can speak," he told me. "So they yell." Then he unleashed a torrent of incomprehensible Arabic so I'd know what they yell.

"What does that mean?" I asked, but he ignored the question. He broke into a scrap of a soccer song as we rolled through the sepia tint of streetlights. We slipped past the billboards of Qaddafi's jowly face, eased into the driveway of the man's villa.

He got out of the car, and lurched into the frame of my open window. His face was panicked.

"I'm sorry to talk so much," he said miserably. "It's the wine."

His fingers wrapped around the window frame as if he wanted to hold us back with his arms, fearful of the control he'd lose when the car backed up and carried us away into the night, taking his words away from him.

"You didn't talk too much. It was nice to meet you."

"Please don't write the things I said," his voice rose through the thick air. "I know about newspapers. They write everything."

Of everybody at the party, this man had spoken the least. Except for his funny little tirade about soccer, he'd barely said a word beyond pleasantries.

"Don't worry," I told him. "I won't write what you said. I don't even remember your name."

"You never met me," he hissed. "We never spoke." He looked into my eyes. All of his dignity had melted into the salty night. He was pleading.

"I never met you," I repeated. "We never spoke."

He stared a minute longer. He sighed. And then he turned his back, shuffled to the gate, and disappeared behind the walls, feet dragging like rocks.

# EIGHT

# SACRIFICE

*On the day of our feast, the black hand came to kill people.*

**—Official statement read on Kurdish television, February 2, 2004**

Violence is a reprint of itself, an endless copy. I mean to say that by itself, violence is not the point. A bomb, a battle, a bullet is just a hole torn in the fabric of a day. Violence is all of the smashed things left behind, and then the things that grow anyway, defiant. Girls move silently behind closed curtains, broken-down schools shut their doors to students, lovers marry in secret. Violence is the babies you have, the jokes you tell, the fixing of windows and mopping of blood. Against that brave human circus of mundane high-wire acts, it is not very important after all, the big empty sound of the bomb, the smell of the chemicals, or the hospital cots where people bleed to death, reeking of burned hair. Anybody who gets close to violence gets a little bit stuck, the gum of it clings to their feet and slows their steps. Iraq was always a tangle to me, a place where there was personal death and also collective death—a city, a neighborhood, a society can get maimed or killed just like a man or woman. The only difference is that cities can be reincarnated, collectives are replenished and resurrected. When the people go, they're gone for good.

As the occupation dragged toward the end of its first year, Saddam Hussein paced in prison and his sons were dead, but the anti-American uprising raged and the first whiff of civil war was rising from the land. Now going into Iraq meant wading into violence. You felt it when they stamped your passport at the border offices, smelled it when you stood at the door of the plane with the hot winds scouring the tarmac. You expected it and it didn't startle you. It was a part of every day. In the first months after the invasion, there had been other things, too. Date palm orchards in summer, restaurants spiked with voices, long, sultry drives in the country. Then you began to realize that the war was surging up, covering things. You looked up one day and saw the place disappearing. It was like watching an eclipse, standing on a sidewalk bathed in strange light, and then noticing all at once that darkness has taken over.

The first time I looked up and felt that Iraq was disappearing was Eid al-Adha, "the feast of sacrifice," one of the most important holidays on the Muslim calendar. It was 2004, a time when U.S. diplomats still had the face to accuse reporters of ignoring all the happy stories of Iraq, and we still ran out to report the details of just about every suicide attack as if suicide attacks were a big surprise.

It was the eve of Eid and I was sitting around the bureau in Baghdad when the stringer in Mosul called. At least nine people were dead in a suicide bombing, she said. Nine wasn't very many dead, not as bombings went, but it was enough. We peeled off into the desert, pushing up the trash-strewn highways that rolled north under a dull metal sky. Raheem was there, and so was Nabil, a lanky photographer who'd drifted to Iraq from Libya. Once we left Baghdad, we were drawn together in a danger we didn't discuss. Bandits roamed. Cars got shot out. A breakdown on a desert highway could kill you. You wanted to get off the roads before night fell. We drove scuffed-up sedans in neutral colors. I wore an *abaya*, and draped a scarf over my head. The idea was to cut a bland profile, to look Iraqi at a casual glance from a passing car.

The bureau driver named Ziad was at the wheel, and Raheem sat beside him. They never said it was a bad stretch, but you could feel the air change. Ziad sucked on cigarettes and Raheem wrapped his silvered head in a checked *kaffiyeh*. Eventually we'd turn into a town, and you could feel a loosening, the stomach unfurling, the lungs expanding. Ziad pushed a worn cassette tape into the dashboard and Mary Chapin Carpenter's voice spilled from the speakers.

*Saturday night and the moon is out*
*I wanna head on over to the Twist and Shout*

There was no sun that day, only a sky sagging under winter's weight and the stretches of dust fields racing away until they petered into a vague horizon. Sometimes I remembered that we were going to a bombing. Sometimes I stared out at the drab earth and daydreamed. You push it away as much as you can. *When the car ride ends, we'll be at a bombing.* "How are your cousins?" I asked Nabil. "They're good, I'm thinking of going back to Tripoli to visit them." *I never want the car ride to end.*

Here is the truth about suicide bombings: They are all the same. At the scene you smell salty blood and burned flesh. You see scorched cars and broken glass and mutilated pieces that you may or may not immediately recognize as human corpses. People there, the bystanders, are hysterical; they scream and weep, and sometimes they yell at you. The people in uniform are officious and struggle to cover their rage. Then you go to an emergency room and interview the survivors, all of whom say exactly the same things, the same quotes, in their own tongues. Their minds linger in those bland seconds before the bomb went off. They were sitting in traffic, shifting weight in line, ordering a coffee. They were thinking about science projects, inlaws, what to eat for lunch. *Everything was normal,* most of them say. *Everything was fine.* And then violence reared up and smacked their little corner of the universe, and nothing was ever normal again, although that is not said, and must be inferred. Many people believe they saw the bomber seconds before he set off his charge. *He looked like a terrorist.* The Israelis said that. It meant, *He looked like an Arab.* Sometimes they describe a man, and the bomber turns out to have been a woman, or vice versa. It happens everywhere: you see somebody you don't like just before the explosion, and in your mind that person is fixed as the bomber. In Iraq, bystanders would swear they'd seen an American helicopter hovering overhead, firing down on the street. It is easier to blame a nemesis than to accept chaos as an everyday condition. *I saw the car coming too fast.* The Iraqis always said that. *I don't remember what it sounded like, I didn't hear anything,* some said, and then I knew they were very close, and lucky to be alive. *It knocked me off my feet. I went flying through the air.* They describe their return to consciousness, limbs and blood and people dying around them. *I saw a man, he was dead. I saw a woman, she had no arms.* At this point, everywhere in the world, survivors inevitably say:

*It was like something on TV.*

Or:

*It was like a movie.*

Fact: The contemporary human imagination cannot confront a suicide bomb without comparing it to pop culture.

There is a collective response to suicide bombings, the way a society toughens itself and rears up like a snake, and that is particular. Israel invades the West Bank or Gaza. Iraqi Shiites, after the walls of Iraq were smeared with their blood for a few years, organized militias and started kidnapping, torturing, and murdering Iraqi Sunnis. But in the moment, the smoky, bloody moment after the bomb has exploded in a fit of shrapnel and fire and force, there are only victims, their lives burned and their bodies broken to make a point. A suicide bomb is a political statement; it is intended that way. But it's hard to find politics in the particular. The particular is a great, dumb wash of blood. Israelis and Iraqis, two peoples with no common political ground or shared grievance, act the same roles, say the same words, stumble through the same grasping emotions.

We nosed into Mosul and roared along darkened streets that twisted and sprawled over the banks of the Tigris. Hours had passed since the bomber had targeted the Iraqi police. We would go straight to the hospital and look for survivors.

Picture them: Men standing in line on streets stained by age and blighted by blast barricades. They are working class, their clothes and shoes are scuffed. It is payday, and as they wait for their salaries, they pass cigarettes hand to hand. Nobody would work as a police officer in Iraq if he could help it. They are marked men, working for the occupation. But they have lived through everything so far and they are ready to keep going. Tomorrow is the holiday. They will spend their salary on a sheep or, if they can afford it, a straggly cow. Their families will gather and cheer as the men cut the animals' throats, offer the blood up to God, and pray for blessings in the months to come. These pleasant prospects hang in the cold, dusty air. And then the bomber's car barrels down out of the day because that is how death comes in Iraq—doubtless and too fast to duck.

The light in the hospital was frail, glistening on things like margarine. The air smelled sour, like medicine and rotten plums and fresh blood. Somebody screamed, the voice bouncing like a ball through the corridors. The ward was one long room, the cots next to each other. In each cot lay a bloody man, and each bedside was hung with faces. There were women in long black robes, and men with rumpled shirttails hanging over work pants. Some families leave the women at home. If the women were there, so were the sacks stuffed with spare clothes, crumbling cookies, hasty plastic things.

The chill of night had been banished by gas heaters. Hot, damp air pressed at the bodies, thinned toward the ceiling, swirled with the perfume of shitty bedsheets and puke-soaked mattresses and antiseptics. Needles jutted incongruously from veins. Men stumbled over IV drips, the old wheels of cots tripped their way over a gritty floor, the ward arranging itself. Sweat pushed through my skin, dampening the wool of my sweater, pooling at the waist of my corduroys.

We stood at a bedside and I forced myself to look at the wounded policeman. His face was cracked, and blood had seeped into the cracks and dried there. It didn't look like a face anymore; it looked like a broken plate that had been plastered back together with blood for glue. There were only his eyes, glittering with fever.

"They are really cowards," he was saying. "If they want to face us, let them do it man by man—but they'll never do that! Let them face me, man by man."

He was thirty-two years old, a checkpoint policeman. "I'd like to make a living for my family. There are no jobs," he said. He knew people loathed him as a symbol of the occupation, but he got up every morning and did the best he could. He complained about the terrorists, and the Americans too. They tell us to come pick up our weapons, he said, and then they never show up.

A relative at his bedside interrupted. Leaned over, butted in, eager to give an American a piece of his mind. I pretended he was not there. I looked at the wounded man, into his eyes. It disgusted me to look at his young, broken face, and I felt guilty. I was afraid he would see me shrink, and so I kept my eyes on him. I did not watch my pen loop across the page. He was getting off topic now, telling me about his work at the checkpoint, but I couldn't find my tongue to stop him. I felt vertigo, as if I were falling headfirst, swan-diving down into bloodshot eyes.

"Sometimes I'm seeing so much that is banned, but I'm forgiving him and letting him go," he was saying. "I'm treating people well."

Somebody moaned. The flesh inside my skin was turning to air, like I might float upward, drift and bump against that scarred ceiling, a dizzy balloon. "What do you remember about the attack?" I swallowed against my stomach. "What did you hear? What did you see?"

"I was standing near the barracks as soon as the explosion happened. I flew and fell down," he said slowly, eyes on the sheet. "I didn't understand anything. It was very strong . . ."

I sucked at the air, but it was full of the smell of the man's fresh wounds, infections fighting for his open flesh, his drying blood. I have a friend who is a doctor. She said to me once, in the singsong of a scientist tough enough to tinker with the truths of the flesh, "If you can smell it, it's inside of you." I have wished ever since that she had kept her mouth shut.

"I lost my sense," the man was saying. "I could only hear the assault rifle firing . . ."

With the salts of a stranger's blood in my nose, I squinted into my notebook, clenched the inner skin of my cheek between my teeth, and made myself write his words. The page looked dim and distant. Darkness started in a ring at the edges of vision and spilled inward, swallowing my sight from all sides. The world was an old movie coming to an end. I was going to faint.

"Excuse me." I staggered through the darkness, bumped into a wall, and slid to a floor littered with crusty bandages. Words punched through the dimness. They were surprised. Raheem stopped translating, embarrassed. The family jabbered, annoyed. The world returned, piece by piece, filling itself in.

"Just a minute," I muttered, raising my head. "I'm sorry. Just a minute."

My eyes collided with Raheem's, puzzled beneath white hair. "You have to be strong. We see this every day."

"I know," I said, staring miserably at the floor. "I'll be fine. I don't know why this is happening."

"Leave her alone," Nabil snapped. "She's sick."

But I knew Raheem was right. There was nothing wrong with me except that all the bombings I'd seen were running together, littering up the back of my mind. My body was shutting down in protest at the parade of broken humans. The same thing had happened a few days earlier, at another hospital. It would keep happening for months to come. I sat there on the floor, waiting for my head to clear, feeling small at Raheem's feet. When I could peel myself off the floor I slunk back to the man's bedside. The men in his family sneered. I asked a few more questions, feet planted on the linoleum, determined not to embarrass myself again. I wrote down the answers and we broke away. To do my job I needed only quotes and color; pieces of description and character. I had enough.

Outside, the night was cold and bright. I gulped the fresh air, grateful for the purity of open sky, the slap of cold on my face.

We spent the night in a drab hotel in Mosul and when morning came, we were finished with the bombing and nobody talked about it. Iraq was becoming a country that swallowed its violence and pressed forward. We were becoming people who did the same. The world starts moving fast around you and you move fast through it, too. One minute slurs into the next; the room and space renew; faces replace one another. You always think you will never forget this one moment, the one you stand in now, but it's not true. I'd forget everything by nightfall if I didn't write the details down. The more chaos, the worse my handwriting, but at least it's there. You snatch up crumbs as you go—a quote here, a bit of description there, moving through events, snorting the world up and swallowing it. At some point you think you have to stop being human or you can't do it anymore, but then you realize that your writing is nothing but your cut and impressed places.

Day creaked up slowly over the hills, and the city lay swaddled in the gentle ache of sleeplessness. Eid had come at last and I wanted to write something about violence, about ritual, about blood sacrifice and Iraq.

You probably know the story of the sacrifice, the centerpiece of Eid al-Adha. Christians and Jews have it too, though slightly modified. This is the story of Ibrahim, the Old Testament's patriarch Abraham. Although he is in his dotage, Ibrahim is finally a father to a beloved son, Ishmael. Just as the child is getting big enough to help with the chores, God puts Ibrahim through a test. He orders the father to slaughter his son, Ishmael. Poor, tortured Ibrahim. What can he do? The Lord giveth and the Lord taketh away. Now the Lord wants the boy back. So Ibrahim informs Ishmael that it's time to die. Ishmael accepts the news stoically, lies down, and offers his throat. Ibrahim holds the knife aloft. Just then, God shouts down from the sky. Hey, never mind! It's okay. I just wanted to see if you'd do it. Look, I'm sending you a ram, kill that instead. The child lives, the ram dies, and Ibrahim is celebrated down the ages as the creator's faithful servant.

The Old Testament has Isaac, not his brother Ishmael, nearly falling under Abraham's knife. And unlike the Koranic Ishmael, Isaac does not know he's about to die. He pipes up and reminds his father that they need an animal to sacrifice. Don't worry about it, Abraham replies darkly, God will provide us with something.

It's a hard story to love. Ibrahim, willing to obliterate his son to obey a voice from behind the clouds. A petulant God, subjecting his servants to loyalty tests. I meditated on Ibrahim in the Middle East and the more I thought about it, the less I liked the story and its suggestion that faith is enough to excuse the stain of violence. Ibrahim's God abruptly demands bloodletting in contravention of his own laws. Maybe it won't accomplish anything grand. Perhaps God would just like to see how far the faithful will follow. As for Ibrahim, he accepts on blind faith that the voice in the sky is not a dream or a hallucination, but marching orders from God himself. This, in fact, is his great virtue—that he doesn't question or argue. This is the moral of the story. Let us proclaim the mystery of faith, the Catholics say. The trouble is that, centuries later, the Middle East is still packed with murderers who believe they are doing God's will, privately attuned to the ring of God's voice. This is still how Middle Eastern battles are fought, by Arabs, Israelis, and now by Americans, too. Blind faith is the footbridge that takes us from virtuous religion to self-righteous violence. That day was the crystallization, a celebration of capricious mercy and murder in the name of faith.

In modern Iraq, families who lost loved ones in Iraq's many wars pour into graveyards to grieve at the tombs on Eid. Saddam Hussein would be hanged on Eid al-Adha in 2006, in an American-occupied Iraq, while Shiites taunted him. It just worked out that way, officials said.

The stringer arrived before dawn to take us to the cemetery. She had cotton-white skin and black robes, and when she came into the room they whispered that her father was a martyr. His name was Ahmed Shawkat; he was a journalist and a Shabak Kurd, a member of an ethnic and cultural minority centered around Mosul. He ran a newspaper and had written a book on the controversial topic of Mosul's founding; his efforts had earned him death threats. One day he climbed onto the roof to use his satellite phone. Somebody stole up behind and shot him at close range. They found Ahmed Shawkat sprawled in blood. There was nothing very unusual in this story, only that he was her father, and now she lived under the martyr's mantle. She had been awake for hours when she arrived at the hotel in the dark. She had already gone to the graveyard alone, to pay her respects.

Sun cracked the horizon at the cemetery, and the land breathed with tides of mourners who pushed and paused, wandering from one family tombstone to the next. Early spring had breathed on the hills, but the tang of cold bit our faces and numbed our fingers. Beggars came, and children, trailing over grass rich as felt. Graves sprouted Iraqi flags, crossed daggers, pierced hearts. Sticks of incense smoked and trashy sweets glistened from the earth. Women keened over graves, singing songs of doomsday: "The God who created heaven and earth can do the same again. If he wants it to be, he'll say, 'be.' "

A twenty-nine-year-old man named Ahmed Younis Muhammed stood over the grave of his oldest brother. Like thousands of his countrymen, the brother had been shot dead in the epic folly of the Iran–Iraq war. Muhammed's family had been suffering ever since: he couldn't find a job, and they could hardly make ends meet.

I asked him whether his family would slaughter an animal that day. He winced.

"We don't have anything to sacrifice," he said, quietly and deliberately. "We have sacrificed enough. We've spent our lives sacrificing. All we do in this country is sacrifice."

Blackbirds circled overhead. Little girls in brilliant dresses blew along the paths like loose petals and, crying and singing, kissed the dirt. Flapping cloth and robes gave the feel of row after row of clothesline. Our heavy-eyed stringer ghosted along before us. The fresh green smell of earth wouldn't leave my nose, life exerting itself on a field of death.

Soon we left the graveyard and went looking for an animal sacrifice. When we saw a truck cruising past with a lamb in the bed, we followed. We lost the lamb, but wound up on a side street where we caught sight of a young cow being led through a gate. This was the home of a merchant named Jamal Almola. He was a mountain of a man with a thick mustache; he wore bright white robes and his family huddled around his table, drinking sweet juices in anticipation of their feast. While we all stood around introducing ourselves, the cow hoofed at the driveway nervously, tied near the marigolds.

What does it mean, I asked Jamal Almola, this blood sacrifice?

"This is like a prayer," he said. "We will give the meat to poor families, to help the poor families."

The cow snorted in panic.

I tried to get Jamal Almola to speak more expansively about the slaughter, but he was having too good a time. He brushed the questions aside, urging juice upon us and begging us to stay for dinner.

The children watched while the men held the cow down on the threshold of the house. They turned its face toward Mecca, and a relative named Rashid cut its throat. The cow did not die quickly. It shivered and twitched. The blood bubbled and surged, swelling over the pavement. The children giggled and knelt down, poking their palms into the blood, playing with it. The men hacked the warm cow into pieces. We kept stepping back delicately, farther and farther, trying to find a spot of dry ground. But the blood grew; it followed us over the soil. It was swallowing everything. Finally I gave up and knew it would stain me, too.

---

The sky was still steel overhead, and the city had the drained-away swoon of a holiday in progress. We would eat, we would leave, we would drive back to Baghdad . . . but the satellite phone rang. It always started like that, breaking through the conversation.

There had been suicide bombings in Kurdistan, at the headquarters of the two main Kurdish parties. There were a lot of people dead. How many? A lot, a lot. Dozens, for sure. Maybe seventy. Maybe a hundred. We were the closest and so we should rush there as fast as we could. In my mind I released the story of sacrifice as I'd released so many other stories when news broke—let go the string and let it rise into the sky until it disappeared.

Driving into the mountains of Kurdistan is like leaving Iraq for another country. The Kurds are not Arabs. They had problems of their own—the civil war fought among Kurdish parties; the armed Muslim fundamentalists the Kurds had allowed to flourish in the hills near the Iranian border. But there were moments when the rest of Iraq came barreling up to Kurdistan, and all their internal rivalries drifted off as light as blown dandelion seeds, forgotten for the night and collected again in the morning. This was one of those times: suicide bombers had blown themselves up at the same minute in the headquarters of the two rival political parties. Because it was a holiday, the party faithful—the men and their children—had called on the headquarters to pay respects. The message was meant for all Kurds, and it was not hard to translate: We hate you, and we will slaughter you.

We found Irbil smothered in thick clouds. A cold nosebleed of rain dripped down over empty streets. By then we knew at least one hundred were dead, maybe more. A middle-aged man limped through the wet dimness, his pants and shirt smeared with blood. He was cut by shrapnel and he was in shock, stumbling homeward.

"We didn't feel anything," he told us woodenly. "The place. It was all fire and smoke. Until now, I cannot hear anything."

He had gone to pay his respects to the Kurdish Democratic Party. He had been caught up in the explosion, and now he wandered the streets.

"Why do you think this is happening?" I asked.

"You understand the matter better than I do," he said coldly, staring at my American face.

It was quiet for a minute. I heard Raheem groping for another way to phrase the question. The man snorted.

"This is the freedom of sacrifice," he said. "It seems we must sacrifice for Iraq's freedom. First we got rid of a bloody regime, and now we must sacrifice still more blood."

And then he limped off, into the rainy night, into the great uncertainty of Kurdistan and Iraq beyond.

A long driveway stretched down and then twisted around to the side of the Patriotic Union of Kurdistan. Kurds came from the shadows, gathered around, and bore us inside. They were angry and they wanted to show their wounds to the world. Tattered party streamers still flapped in the naked winter trees. A green banner announced: *We welcome our respected guests.*

A hurricane had been locked inside the main hall. The couches were blasted open, the tiles peeled down from the ceiling, speakers thrown askew, empty plastic chairs strewn like toys. Plastic flowers oozed on the ground, scorched and gummy. There were tangles of ribbon, hats, and shoes that had been blown off the victims. Children's shoes, too, and gaudy little hats like Easter bonnets. I looked at all those hats and shoes and knew the people who had put them on this morning were probably dead. We were stepping around in wet puddles, and in the back of my mind I was remembering the cow, and the spreading tide of its blood. It seemed like a long time ago. But this is not blood, I told myself, this will be . . . water from broken pipes, or gasoline, or just anything else, something ordinary, the fluids of a building. But then I looked down and saw what I'd already known: Blood. Puddles of blood spread over the floor, and pieces of flesh floated in the red slicks. It was on my shoes; I waded in it. Animal blood in the morning and human blood by nightfall. The blood was fresh under my feet.

One day killed the next in Iraq, and the months rose up to murder their forebears, and it all piled up into one year and then the next. The blood kept flowing until it covered everything.

It was getting harder and harder to find a piece of dry ground.

# NINE

# WE EXPECTED SOMETHING BETTER

What kind of place would Jordan be if it weren't marooned on the map between the West Bank and Iraq? By now the country has been shaped by neighboring wars—census redrawn by the massive resettlement of Palestinian refugees, politics defined by making nice, memories stained by spillover fighting. And yet, in itself, Jordan doesn't leave a deep impression. As capital cities go, Amman is bland: A spread of hotel lobbies and snips of desert and sleepy hills; a sand-hued turnstile churning the somnambulant traveler from one vivid elsewhere to the next. It is a city trading on its placid nature, destined and designed to be passed through on the way to, or from, bigger problems.

It was 2004, the time of year when gritty winter still clings to the landscape, and the sky sagged heavy as a damp sheet onto Amman's seven hills. Nora* shushed up to the curb in a car thick with perfume and pop music. It would have to be Mecca Mall, she said. We didn't have much time.

"Hey," she pointed at a minivan up ahead. "I think that's a *mouse*." This was Nora's code. It meant "I think that's an intelligence agent."

"How can you tell?"

"The picture of *flower*. Look how big it is. The *mice* love those pictures. They all have them." ("The picture of the king. Look how big it is. Intelligence agents love those pictures. They all have them.")

---

* A pseudonym.

"I see them everywhere."

"Well . . ." She tugged at the wheel. "There are a lot of *mice*."

I knew something was wrong when I sat across from her at the café. Nora's face played emotions like a movie screen—the jellyfish squeeze of her pupils dilating and contracting, catching pieces of light, the half smile that hung on her lips, always about to stretch into a shout of laughter that would rock her frame and squeeze her eyes shut. Today her shoulders hung low and her features had a vacant look. She had pulled her personality back, buried it deeper in her head.

"Are you okay?"

"Yes, Megan," she said with rote cordiality. "I'm fine. How are you?"

I laughed. "I'm fine, too." She laughed too, a quick stab, and then her face sank back into ashy stillness.

"I can't believe this about Abu Ghraib," she said.

So that was it.

"I know," I said.

I wasn't supposed to have met her at all; it was a mix-up from the start. That had been more than a year earlier, when the invasion of Iraq was just beginning. I was stranded in Amman, waiting to go to Baghdad. For the time being everybody was frozen in place, the border closed, and the road to Baghdad a cemetery of bombed-out cars. Reporters stuffed Amman's hotels, steaming and scheming into their beer at night. They twitched with plans to sneak into Iraq, or they had been in Baghdad already but lost their nerve and fled Saddam and his alleged arsenal of mass destruction. We all had the smell of meat in our noses, close but out of reach; we were crazed with hunger, not for a story, but for *the* story. Reporters begged for Iraqi visas from the embassy of a nearly defunct government, and waited for permits from the Jordanians to drive to the Iraqi border. We hunted for generators, stocked up on Cipro, piled helmets and flak jackets against minibars.

Spring came too early and too hot that year. Sandstorms clawed at buildings and machines. Fog came in the morning and bound the city blind, wrapped like bandages around the buildings. In these glaring, wilting hours, the televisions squawking nervously about collateral damage and new world order were as obscene as anything you can imagine. The invasion began and blood wafted over the sands, over the border, on eye-stinging winds. Amman filled with people and the people kept talking and all that gas built into pressure, sizzled like carbonation through the nightclubs and bars, hissed down the highways at night and punched lonely border outposts. Jordanians, aid workers, Iraqis who'd gotten out all mixed together, everybody on edge, angling and outraged. There were no proper nouns except Iraq and the Americans, Saddam and Bush and Blair. Waitresses plodded up behind glazed faces; sad hotel clerks stared over teeming lobbies; cashiers dropped coins into white hands with a sneer. The truth of the invasion was new and angry. It had been a suggestion that seemed impossible until, with the smooth birth of enormous news, it became real. Some faceless pilot dropped the first bomb into Baghdad and the war had come. Arab countries melted into pure rhetoric. People shouted about the Americans and spat on the ground to clear their mouths of bile. The Americans would take over all Arab lands. There was no more United Nations, no more decency, no more rules. This is terrorism! They are the terrorists! George Bush is a terrorist! The Americans wanted land and oil, they hated Muslims, and they were doing it all for Israel. This was the new face of colonialism. American power would redraw the borders. And the Arabs wouldn't stand for it. They would fight to the bitter end, every last one, the portly man smoking in his great-grandfather's coffee shop, the pampered middle-aged princess with her Botoxed forehead and husband's crooked bank accounts, the calloused farmers of the Nile Delta.

Earnest aid workers rigged refugee camps in the eastern desert. They thought it would be that kind of war, that refugees would straggle out and live in tents. Everybody imagined how the war would be and set things up for the war they had conjured. But you can't see a war before it's happened. Those tents stood nearly empty for months, irrelevant crusts on the edge of a sinking country. The first refugees cruised into Amman in gleaming cars with smoked windows. They sweated filthy dollars, bought posh flats, and drove the price of real estate through the sky. Saddam's daughters flounced through the beauty parlors. It was that sort of war. But in the beginning nobody knew.

Then the twitching, sand-blind city stared down the first Friday after the U.S. invasion began, and news spread: The clerics would sermonize about the evils of war, and then people would rampage in the streets. It was a useful idea, because inaction was driving everybody crazy. Maybe the government could have stopped it, but then a clever regime bends so as not to break; this is otherwise known as staying power. All that anger shouldn't fester; it had to find release. So it would go into the streets, but only in a flash, as a quick demonstration of the travails the monarchy faced in keeping the people's passions in check. It would show the Americans how their invasion made everything harder for this benevolent government with the pretty, plucky queen, and let the Arab brethren see that Egypt and Syria weren't the only ones who got into a lather for the Great Arab Cause. Yes, Friday riots were the answer. Everybody had something to gain, and so did we, because the reporters were pent up and chomping for a story. Friday is the Muslim Sabbath, and everybody goes to the mosque to hear the sermons. It was a good day to whip up the crowds.

Friday came and I overslept, woke up, and called the *L.A. Times* translator, Nour.* She was snippy. We had never met. "I'll be in the street with some other journalists," she said. "You can meet me there." I heard small children yelling in the background.

"What street?"

"Near the al-Husseini mosque."

"*What* mosque?"

"Al-Husseini!"

"Where is it?"

"It's—it's downtown," she sighed heavily. "The taxi drivers will know. Okay?" She hung up.

Creaking cars and tinted Mercedes and policemen jammed the streets. Koranic verses moaned from streaked windows. The taxi wove and wheedled downtown until the driver's weary gestures indicated it would be faster to walk. As I pushed through the crowds in the shadow of dingy apartment blocks and dreary offices, I dialed and redialed Nour, hearing busy signals.

Then I saw them: a cluster of jeans-clad foreign journalists, cameras

* A pseudonym.

swinging from their necks, all of them clumped around a young Arab woman who chattered into her telephone as if she were alone. I planted myself in front of her and stared until she hung up. "Hello," I said.

"Hello," she said.

"Are you Nour?"

"*Nora*," she said archly. "Do I know you?"

"I'm Megan. From the *L.A. Times*. We talked a while ago. We were supposed to meet."

"I don't think so."

"You were supposed to translate for me."

"I don't know who you are," she said lightly. "But I'd be happy to help you."

I sighed. "We just talked on the phone."

"Well," she said, "Why don't we walk together anyway, and I'll help you out."

She had been herding us along as we talked, Nora the Pied Piper of pale and gangly journalists, and now we had reached the old mosque. Piled rose-and-white limestone in the oldest quarter of Amman, the mosque is not far from the skeleton of the Roman amphitheater, and they say it was set on the ruins of the Temple of Philadelphia. But whatever splendor graced this valley in the days of the Romans has been rubbed away by centuries. Wealthy Jordanians didn't stay in the tight, shabby streets of downtown; they climbed up the hills and into the desert to build lavish white houses. At the al-Husseini mosque, poor men peddled slabs of cardboard for makeshift prayer rugs and knelt down like ragged flowers in a stained concrete garden. The voice of the preacher piped through a loudspeaker.

"The Arab nation is being humiliated because we are not religious enough," Nora translated. "The Arab nation tasted humiliation because we do not pray enough.

"If we unite as Arabs, we will win this war. This war is a sign for us to move forward and do something about our nation."

Not very radical, I thought. Whatever happens, this cleric will be able to say it wasn't his fault. Rings of praying men radiated from the mosque, a field of timeworn carpet and bowed heads. Everybody was tensed. It was coming and we waited. The prayers ended and the men stood, dusted off their dishdashas and the knees of their slacks. The street was crowded as a circus and silent as a cemetery. More men poured from the dim recesses of the mosque. Eyes flicked around, wary. Who would start the demonstration? They had so little practice.

A knot of men broke from the shadows and charged into the street, words in their throats and fists in the sky, screaming the timeless incantation of Arab dictatorship:

*Bil roh! Bil dam! Nafdeek, ya Saddam!*

With our souls, with our blood, we will sacrifice for you, O Saddam. This is shouted in every single Arab country; only the name changes. We will sacrifice for you, O Mubarak, we will sacrifice for you, O Rafik, we will sacrifice for you, O Bashar, we will sacrifice for you, O Islam, O Nasrallah, O Sheikh Yassin. In every Arab country, crowds of young men rush into the street to holler about sacrificing soul and blood for a dictator. It's the cave art of political discourse, done as automatically as American students pledge allegiance to the flag of the United States of America and to the republic, etcetera. Except these men are not passive, muttering their lines, hands limp on their hearts. They flame with rage and fierce pride. And then, through some alchemy, it cakes off like dried dust and blows away. The feeling is there, and then it is not. I looked many times at these skinny men with their thin mustaches and injured eyes, watched their mouths stretch and snap around the words. They looked back at me with hatred and yet it was tainted with confusion over which they hated more: themselves and their circumstances, or me standing there staring. Could they even say themselves, could they sort through the palpable indignity of having to cheer for an abusive power, through the vague pride and eagerness to please authority that rang in their voices?

*With our souls! With our blood!*

Disorder had been induced, the shouting scared away the pigeons, and after that nobody needed a prompt. The men who lurked cagily on the stained old streets, waiting for somebody else to get things started—they joined in, too. They punched at the sky, screamed for Iraq and Saddam, cursed America and Israel. The protestors emptied the dirty air from their lungs, the chains loosened for just this one afternoon, just this hour, just this place smeared with sun until it looked like a dream of itself. Nora stood unabashed in her short sleeves and blue jeans, hair knotted back into a ponytail, bangs dripping into her eyes, translating the chants, matter of fact and unreadable.

Rows of riot police stomped up a side street, gripping shields and clubs for beating. The demonstrators marched toward them, screaming their chants.

I put my hand on Nora's back. "We're in the wrong place," I had to yell. "We're going to get stuck in between them."

"I think it's okay," she said. "So far it's calm."

"It won't stay calm. Watch."

The crowd had thickened by then, swollen and scraping against the shuttered market stalls, too big for the cramped stone streets. The police sticks pointed skyward, and the afternoon collapsed in running. Shoes slammed on hard streets. Every shop was a blank eyelid, screwed tight. There was nowhere to escape and so we ran with the demonstrators, riot police at our backs, swinging their clubs, thwacking at any limb, any spine. These were not hardened activists; these were middle-aged Arab men whose resolve vanished at the first smack of club on skin. Their hands thumped against our shoulders, shoved us aside. Panic turned to stampede and we raced blind through bodies slamming blindly into bodies, bone on bone and muscle on muscle, ragged breath, and clothes snagging on the sides of buildings.

Somebody was shouting and we turned to see a shopkeeper holding a demonstrator by the collar, punching him in the face, over and over. "Get out of my store!" he yelled hysterically, thrusting the man into the stampede. Somebody had found an open door and we jammed ourselves through, ran up one flight of wobbling stairs after the next, hunting for a window. Sweating, shaking, laughing. Nora was silent. Her enormous brown eyes flickered.

"Are you okay?" I asked.

"Yes," she said. "This is great."

I worked my cell phone out of my jeans pocket. I had a message from Nour: Are you here? I stared at it, frowning.

"Wait," I said to Nora. "So you're not Nour."

"I'm Nora."

"You don't work for the *Los Angeles Times*."

"No."

"And we didn't talk on the phone this morning."

"No," she said, and a laugh spread across her face.

"Oh my God. I'm so sorry. You must have thought I was crazy. I thought you were somebody else. I never met our fixer here, I don't know what she looks like."

"Megan," she cut me off. "It's no problem."

She started giggling. I started giggling.

"Hey," I said, "we can't really see anything from here. You want to go back out?"

She did.

It took police half an hour to haul the last diehard protestors into paddy wagons. When they finished, the shopkeepers unlocked the metal screens and threw open their dens. Clumsy racks sprouting feather dusters and baseball caps resurrected themselves from the bed of concrete. The men hauled out old chairs, lit coals for their water pipes, and sat smoking, eyes fixed over the street as if nothing had passed.

Nora packed us into her car and whisked us off to a café. Here the Jordanians were young and lithe with designer eyeglasses, tight jeans, and flirty glances. Pop music bounced off walls the color of watermelon. It felt insane to be here, insane that this was the same country as the sweaty, tumultuous warrens of downtown an hour earlier. Do these kids even know about the demonstration? Nora shrugged. They are not interested, she said.

One of the journalists in our group is talking about the men who follow him from his hotel.

Nora frowns. "Shhhhhhh."

"It's not safe to talk here?"

"It's not safe to talk *any*where."

We fall quiet. Then Nora says, "Here's what we do, guys, okay? My friends and I have a system we use so we can talk. It's like a code. Like, we say 'flower'—what do you think that means?"

The queen? Somebody guesses.

"Her husband."

*Flower* means "king."

*Mouse* means "intelligence agent."

These days, Jordan is full of *mice*. Everybody is afraid of them. They have never been so prevalent, or so powerful. Why? Because *flower* is scared. He's very close to the West, which is not popular, especially since the Palestinian intifada, the war in Afghanistan, and now this war in Iraq. *Flower* was educated in English, people criticize his Arabic. Since September 11, it seems like everything is illegal. There are a lot of things the Jordanian newspapers won't print; they just can't. After September 11, there were even more red lines and topics that angered the government.

What are the repercussions, we ask.

Actually, she says, it's like a point system. The first time, if you mess up, say they know you said something bad about *flower*, you get called in. They might give you a warning. The second time, they might give you a beating. The third time, you're going to prison. Roughly like that.

Nora closed her mouth as the waiter drew near. The girl at the next table wiggled her shoulders and sipped through her straw, eyes locked on her boyfriend. The music pumped on.

After the United States invaded Iraq, my job got more complicated. Suddenly it was a tiresome problem, being an American. My nationality invaded every interview. If I wanted to talk about agriculture or mosque renovation, we'd end up dissecting America first. Every Arab had a detailed critique of U.S. foreign policy, and no intention of missing his chance to unburden all that outrage into the ear of an honest-to-God American. If I were strategically smart, I'd listen sympathetically to the complaints about America's basic moral unseemliness, my silence a delicate, implicit apology. And then, after I'd scraped and nodded and mm-hmmed, I could wedge in a few questions. Stay cordial, I'd remind myself. You catch more flies with honey.

But I couldn't always do it. I didn't have the patience.

"You don't really have a democracy in America. I know you're not free to write what you see. You can only write what the government allows you to write. You don't have to pretend with me. I know how it works."

"America used to be a great, powerful country. Now you let the Israelians run everything. The government and the business, too. The Israelians knew about September 11. Why is America so blind?"

"How did the United States elect this Bush? We thought Americans were intelligent but now we see that they are not."

Sitting there, I'd get agitated. I didn't rub this man's nose in his country's corrupt, cruel leaders, or remind him of the shame of living quietly inside a dictatorship, impotent amid torture and censorship. I did not force him to represent his government. And yet I could not expect the favor to be returned, because my own government dripped with strength. As a citizen of an invading power, I could be called to account. My leg bounced wildly, my eyes narrowed, I dropped the pretense of taking notes. When you stop writing, people always notice.

"Write this down, please," he intoned condescendingly.

"I don't need to. I've heard it before, and it has nothing to do with the story I'm working on."

Then a flash of shame, seeing myself through his eyes, brittle and snappy. I'd try to smooth things down.

"Look, I understand what you are saying. But we are not in Baghdad and I am not here to write about the invasion of Iraq. I'm writing about this other thing. So please, I am asking you, can we talk about that instead?"

It was hard to stomach. People who lived under the thumbs of dictators could look at America with a gleeful sneer: Look how your strong country has been drawn into a trap that will cost you dearly. Now we see that America, too, is criticized by the international human rights organizations. Now we see how America can sap its own strength. Now we see how the mighty stumble.

But there was always Nora. I'd find her leaning in the marble corner of some hotel lobby, in the shadow of lily stalks. Her car was with the valet. She did not so much drive as slide through the city, slipping crookedly over lanes, giggling when the horns honked. Somebody would pull up and wave. "Oh, it's a friend of my father's."

As soon as we were in the car, she was spilling out the things she'd saved to say. "Did you see that story in *The New Yorker*? What did you think?"

Nora had earned a bachelor's degree at a small university in the United States, and she filled my ears with stories about the professors she missed, nights out trolling the clubs, her visits to New York City. She had an imprint of America on her—not the menacing America in fatigues and boots, but the America that Americans know instinctively, the open, eager, optimistic one.

Nora was in her mid-twenties then but she seemed even younger. She moved slowly, looking and listening and drawing everything in to someplace deep and out of reach. She seemed to have no convictions, but in a good way, in a young, deciding way, and she met all people and scenes with flat frankness, dutifully picking up more material to put on her scales, to weigh out her beliefs, as if this were a lifelong project, as if it might take decades. She asked questions about everything, and she read religiously, especially American coverage of the Middle East. She was always dressed expensively, her makeup carefully done. Her family had money.

"Okay, where do you want to go?" Very serious all of a sudden, fiddling with the radio. Businesslike. That made me laugh. Whenever I laughed, she laughed. I could feel the weight slipping off—the airports and strangers and long, sleepless nights. I was so often with people who made me nervous, and now I laughed with relief, she laughed for company, we'd laugh constantly. We'd trade stories about what we'd been up to. Telling Nora about things, they didn't seem so bad.

"What are the choices?"

"Maybe Italian. There's a new place. Or the Blue Fig, you know that. Or we can have sushi."

"Is the sushi good?"

"Yes, it's very good."

"Then I say sushi."

"There's one thing, though, Megan. You might think it's strange."

"What?" I was laughing already.

"It's at the Best Western!"

"The Best Western!"

"But I swear, it's good, you'll see. If you think it's bad we'll leave."

"I'm sure it's great." Laughing from low in my seat.

Through the yellow light of a cramped lobby to a creaking elevator that pushes us up. The doors open and we hear tinkling china, braided voices. Every wall is a great window. Amman is spread at our feet, a winking, bejeweled carpet. Fish gleams under glass.

"What do you think, is it all right?"

"It's all right."

Late one sticky summer night, Nora and I walked through Abdoun Circle, looking for ice cream. At this hour the shops and cafés were crammed with Kuwaitis, Emiratis, and Saudis. They shrank from the heat of day; it was never too late for them to pace the streets, thobes swishing around their legs, fidgeting endlessly with their red-checked headdresses and unfathomable cell phones. They rented luxury cars and choked the roads with late-night traffic. Cigarettes dangled into the dark; hubcaps gleamed wicked under the streetlights; 50 Cent and Amr Diab churned in the desert air. Some of them drove all the way here from Saudi Arabia or Qatar. These were not the richest Gulf Arabs, because if they had serious oil money, or the kind of influence known as *wasta,* they'd be in Europe. But they were plenty rich all the same, and they came every year to hide from the Persian Gulf summer in the cooler places—Cairo, Damascus, Beirut, or Amman. They are an invasion and the locals complain, but only behind their backs, because you can't insult their cash. In Egypt I'd had my ass squeezed in an elevator, with a hissed "What are you doing tonight?" I'd watched a drunken Saudi yank sadistically on the testicles of the emaciated and crumbling singer at a cheap, smoky bellydance club, and the guy was so broke and beholden he just doubled over and smiled, sickly, as his cracked voice creaked on. They sat in horse-drawn carriages and threw firecrackers at the poor Egyptian kids who hung out on the bridges over the Nile, watching them scatter and screaming with laughter.

We passed a pair of twenty-something Saudi guys, wandering along in their robes. As soon as we were out of earshot, Nora turned her face to me in astonishment.

"Do you know what they just said?"

"What?"

"One of them said to the other, 'Look, they are from the enemy.' They were talking about us. They thought we were Americans because we were speaking English."

"I am American."

"Megan! That's so crazy."

"No, you know what's crazy? That they were eating McDonald's."

"Oh my God."

We laughed and laughed under the trashy neon stars.

And now we were here, Nora with her slumped shoulders and drawn face, looking empty because of Abu Ghraib, and I trying to find, not the right words, but first the right feeling.

By that time, I was steeped in torture. The Middle East was divided into three classes: the torturers, the tortured, and those who stayed out of the way. Filthy things happened in back rooms, people were driven mad by torment, and slick rulers lounged on top of it all. It seemed like half the people I interviewed had been tortured. Worse, half the people I hired had been tortured. The news assistant in Cairo, Hossam, had been tortured for organizing political demonstrations when he was a student at the American University in Cairo. A translator in Morocco had been tortured so hard for so long that he could hardly walk, and one awful morning he started yelling about it in the middle of an interview. You got tortured for being too religious, for being too left-leaning, for being gay, for marching in protests, for blogging, for refusing to pay a police bribe. People were raped and sodomized; waterboarded; electrocuted, cut, beaten, frozen, burned. I met an Iranian blogger my age who made me cry, talking about how he'd been broken behind bars, about how even in freedom he lay sleeplessly in his bed and wept, too ashamed to tell his mother the truth of what had happened to him. Torture lurks at every single level of the Middle East. It's in the fiber of the place.

"It's pretty bad, huh, Megan."

"Yeah. It's bad," I said. "But are you really surprised?"

Her eyes flickered. "Yes," she said. "Of course!"

"But Nora, it's a war. These soldiers are kids. What do you think happens?"

"But Megan," her habit of repeating my name sounded, now, like an accusation. "This is the Americans."

"But at least it's coming out. At least at some point the system worked. It got found out by investigative journalism. And now people will get punished."

"Yes. I know that's true. But Megan, don't you think this is really bad for the United States, to have people seeing these photographs?"

"Worse than invading Iraq in the first place?"

"This is different."

"Why?" Why was I doing this? Of course it was bad for America; of course, in its way, it was worse. The photographs had made me feel sick. But I could not bring myself to tell Nora, and I couldn't understand why.

"This is worse. It makes everything that's happening in Iraq worse. It shows it in a different light." She said the last sentence slowly, like she was reading it from a paper.

"But Nora . . ." The sentence fell off in a sigh. All the questions were piled up in my throat: *Did you really believe in us? Did you think we came to Iraq to fight a noble war, did you honestly think that? Don't you see what we have done?* It felt foreign, suddenly, the two of us. After all our conversations about war, about Israel, about America, these photographs were stuck between us like a thorn tree, pricking our hands when we tried to reach through. Her fingers twisted and worked, and a forgotten coffee steamed into the afternoon.

"I mean . . . Nora, what did you think would happen when the U.S. started a war with Iraq? It's a *war*. And—God, I sound like I'm defending what these soldiers did. I'm not. I'm absolutely not. But—I guess I'm just surprised by your reaction. It's not like you were supporting the war until now."

"They said they were coming to bring something better than Saddam Hussein."

"Is that what you think this war is about?"

Nora studied her sleeves.

"I interview people every day, all over the Arab world, and I never meet anybody who thinks the Americans invaded Iraq because they don't like dictators."

"But Megan, people believe in the Americans."

"Who?" My voice was bitter. "Why? Where?"

Then I looked at her, and I understood what she was saying. In fact, people did not believe in the Americans. But Nora had. Nora had loved America, and she had stood up for it, not so much in words as in deeds. She had embraced the Americans she met, aspired to American-style journalism, traveled to America to be educated.

"Americans are the ones who always say that America is the model," she said weakly.

There were a lot of things I wanted to say, but it was all wedged too deep. I wanted to tell her about rural America, about all the different classes and experiences and geographies she hadn't penetrated when she'd studied in New York. About the cruelties and brutalities of American history that she could not intuit, the things that dragged behind my country. Just as I could not hope to understand the men who hollered for Saddam, she could not make any sense of the soldiers at Abu Ghraib. We were both just crusts of deep and complex icebergs, the small pieces that poked over the water and showed themselves to one another. At the end we were standing side by side, just standing there and looking, like that first day when we'd met, Nora with her bangs in her eyes and her bright red T-shirt watching the praying Muslims at the mosque and waiting for the riot to begin. I was thinking of police beatings, prison rape, racial tensions; about lost suburban youth; about senseless, sadistic crime I'd covered in stifled, silent, dying small towns, the America that Nora didn't see, in all its ugly complications and rotting institutions. I wanted to say, if you believed in the place before, don't stop because of this. But it was more, too, and all these thoughts and memories spun through, fast, and so I started blurting things out.

"You know, I really don't understand the Arab reaction to all of this. I just don't. In these countries, people get tortured every day. And nobody says a word about it. And then the Americans are exposed and everybody wants to talk about that. Why don't all these Arabs who are so angry at the Americans deal with their own leaders? Why don't they demand something better from their own governments?"

Nora gave me a look I'd seen many times, but never on her face. It was resentment, impatience.

"But *Megan*," she said slowly, "that's the point. We don't expect anything from the Arab governments. We expect something better from the Americans. That is the *idea* of America."

"After everything that's happened? Seriously?"

"I thought so," she said. Then she got quiet. Her eyes were down again, and I thought she was about to cry.

But she held it together and we sat there while piped music wove its canned dreams through sterilized air. Boys in spiked hair and slender women in *hijab* poured through the shining caverns of this shopping mall named after Mecca—rich Iraqi refugees and the rich Jordanians who resented them, buying American sneakers and Chinese microwaves with their British credit cards. Nora was an Arab and I was an American, after all. That distinction grew up like a wall, and we each sat on our separate sides, sipping at our cappuccinos, groping around for words, both of us polite to the end but not bothering to pretend this could be repaired.

I saw Nora again the next time I came to Amman. We ate sushi and neither of us breathed a word about Abu Ghraib. Not too long after, Nora left Jordan to go to graduate school in the United States.

She didn't like it nearly so much the second time around.

## TEN

# A QUESTION OF COST

It was the kind of lazy, sun-dappled day made for lemonade and swimming pools, and kids all over the compound banged through screen doors with the taste of summer freedom in their mouths. It was the weekend, and men in primordial hunches grunted along sidewalks in headphones and jogging shorts, teenagers wheeling past on bicycles.

"I can't get over how American it is here," I said vaguely to Valerie. She laughed an airy laugh and said, "Yeah, that *Leave It to Beaver* thing." Yeah, I thought. A world bleached clean of traffic and bad moods and fights that couldn't be set right within half an hour—the America that America had never been.

Valerie was an aerobics instructor and the wife of an American oil worker. I'd gotten her name from a woman in Riyadh; they had met at a Girl Scout convention in Kuwait. Well, great, come on over, Valerie chirped when I called. A towering blonde with bright blue eyes, fine features, and a southern lilt, she picked me up from the front gate in a Land Rover. Her yellow hair gleamed and bounced, fresh from a hair dryer and unwilted by a head scarf. The bronzed run of flesh from her fingertips to shoulder stretched bare. Outside the gates, back in the real Saudi Arabia, she could have been caned and jailed for any number of sins. But we were in the compound now. I slithered out of my *abaya* and felt my limbs go suddenly light, as if I had peeled Saudi Arabia itself off my back.

Here in the far stretches of the kingdom, the compound was a hologram of America complete with baseball diamonds, a cheery library stocked with English titles, and lawns sprinkler drenched in defiance of a withering Arabian sun. Smooth, flat streets vein the desert with implacable American nomenclature: Rainbow Road, Golf Course Boulevard, and Prairie View Circle. On the edge of the Persian Gulf, near the hardscrabble towns of chronically disadvantaged Saudi Shiites, the compound cradles the workers of the Saudi Arabian American Oil Company, Saudi Aramco for short, the government-owned corporation trafficking in the world's largest proven oil reserves.

For decades, thousands of foreigners have hidden behind walls in Saudi Arabia, barricaded against the kingdom's stringent code of public morals. The compounds boasted smuggled whiskey and bathtub gin, outlawed Christian services, and pools where men and women mingled illegally. Saudi Arabia stayed outside the gates; within, the capitalized West thrummed along. But now, in the summer of 2004, an insurgency battered Saudi Arabia's expatriate housing compounds and oil facilities. Militants rammed car bombs into apartment blocks, attacked government ministries, and gunned down BBC reporters. It wouldn't be long before they sawed the head off an American helicopter engineer and stored it in a refrigerator. One bright day in May, they had dragged a dead American oil worker into a schoolyard to preach about the murdered Muslims of Fallujah. The insurgents worked languidly, as if time meant nothing, and everybody was muttering about whether Saudi law enforcement was infiltrated by jihadis. Answers and information were scarce. This is a Saudi problem, inscrutable Saudi officials said, and only Saudis know how to handle it. They droned on about tribes and families, swore that everybody was against terrorism and that, despite appearances, everything was under control. Still the violence kept coming, cracking the calm of desert life and turning the compounds into strategic forts. The walls and guards, once a protection from the cultural nuisance of strict laws, were now a barricade against mayhem. America was fading into armed fortresses, first in Iraq and now in Saudi Arabia.

A few days before I visited Valerie at Aramco, insurgents had stormed the nearby Oasis compound and killed twenty-two people, almost all of them foreigners. The Oasis was an unremarkable warren of palm groves and condominiums under red tile roofs. The gunmen stalked the grounds hunting for non-Muslims, and spared the infidels no mercy. An Italian and a Swede were butchered, their throats cut like animals. Others were shot dead. When they tired of slaughtering non-believers, the insurgents simply scrambled up an artificial waterfall, clambered over the back wall, and evaporated. This should have been impossible. Eight hundred Saudi commandos ringed the walls. Had security forces helped them slip away? There were other questions, too—disputes over how many men had been involved, things that gave the distinct impression that Saudi officials knew more than they said, that there was a deeper, hidden truth even more frightening than the version of events we were encouraged to accept as fact. I reported often in Saudi Arabia, and the only thing I believed with conviction was that I knew very little. Truth was buried like oil under blank sands. I still haven't heard a coherent explanation for why the insurgency turned so intense that year, or why it later petered out.

The Oasis attack drove oil prices to a record high of $42 a barrel. Back then, a $50 barrel of oil was unimaginable. It took another four years of regional chaos to drive the price to $100, and then higher still.

"Every society secretes its evil." That's what the Saudi president of Aramco told me. His office had inlaid marble floors, and pieces of sky flickered through windows and were refracted in glass columns. "We have our share, you have your share. This is our share."

As we pulled into Valerie's driveway, her husband was headed out the front door, hauling a Labrador by the collar. "We're out riding around," he told Valerie. "Okay," she sang. The living room was sunny and cool. Three of her friends nestled in leather sofas, sipping Diet Pepsi on the rocks and glowing in vibrant floral cottons, the plumage of the suburbs.

"I made iced tea." Valerie slid a platter of homemade chocolate chip cookies and cranberry cake onto a low-slung coffee table and collapsed into a sofa. Awkward quiet ensued. We all looked at each other, wondering who should start. Then Valerie lifted her chin.

"The other day should never have happened," she cried indignantly. "They knew it was coming. They knew it was inevitable for these guys to get away with it."

She meant the massacre at Oasis. Where was the security, she demanded. "For that matter," she added in rising tones, "where is *our* security?

"I go to the pool, and those guys are sitting there smoking cigarettes and drinking tea," Valerie said. "They're not going to stop me if I blaze in there with a gun."

Give the Saudis a break, interrupted Cora Lee, a forty-four-year-old accountant. Security was getting much better and, after all, you couldn't expect them to have anticipated this sort of carnage. "They really haven't had a need to invest in security until now."

The other women groaned as if they'd heard that old excuse a thousand times. "Since 2001 they should have had it covered." Valerie's blue eyes flashed. "You don't have to be the head of the country to figure that out. It's common sense."

Tracy Thompson nodded vigorously. A substitute teacher and the wife of an Aramco worker, Tracy wore a Miami Dolphins visor and capri pants.

"Even if they catch these two guys, so what?" Her voice sounded rough. "There's another two hundred. It's frustrating, too, because we know there could be a sympathizer living next door."

"We know they're on camp," Valerie chimed in.

"We know they're on camp," Tracy echoed, nodding as if she were giving an "Amen."

"But are there really people like that living here?" Cora frowned.

"Those Palestinian-American kids walk from school with our kids and they're telling them that America is evil, America is the enemy." Tracy looked at Cora as if she were hopelessly naive. "It's here, and you just don't know it. And they have American passports. Immigration laws, that's another thing. Why do we give visas to pregnant women from these countries?" She addressed that one to me. I kept my mouth shut.

"You know it's there," agreed Amy, a preschool manager.

Until recently, these women were living what they called "the good life." They were middle-class wives and mothers who'd caught the elusive American dream here in Saudi Arabia, and they were determined to cling to it. They'd found a corner of the planet where salaries were high, streets safe, and neighbors friendly. Within Aramco's gates the sun shines day after day and there is no unemployment or homelessness, there are no uninsured. Ensconced in a sort of corporate resort and military base rolled into one, utterly removed from the severe desert kingdom that they called home in only the most theoretical sense, they enjoyed the romantic mystique of expatriate life without the inconvenience of foreign language, unfamiliar mores, or strange cuisine.

"Security here is so bad," Tracy griped. "Wednesday and Thursday nights we have all these youths here, and they don't belong here."

"Why not?" demanded Cora. "They're friends of the kids here."

Pamela caught my eye across the table. "Life here is so great for those of us who are here," she said breathily, with a faint smile that cracked and immediately slipped.

There is oil under our feet, and these are prairie women. When the topic of the kingdom outside the gates comes up, they turn questioning faces in my direction. They had carted themselves along, Americans swaddled in Americana. Maybe this is the essence of the Saudi–American relationship, I thought. We need one another, and we are braided together. But we don't try to become one another, and maybe we don't even try to understand one another, because what each sees in the other provokes visceral disgust. In Saudi eyes we are a nation of whores, drugs, broken families, and guns; we swing our power like a club and the world bides its time until our ignorance strips us of our glory. To Americans, Saudis are fanatic, brutal, sexist, materialistic, modern-day slave owners. But we have been wrapped up in the Saudi oil industry since Americans struck black gold in 1936 and on down through the twentieth century, as riches welled up and transformed an illiterate, impoverished backwater into an opulent kingdom. Americans needed Saudi oil, and Saudis needed American expertise and political cover. All of that weird codependence revolved around Aramco. America is here, absolutely, but hidden so as not to anger the locals, walled off because otherwise who can stomach Saudi Arabia? We will coexist but neither side will sacrifice its character. We will not show our faces and we will not look one another in the eye. These women do not know what I know, because they have not lived outside the gate.

One afternoon I had found a Starbucks in a fancy shopping mall in Riyadh. I filled my lungs with the rich perfume of coffee, and it smelled like home—caffeinated, comforting, American. I asked for a latte and the barista gave me a bemused look; his eyes flickered and he shrugged. The milk steamer whined, he handed over the coffee, and I turned my back on his uneasy face. The Saudi men stopped talking and watched me pass with hard stares. I ignored them and sank into an overstuffed armchair.

"Excuse me," hissed the voice in my ear. "You can't sit here." The man from the counter hung at my elbow, glowering.

"Excuse me?"

"Emmm . . ." He drew his discomfort into a long syllable. "You cannot stay here."

"What? Why?"

Then he said it: "Men only."

He doesn't tell me what I will learn later: Starbucks has another, unmarked door around back that leads to a smaller espresso bar, and a handful of tables smothered by curtains. That is the "family" section. As a woman, that's where I belong. I have no right to mix with male customers or sit in view of passing shoppers. I must confine myself to the separate, inferior, and usually invisible spaces where Saudi Arabia shunts half the population.

I stand up. It's the only thing I can do. Men in their white robes and red-checked *kaffiyehs* stare impassively over their mugs. I drop my eyes, and immediately wish I hadn't. Snatching up my skirts to keep from stumbling, I walk out of the store and into the clatter of the shopping mall.

Futilely I would count down the days until I could flee westward on sterilized jets, only to remember, over and over again, that there was no escape. Saudi Arabia stuck to me, followed me home and shadowed me through my days, tainting the way I perceived men and women everywhere. Back home in Cairo, the cacophony of whistles and lewd coos on the streets sent me into blind rage. I slammed doors in the faces of delivery men; cursed at Egyptian soldiers in a language they didn't speak; kept a resentful mental tally of the Western men, especially reporters, who seemed to condone, even relish, the marginalization of women in the Arab world. If a man suggested I take a shawl to dinner, I demanded to know why he was telling me what to do, did he think he owned me?

I first visited Saudi Arabia during the fasting month of Ramadan, prepared for even greater holiday inconvenience than non-Muslims encountered in Egypt—no eating in plain view until after sundown, dry throats, and the gassy stomachs of midnight feasts, everybody jagged and jonesing for nicotine and caffeine. But in pious Saudi Arabia, I learned, Muslims follow the letter of the daylight fast while subverting the spirit. They sleep all day and start work at sundown, when eating is no longer *haram*. I couldn't make calls until five in the afternoon, and sources offered appointments at two in the morning.

And so one lost night I slumped limply on a hotel sofa as the clock neared three a.m., screwing my eyes open to interview a lawyer known for his links to Saudi insurgents. He'd brought along a man with a big hammy face and bushy beard frazzled orange with henna. Redbeard, it turned out, was a veteran of the Afghan jihad. He told me about how he'd been sent to Afghanistan, a warrior in the Saudi-American project to fight the USSR with Islamic fundamentalism. Back then, he told me, his government and my government had been on the right track. "The government betrayed herself," he snarled.

"So what did you think of September 11?" I asked him.

He spread his face into a grin and showed me a thumbs-up.

"I hope it is repeated every second," he said deliberately. "And I enjoy the picture of the falling Trade Center every time it's shown on TV."

Veterans of Afghan jihad had molded Saudi society and made holy war trendy, and their ideologies festered until they eventually helped birth September 11. Now Iraq seethed and boiled next door, and Saudi clerics whispered of jihad in Fallujah and Ramadi, and all that rage turned against the Saudi government itself, the corrupt, filthy, apostate government that had sold its soul to Washington and let Western infidels roam the Land of the Two Holy Shrines. And all the while, the Saudi-American friendship marched forward.

Saudi Arabia was always, to me, the place that most maddeningly displayed the mystery of jihad. People got radicalized in Gaza City, where they lived like rabbits in a squalid little cage while Israeli settlers rolled past on private highways to beachfront homes. They got radicalized in Afghanistan, where war was printed on the landscape, and in Baghdad, where a foreign occupation unleashed deep political fears of disenfranchisement. On a human level, all of that made sense; there was a logical scheme that you could follow.

In Saudi Arabia, it was rich boys and men, nestled in material comfort in a sovereign country, railing about how their brutally Islamic government wasn't Islamic enough. In Jalalabad or Gaza, people stood in the street and told you how they felt. In Saudi Arabia, radicalism was tamped down behind obfuscations. It was packaged in fancy cars and expensive sunglasses; hidden behind the high walls of mansions. They didn't spread it out and say, this is what it is, and this is why it is. The heart of jihad looked as smooth and American as anyplace I could ever imagine, full of Saudis who had studied in Kentucky and Wisconsin and Americans enthusing about the wonderful Saudi hospitality. And they didn't trust each other at all. There was a place where the East and the West joined, and that place was the dark slick rush of oil money. It was in the greed of Americans and the cold calculations of Saudis.

The rules are different in Saudi Arabia. The same U.S. government that drummed up public outrage against the Taliban by decrying the mistreatment of Afghan women goes to Saudi Arabia and keeps its mouth shut. McDonald's, Pizza Hut, and Starbucks make women stand in separate lines. Hotels like the InterContinental and Sheraton won't rent a woman a room without a letter from a company vouching for her ability to pay; women checking into hotels alone are regarded as prostitutes. Saudi Arabia is still the place where America colludes, where we have quietly decided that women's rights are negotiable.

Terrorism and security are questions of cost. That's what a Saudi oil official told me when I interviewed him that summer. He was irritated with America for urging its citizens to leave the kingdom.

"The U.S. government is discouraging people from coming to Saudi Arabia, and at the same time they're recruiting people to go to Iraq," he snorted. "As if that were safer."

We were sitting in a Riyadh skyscraper, one of the many anonymous towers hemmed in by webs of freeway. Far below Mercedeses and Hummers coursed through the dusk toward a flat horizon, along corridors of shop windows asparkle in silver and silk.

"I believe in the human capacity for making good things and making bad things," he said. "At the end of the day, it's a question of cost. It's an economic issue."

---

Saudi men often raised the question of women with me; they seemed to hope that I would tell them, out of courtesy or conviction, that I endorsed their way of life. They blamed all manner of Western ills, from gun violence to alcoholism, on women's liberation. "Do you think you could ever live here?" they asked. It sounded absurd every time, and every time I would repeat the obvious: No.

I was there when, inspired by the war in Iraq and a general enthusiasm for Arab voting, the kingdom called for municipal elections. Women couldn't vote, let alone run, in elections that filled just half the seats on impotent city councils. Still, in a simulacrum of democracy, candidates pitched tents in vacant lots and hosted voters for long nights of coffee and poetry readings. I stepped inside a tent one night; men milled around on thick layers of carpet, sipping thimbles of coffee in white robes bleached spotless by a hidden army of women. When they caught sight of me, they turned their backs and muttered. The campaign manager, who had invited me to the tent in a flourish of liberalism, rushed to my side, apologies spilling from gritted teeth. The citizens were angry at the sight of a woman, he said. I was costing his man votes; if I stayed, he'd lose the election. So I picked my way back out of the tent, eyes dazzled by portable lights, and waited in the vast desert night for one of the men to drive me home.

A few days later, a U.S. official from Washington gave a press appearance in a hotel lobby in Riyadh. Sporting pearls, a business suit, and a bare, blond head, she praised the Saudi elections.

"[The election] is a departure from their culture and their history," she said. "It offers to the citizens of Saudi Arabia hope . . . It's modest, but it's dramatic."

The American ambassador, a Texan oilman named James Oberwetter, chimed in from a nearby seat.

"When I got here a year ago, there were no political tents," he said. "It's like a backyard political barbeque in the U.S."

One afternoon, a candidate invited me to meet his daughter, a demure twenty-something who folded her hands in her lap and spoke fluent English. I asked her about the elections.

"Very good," she said impassively.

So you really think so, I said, even though you can't vote?

"Of course. Why do I need to vote?"

Her father interrupted. Speaking English for my benefit, he urged her to be candid. But she insisted: What good was voting? She looked pityingly at me, a woman cast adrift on rough seas, no male protector in sight.

"Maybe you don't want to vote," I said. "But wouldn't you like to make that choice yourself?"

"I don't need to," she said, slowly and deliberately. "If I have a father or a husband, why do I need to vote? Why should I need to work? They will take care of everything."

Some Saudi women are proudly defensive, convinced that any discussion of women's rights is a disguised attack on Islam from a hostile Westerner. But some of them fought quietly, like the young dental student who sat up half the night for months to write a groundbreaking novel exploring the internal lives and romances of young Saudi women. Or the oil expert who scolded me for asking about driving rights, pointing out the pitfalls of divorce and custody laws: "Driving is the least of our problems." I met women who worked as doctors and business consultants. Many of them seemed content enough.

But they are stuck, and so are the men. Over coffee one afternoon, an economist told me wistful stories of studying alongside his wife in the United States. His wife drove herself around; she was an independent, outspoken woman. Coming home to Riyadh had depressed both of them.

"Here, I got another dependent: my wife," he grumbled. He chauffered and chaperoned her as if she were a child. "When they see a woman walking alone here, it's like a wolf watching a sheep. 'Let me take what's unattended.' "

Both he and his wife believed, desperately, that social and political reform needed to materialize. Foreign academics were too easy on Saudi Arabia, he argued, urging only minor changes instead of all-out democracy because they secretly regarded Saudis as "savages" unsuited for a surfeit of freedom.

"I call them propaganda papers," he said. "They come up with all these lame excuses."

The couple had already lost hope; their minds were on the next generation. All they could do, they thought, was speak frankly.

"For ourselves, the train has left the station. We are trapped," the economist said. "I think about my kids. At least when I look at myself in the mirror I'll say: 'At least I said this. At least I wrote this.' "

The story was on the front page: A nine-year-old girl had been stabbed to death by her father and stepmother. It happened in Mecca—Islam's most sacred city, home to the holiest of holy shrines.

I sipped Nescafé. I chewed on a sweet roll. I was in the oil-rich eastern provinces, in a stuffy hotel breakfast lounge with big glass windows and the flat sprawl of desert below. My eyes flickered down through the article. I swallowed, and the bread stuck in my throat.

> The mother and the father divorced a long time ago after she suffered physical abuse at his hands. She kept custody of the girl under Islamic law until the girl turned seven . . . The father won custody last year . . .
>
> When the mother did get an opportunity to see or speak to her daughter, she noticed signs of abuse. When she reported this abuse to authorities, she was ignored . . .
>
> After stabbing his daughter and realizing that she might have died, he and his wife washed her blood with Clorox and took her to the hospital where he told the emergency personnel that he doesn't [sic] know what is wrong with her. When they examined her, they found she was already dead and that she had suffered multiple fractures and stabs . . .
>
> A few days before the incident, the biological mother had sent a letter to the Mecca municipality begging the governor to intervene before the father killed the girl . . .
>
> The rights of the parents are granted priority over the rights of the child. The father, who is more often the perpetrator of domestic abuse, is also favored under the current system in accordance with social norms . . .
>
> Police do not have the authority to enter homes and bring abused children under public protection . . . according to law,

> wives cannot report domestic abuse by husbands to the police . . .
>
> According to Islamic law, a father who kills his child is not eligible for the death penalty . . .
>
> The father is likely to serve a jail sentence of a number of years if he's found guilty. The mother may receive monetary compensation for the death of her daughter.

I looked up from the page. All around me sat men—men from America and men from Great Britain and men from France, men eating their breakfasts and preparing for business meetings. Men who'd already begun their meetings, hunched with jovial, berobed Saudi men over platters of scrambled eggs. Men meeting for oil in this land of invisible women.

Pundits like to talk about Saudi reform. About how maybe women will be allowed to vote, or to drive. But after years in the Middle East, the word *reform* signified, to me, the tangled, unholy alliance between America and the Arab dictators who grant and revoke press laws, women's rights, and political party laws on a whim. The flaw in the notion of Arab reform is the idea that people who lord over their land in autocratic splendor will voluntarily relinquish power. In truth, progress is doled out and taken back at the king's pleasure. Rulers take one step forward and holler about it, wait until the world is busy elsewhere, and slide back to where they started. Generations of diplomats and journalists talk about reform, and in the meantime the stories pile up:

> Fatima and her children have been languishing in prison for the past three and a half months. Her crime: She wanted to live with Mansour, her husband and father of her two children.
>
> A Saudi court had forcefully separated them. Fatima is free to leave jail if she is ready to return to her family, and not her now ex-husband.
>
> It was her brothers who initiated a lawsuit demanding the couple's marriage be nullified on the grounds that they were incompatible on tribal grounds.
>
> Fatima refuses to leave the prison or go to a shelter home for

> fear of retaliation from her brothers, who are her legal guardians since their father's death.
>
> Or:
>
> According to the allegations, the daughter, now 22, has been a victim of her father's deviant sexual behavior since she was three. She claims her father raped her when she was 13 . . .
>
> There is no specific sentence for sexual assault, so it is up to the judge's discretion and opinion . . . There are no laws in place that automatically revoke a father's custody of children—even if the father turns out to be an incestuous rapist.

The word *woman* is not popular in Saudi Arabia. The going term is *lady*. I heard a lot about *ladies* from Saudi officials. They talked themselves into knots, trying to depict a moderate, misunderstood kingdom, bemoaning stereotypes in the Western press: Women banned from driving? Well, they don't want to drive anyway. They all have drivers, and why would a lady want to mess with parking? The religious police who stalk the streets and shopping centers, beating "Islamic values" into the populace? Oh, Saudi officials scoff, they aren't strict or powerful. You hear stories to the contrary? Sensationalistic exaggerations, perpetuated by outsiders who don't understand Saudi Arabia.

On a morning when glaring sun blotted everything to white and hot spring winds raced off the desert, I stood outside a Riyadh bank, waiting for a friend. The sidewalk was simmering and I sweated in my black cloak, but I couldn't enter the men's section of the bank to fetch him. Traffic screamed past on a nearby highway, and I wobbled when wind spread my polyester robe like the wings of a kite.

The door clattered open and I looked up hopefully. No, just a security guard—stomping my way and yelling in Arabic. He didn't want me standing there, I gathered. I took off my sunglasses, stared blankly, and finally turned my face away.

He retreated, only to reemerge with another security guard. This second guard looked like a pit bull—short, stocky, and all flashing teeth as he barked: "Go! Go! You can't stand here! The men can *see*! The men can *see*!"

"Where do you want me to go? I have to wait for my friend. He's inside." But he held his ground, arms akimbo, snarling and flashing those teeth.

"Not here. NOT HERE! The men can *see* you!"

I lost my temper.

"I'm just standing here!" I growled. "Leave me alone!" This was a slip. In a land ruled by male ego, yelling at a man only deepens a crisis.

The pit bull advanced, lips curled, pushing the air with little shooing motions. Involuntarily, I stepped back and found myself in prickly shrubbery. In the bushes, I was out of view of the window; the virtue of all those innocent male bankers was unbesmirched. Satisfied, the pit bull climbed back onto the sidewalk and stood guard over me. I glared at him. He showed his teeth. Finally, my friend reemerged.

A liberal, U.S.-educated professor at King Saud University, he was sure to share my outrage, I thought. Maybe he'd even call up the bank—his friend was the manager—and get the pit bull into trouble. I spilled my story, words hot as the pavement.

He hardly blinked.

"Yes," he said. "Oh." He put the car in reverse, and off we drove.

People asked, always: What's it like, being a woman there?

You are supposed to say that it doesn't matter a bit. *Gender? I never give it a second thought!* You are supposed to say that you navigate as a third sex, the Undaunted Western Reporter, clomping around in trousers and ponytails and clumsy head scarves slipping perpetually over your eyes. You are supposed to say that you were privileged, because you had a pass to the secret world of local sisterhood, to a place where faces showed and words were honest, where there was no husband to interrupt and bully. You are supposed to say, in an almost mystical voice, "I could write about the *women*." And then you should pause and add, smugly: "Which the male correspondents could never do." You leave the mythology intact lest you admit weakness and undermine the other women in the field.

And then, too, the truth is not really easy to admit or articulate. You can't admit how dirty it made you feel, the thousand ways you were slighted and how flimsy your self-assurance turned out to be, how those little battles bit at you like acid. Men who refused to shake your hand; squatting on floors with men who refused to look at your face because you brimmed with sin, not one glance in an hour-long interview; the sneering underfed soldiers who hissed and talked about your ass when you walked past. You can't admit it made you so bitter that, for a time, you looked at any woman who hadn't been where you had been as if she were an ingenue who didn't understand the world she occupied. She was blind to the dark, ruthless fraternity of men—all men, all around the globe—how luridly dangerous they were, how we had to keep pushing against them or we'd wind up where we began hundreds of years ago. You are not supposed to say any of that. It proves you were never really up to the game, that you might as well have stayed home. So you pretend it's nothing, you tell everyone that you were lucky because you could talk to the women.

In the end, you can't lose yourself. You can drape your body in black, you can smother your breasts and cover your face and drown yourself in expensive perfumes until your smells, too, are submerged. You can do all of that, but you will still be a woman, and you chose to be there. You can hide but you can't disappear. Like America itself, you have done a calculation, you have accepted a condition, because you wanted something out of it. You can build walls, cower in the Green Zone, hire armed guards, and never, ever set foot outside the fortress, but you are still an American. You have still chosen to be there. What does it mean that your choice is between being isolated in your own place, and hiding in some other place?

"I left in mid-June and stayed out 'til school started this year. Because of the bombing," Cora said wearily. "Now people say, 'Why'd you leave last year and not this year?' "

She sighed.

"We're putting our kids at risk. My husband and I feel like we're old, we've lived, but they have life ahead of them. If we're so greedy to stay here and put our kids at risk, what does that say about who we are?"

"Exactly," said Tracy emphatically.

"To me, it's not the money. It's, if you knew for certain, you'd go," said Amy. "But you're pulling your kids out of school, and they have games, and they have ballet recitals. And you see all these terror warnings in the U.S., and nothing happens. So how can you know?"

"My daughter was crying because she did not want to go back to the States, it's too dangerous," Tracy said.

"The quality of life is incredible here," Cora said.

"We are so spoiled here," Tracy agreed.

"Here it's real friendly," Pamela said. "We have ballet, soccer, softball."

No pork is allowed, and the drinkers are reduced to making moonshine with woodchips. But there were consolations: you could cruise the desert on a Harley or in a golf cart, then go home to mingle with like-minded international neighbors. They all underwent background checks and medical exams before arriving, the women said.

"You have to be perfect to be here," Tracy told me. "It's like Stepford—everybody's healthy, smart, good-looking."

"Oh, don't say that!" Valerie interrupted. "Now it will be in the paper, the Stepford Wives of Aramco."

"It's true," Tracy cried. "My mother came here and she was like, 'This is kinda weird. It's too perfect. It's like the Stepford Wives.' "

But now the American embassy had issued a blunt warning to leave the country, and the women believed the bloodshed they'd already seen was just "the tip of the iceberg," Valerie said.

"My husband isn't ready to go yet, and I'm like, 'When can we go?' " Tracy said. Her husband was urging her to take the kids out, she said, "but I didn't sign up for this single mom thing."

"I told him, 'We can go back and you can flip burgers if that's what you need to do, but we need to stay together.' And then my daughter said, 'If he's here alone, maybe he'll get a girlfriend like Mr. So-and-so.' "

"She did not!" the other women cried with one voice.

"She did!" Tracy said.

"She did," another woman confirmed.

"There's this tribal mind-set that more information is dangerous," Pamela said. "They don't know how to give information out. It's not in their nature."

"You've got people who say we need the expats gone, but then the whole country will really go down," Cora said. "All of us have known for years there was a lot of civil unrest. If we all leave we just hurt ourselves."

"Are people resigning?" I asked.

"They may not be resigning, but they're job hunting," said Amy.

"Everybody says, 'I'm not leaving, but I'm looking,' " said Valerie.

Cora sighed again. "Every night, every mom, we say, 'What'd your friends say at school? What'd they say on the bus?' I was on the phone all day with people at the Oasis."

Sitting there with these women, I could feel their reluctance. None of them would ever manage to duplicate their sumptuous lifestyles back in America, and they all knew it. In a sense, they were living out their own childhood dreams—they talked about the things they'd pined after as little girls, and finally found here. Valerie, who once dreamed of ponies, shared a horse with her daughter at nearby stables. Their children trooped off on field trips to Nepal and South Africa. They are so sophisticated and worldly, the women said of their broods, smiling immodestly.

"What do your kids think about leaving?" I asked.

"My son's twelve and he's not at all pleased about it," Tracy said. "It's a way of life for my kids and they feel safe here. We went to Switzerland on spring break. How many middle-class kids go to Switzerland? My kids have studied the Nile and been down the Nile."

Tracy was bragging now, bare feet bouncing on the floor like a child gloating over a stash of sweets.

"They know how to sign their room numbers for drinks at the hotel bar," Valerie said. "It's unbelievable. They're not going to Pinewood Whatever, Wherever."

"Camping on vacation!" scoffed Cora.

"Commuting," Tracy said. "Going to Grandma's. I mean, we like Grandma's, but we want to see New Zealand!"

Tracy had hoped to treat her nieces and nephews to overseas adventures, inviting them one by one to join the family on vacations. "I'm trying to hang on for that," she said, as if she had not, five minutes earlier, said she was yearning to leave.

In Amy's childhood, the greatest excitement of summer vacation was putting coins into vibrating beds in roadside motels. The room erupted in laughter.

"My son is like, 'Oh, Mom, do we have to go to Europe *again*?' " Tracy said. "And I'm like, 'You little . . .'" she flapped her hand in the air as if she were slapping her son.

The afternoon wore on. The women kept forgetting about the terrorism. Then they would remember again, and the room would grow quiet and they'd fidget uncomfortably.

But only for a minute.

ELEVEN

# LODDI DODDI, WE LIKES TO PARTY

*There are known unknowns. That is to say, there are things that we now know we don't know. But there are also unknown unknowns. There are things we don't know we don't know. So when we do the best we can and pull all this information together, and we then say well that's basically what we see as the situation, that is really only the known knowns and the known unknowns. And each year, we discover a few more of those unknown unknowns. It sounds like a riddle. It isn't a riddle. It is a very serious, important matter.*

**—U.S. Secretary of Defense Donald Rumsfeld, June 6, 2002**

I went to Yemen looking for a revelation. I wanted to know what got traded, and at what cost, between American and Yemeni intelligence. In the untamed mountains and deserts clinging to the tip of the Arabian Peninsula, I hoped to turn up stories of CIA renditions and the dirty work the cash-strapped government did for the United States.

I didn't find those stories. Instead, in Sanaa, I found Faris. He loped through the hotel lobby, a glint in his eye, knowing everybody. A sharp little mustache peppered his lip, and white teeth flashed beneath changeless eyes. He was aide and friend to the president, the owner of an English-language newspaper, and the official who talked to CNN on the rare occasions when international curiosity about Yemen's motives coincided with Yemen's willingness to explain itself. Faris had gone to college in America's Midwest, and I'd heard he was the key to getting anything out of the government. "Promised a lot, didn't deliver that much. But he can be helpful, if he wants to be." That was the note I'd gotten from a colleague. Upon hearing the name of a large American newspaper, Faris was most obsequious. *Let's talk about it, about what your stories are. I tell you what—you've never been here before. How about I pick you up, show you around, and you can tell me what you're covering, what your objectives are. So you get a feel for Yemen.*

"So much misinformation printed about Yemen in the American press," he griped as his SUV groaned over the cobblestones. I stared out the window at crooked clusters of fairy-tale towers, stained glass ringed with gypsum, the cut of minarets against a darkening sky.

"It's like they cannot mention Yemen without saying it's the ancestral home of Osama bin Laden. Why? Okay, so some of his family lived here. Do you know what it's like up there in the north? You can't even see the border between Saudi Arabia and Yemen. It doesn't mean anything."

"I'd be interested to get up there," I said.

"Oh no," he barked. "You can't go."

"Why not? It's impossible?"

"Well, not impossible," he smiled a cat's smile, eyes lingering on the road. "Not completely impossible. But, you know, you're getting into the tribal areas—"

"And you don't have control over the tribes."

"We *do* have control. But these days we have this situation with the rebels up there. There's a lot of fighting."

"You mean Houthi."

I'd been reading about the Houthi rebellion—at least, reading what few details managed to squeeze out of the government's grasp. Hussein Houthi was a Zaydi Shiite cleric who'd led thousands of followers to wage a guerrilla war against the central government, angered by its ties to America and keen for Islamic rule. The government blamed the insurrection on "foreign sponsors," whispering that the Houthi clan was backed by Iran. The fighting dragged on for months and the death toll swelled, but journalists couldn't get to the Sa'ada region to investigate. In the reporter-saturated Middle East, here was a rare wilderness still hidden from cameras. Only sketchy rumors of war rumbled down from the hills.

"Yes," Faris said tensely, all of that hiddenness blackening his voice. "The Houthi."

"I don't mind. I wanted to write a story about the Houthi rebellion, anyway."

"We can't guarantee your safety."

"It's not your responsibility."

He puffed his cheeks and laughed nervously. "Okay. It's impossible."

"Are you telling me I can't go?"

"I don't put it like that."

"What if I go on my own?"

"You'll never get up there."

"Why? Because I'll get kidnapped?"

"There are checkpoints everywhere. You can't even get very far out of Sanaa unless you're on a tour bus with a special permit. We're very careful with the tourists. But, no, the kidnappings aren't really happening these days."

"I see."

"Anyway, you know, people don't really understand about Yemeni kidnappings." His face muscles loosened; he had found his way back to more comfortable talking points. "It's just what the tribes do if they want something from the government. They want a new water pump or a road. So they might kidnap a foreigner to try to get attention, to start negotiations. But it's not a bad thing, to be kidnapped. Actually, under tribal tradition, you are a guest, so they treat you very well."

"Except that you can't leave."

"Except that you can't leave. But you may not want to. They prepare feasts, and everybody wants to meet you. You're the guest of honor. There is a story, actually, about a tourist who was kidnapped by a tribe, and then the government finished negotiating with the tribe so they released him. But then the tribe got sad, you know, because they were planning a big feast for that night. So they went back out and kidnapped him again so he could come to the feast. Then afterward they released him again. That's a true story!"

"Funny. Wow. Maybe I should get kidnapped."

"One time—this is so funny—this guy came to Yemen and, you know, he really wanted to get kidnapped. He was wandering around all by himself on the roads, and nothing. He was so angry about it. He came down to the paper and said, 'I'm trying to get kidnapped and nobody is picking me up! What does it take to get kidnapped around here?' We wrote a story about him."

Faris, armed with documents that made the checkpoint guards fall back respectfully, was a solicitous tour guide. We watched grooms prance to the rumble of drums on the craggy bluff traditionally visited by wedding parties, curved, phallic knives strapped to their bellies. At a rooftop café in the slumbering towers of Old Sanaa, we looked down at the spread of ancient walls, dark mountains rising on the horizon and stars smearing the sky. All the while, Faris dangled promises of exclusive interviews he was allegedly working to arrange. When pressed, he'd gloss into vagueness. "I have to call my friend," he'd say.

"Why don't you call him now?"

"Oh, I can't right now because they have a meeting. Don't worry. I'll call him tonight."

"You have to meet this woman," he announced. It was Friday, my second day in town. "She's incredible. Her family was poor so she started cooking for people, to support the men in her family. Now her place is famous. This one illiterate woman, and she started the most famous restaurant in Yemen. Can you imagine? Now the whole family works there."

"That *is* interesting."

"It's a good story, don't you think?" he said suggestively. "You should do a story. It's interesting, how a woman can do that, even in a traditional society."

I laughed. "Yeah, right."

"Anyway, you have to try her food. It's amazing."

Scratching chickens, bleating goats, and black-shrouded women picked their way through dust and trash at the squalid market in the provincial town of Shibaam Kawkaban. We slipped down an alley and into a courtyard. A silent girl smiled and led us up a sagging and shadowed staircase, and into a light-flooded lounge. Windows yawned open on all sides, to rocks and mountains and hawks dipping in air.

We sat on pillows and the woman laid down a spread of meats, eggs, vegetables, and hot, rich bread. When the tea arrived, Faris pulled out a bundle of qat. "You said you were interested in qat," he said, passing me a handful of branches.

"I am."

"Well, it's Friday. Everybody chews qat today. Break off the smallest leaves, the green, flexible leaves. Chew them but don't swallow them. Push them over into your cheek and suck on the juices."

This was the last day Faris would waste, I coaxed myself. The translator I'd hired the night before was already fixing appointments. It was Friday anyway, a futile time for work. I stuffed my mouth with qat, sucked on bitter juice, and watched the hawks rise and fall, suspended against a sky blasted white by sun.

"It's very good for you to spend time with Faris," Mohammed, the translator, had told me hesitantly. "He can help you a lot, if he wants." *But he probably won't.* Those words hung, unspoken, in his tone.

Black birds wheeled, shadows thinned, and the monochrome glaze of a sun tacked straight overhead coated the mountains. Soggy qat burrowed into my cheek. Leaves slipped off down my throat. Then my head began to hum and I didn't care. I'd let go of terrorism and burn a day in this forgotten place.

We rode through long plains and valleys, back toward Sanaa, and Faris talked about his kids and the foreign wife he'd married and divorced. He'd settled now with a Yemeni wife and that was working because she understood him. We drew to the edge of the capital and I leafed through his CDs until I found a Snoop Doggy Dogg album, *Doggystyle*. "You like this?"

"Yeah, I love Snoop," he said.

"I haven't heard it since high school," I said.

"Let's listen to it."

The sun slanted down on the old city and Snoop Doggy Dogg slurred, "Loddi doddi, we likes to party . . ." and the music spilled out of the car windows and puddled in the streets, drawing eyes after us. Men in tribal skirts stood still and stared out of hard-edged faces, as if they had been standing there for all time, legs gnawed down to the bone, bunches of foliage big as baseballs bulging in their cheeks. They stood, stared, and sucked on their leaves. I was lost in glittering futility now, coming to the end of the first dead end, the great waste of trying to know something of Yemen and know it quickly, know it now. Glazed by Arabian sun, sheened in dust, estranged from facts, I was looking for things I could not see. The war on terror was happening now, on all sides, and lives were slipping past us unseen. "Murder was the case they gave me," Snoop murmured, and day crumbled into night.

Back in Cairo, the Yemeni foreign minister had boasted to me that American agents had free run of Yemeni prisons. They could watch the interrogations and, presumably, absorb any information spilled under torture. Why would the United States bother kidnapping people and spiriting them into hidden prisons if they had a setup like that? Of course, they had rendered Yemenis anyway—presumably those the government wouldn't relinquish. America had given Yemen plenty of money and military equipment to fight terrorism at the turn of the new century, after the USS *Cole* was bombed by Yemeni Islamists while refueling in the harbor of Aden. Seventeen American sailors died in the attack. More American cash flowed to Yemen after September 11. There were rumors that bin Laden might be hiding here, embedded among his tribe. Nobody believed it. And yet when you got to Yemen, torn by civil war and crippled by poverty, you felt yourself so far off the map, so deep in a lawless land, that anything at all seemed potentially true.

The next morning in Sanaa, I watched a human rights lawyer named Mohammed Naji Allaw take down file after file, spread them between us, and read off the names of men who'd been detained, disappeared, or opaquely incarcerated. The government had warned him against investigating renditions, he said. He seemed at a loss for whom to resent more, the Americans or his own government.

"The governments in the Arab and Islamic worlds work as police stations now for the United States, and still they are bad police stations," he sighed. "A police station in New York is more able to say no to an order from the American government than any government in this region. The governments don't even follow their own constitutions."

Yemenis had vanished while traveling overseas, only to turn up in Guantánamo. Forty families had been arrested and interrogated by

Yemeni intelligence because they had relatives in Guantánamo. Yemenis were being held in Yemeni prisons without charge because the Americans wanted them in custody, he said.

"They keep people hidden and don't allow people to visit relatives. Solitary confinement. Sleep deprivation. Kicks and slaps. They threaten to attack their families."

I wanted to talk with the families. He sighed and shook his head. He would try, he said, but they were afraid to talk, because nobody knew how far this would go.

"This is totally different from what was going on before September 11," he said. "The United States used to put a lot of pressure on governments to improve human rights. It was believed to be the country that protected human rights. Activists and journalists used to use the United States as a backup, as something to keep them strong against their governments, and the governments tried to beautify their images before the Americans. Now the United States turns a blind eye. The State Department issues an annual report, but there's no punishment behind the report. Now, when we try to challenge our government about a detention case, they say, 'Look, see, there's your glorious example at work.' They say, 'Because we are not strong enough to face the United States, we are obliged to do what they ask.' It's not acceptable to anybody, but this is really happening."

"This is an important interview," Mohammed the translator announced as we drove through the dust and clotting darkness. Hamood Abdulhamed Hitar was a prominent judge and head of the newly formed theological committee. "He is a very big judge, an important man," Mohammed told me. A proudly displayed sheep pelt slid along the dashboard as he swung the wheel. "He can answer all of your questions, about terrorists, everything."

"And renditions?"

He tightened his lips.

"I think so, yes." He paused. "Maybe he will talk with us quickly, because now it's time for chewing qat."

Each Yemeni afternoon dissolves into qat, the balm and consolation for another day endured. "Did you chew qat before?" he asked.

"A little the other day."

"Did you like it?"

"Yes." It wasn't polite to admit that it had given me a mediocre buzz and a splitting headache.

Frames of light etched the windows and doors of the judge's house, chasing off the gloaming. We doffed our shoes at the threshold and padded into the *mafraj*, a qat-chewing salon swaddled in carpets and strewn with cushions. There he was, the high court judge and soon-to-be cabinet minister, luxuriating on thick pillows, the spoils of trees spread about.

"*Salaam aleikum*," I said.

"*Aleikum salaam*," he replied.

Islamic greetings thus dispensed, I sank down into the cushions. Mohammed pulled out his own bundle of qat, and handed me a few branches.

"Tell me about the work you do." I tried to poke the leaves out of the path of my tongue.

The judge combed his fingers through glossy leaves. "I'm in charge of holding dialogue with those returning from Afghanistan and those with extremist ideas which are uncommon to people . . ." He trailed off. I slid my eyes over to Mohammed, who stared serenely at our host. Head hung low, the judge pored over the qat branches. Then he roused himself with a shake, and slipped back into the interview:

"I talk to people with extremist ideas whether they went to Afghanistan or not," he said by way of clarification, and gazed indistinctly at the air between us.

"When they came back they were under security supervision and security knows that and from the way of common speeches and ideas it's obvious they have extremist ideas," he finally said.

I copied this incoherency down and looked up to find his bloodshot eyes flickering expectantly. The question, his gaze announced imperiously, had been duly answered. I looked at him. He looked at me. Mohammed chomped away at his leaves.

As qat speeded the judge's blood, his words crowded and leapfrogged from his mouth. My pen chased his runaway thoughts over the page in long, broken sentences. Acid juices trickled down my throat, and my head thickened. When the judge said things like: "We work in three stages. The fourth stage involves two types of dialogue . . ." I just scribbled away.

The judge thought he could talk the terrorists out of it. That was the upshot. He met with militants and argued with them, trying to debunk their extremist ideas with theology. This was trendy in Saudi Arabia, too—a dry and Socratic strategy of undoing extremism. It always sounded bogus to me, this idea of coaxing bombers back to normalcy. I wondered if theological redemption was a circumspect way to protect criminals with the right family or tribal connections from going to jail. Not everybody was eligible to pay penance by chatting with religious scholars. Others languished in prison, were executed, got disappeared, and wound up in CIA custody. Who decided?

"So who, exactly, are you having these dialogues with?"

"People who have ideas based on the Salafi creed or people suspected of involvement with Al Qaeda or the Aden-Abyan Islamic Army and people suspected of involvement in the jihad movement and any other people who have some thoughts different than Islamic scholars," all in a single breath.

One hundred and seven suspected Al Qaeda members had so far been reformed, he told me. He'd also reached out to 350 of Houthi's followers, and brought 176 of those to "positive ends." We were all ramped up and the air popped with exclamation points, statistics glinting like beads in my notes.

"All of them," the judge said grandly, "undertake to denounce extremism, terror, and violence, to be good citizens and follow the constitution and maintain security and respect the rights of non-Muslims in Yemen and undertake not to harm foreign embassies in Yemen."

I mentioned the Aden-Abyan Islamic Army, a group that had kidnapped foreigners and was linked to the bombing of the USS *Cole*.

"The Aden-Abyan Army is dissolved already," the judge said hastily. "People who were involved are good citizens now and they never think of it at all."

I blinked. He had just said he was holding dialogues with members of that group. The judge blustered forward in his monologue.

"There is no so-called jihad movement at all," he announced grandly.

"Those people who were members of Al Qaeda and sympathizers of Al Qaeda. From December '02 to now there is no terrorist threat."

"No terrorist threat . . ." I muttered. "But—what happened in December '02?"

"They formed the theological committee," Mohammed whispered helpfully.

"Yemen suffered from terrorism more than any other country." The judge jabbed a finger in time with the clatter of consonants. "I believe there is no threat from extremism. There might be people with extremist ideas but they pose no threat. We are on the right path now, to stability."

"But you just said . . ." I shuffled unhappily through my notes. "You just *said* you're meeting with members of those groups. How can you now say they don't exist?"

"Eighty percent of the danger has been removed," he said, and nodded slowly. He cleared his throat, looked at Mohammed, and said something like "Well . . ." We were being cordially invited to clear out.

"How can you possibly quantify that eighty percent?" I asked desperately. "What does it even mean?"

"Eighty percent," he replied dreamily, smiling a close-lipped smile. "More or less."

Empty statistic ringing in my ears and diffusing on the surface of qat-muddled thought, I stepped back into the dark, cold mountain night.

The truth is, precious few people know what the United States is doing in Yemen or Saudi Arabia or even Jordan. And by all signs, journalists are not among them. People in the embassies know, theoretically, at least about their own bit, but they are unlikely to share with a reporter unless there is some public relations benefit, which in turn renders the information suspect. There are people like Faris, who talk to reporters while spinning a protective gloss over the rest of the country; and people who know a lot but don't talk to you. And there are people like the human rights lawyer—living on the margins, shuttling in and out of jail, relying on attention from abroad as a weak shield. I recently read that he was beaten and gun-butted in a courtroom by soldiers and bodyguards.

You get a translator and people whisper, don't trust him, he's compromised, he works for the government. Everybody said that about everybody else; and although they didn't usually say so, many of them believed that journalists were also spies. Somewhere behind all those walls and obfuscations, the war on terror was fought. The CIA flew a drone over the Yemeni countryside one day, shot a Hellfire missile down, and killed six people. One of them was a U.S. citizen. No safe harbor, as they say. Yemen was a ward stuffed with all of those disorders—the hidden war, the crazed tribesmen, the jihad, the debts owed to America, the secret operations. It was all there, sensed but not seen, palpable but intangible.

There was so much lying and hiding going on that you couldn't believe much of anything unless you saw it yourself, and the things I saw never seemed to match what people said about them. My job would have been easier if I could have been more credulous. "I think maybe this is happening," says one reporter to the other, who will likely reply, "It can't be, because so-and-so told us X." Nobody tells you how to proceed if so-and-so is lying to you, if X is false. Still, you have to file something. The newspaper bawls its big, inky hunger. If you think you know one tiny thing, if somebody has said something, at least it's something to write about. So you write.

The public affairs officer at the U.S. embassy begrudgingly agreed to a meeting, but it came studded with conditions. "I don't know how helpful I can be," he warned grimly.

I breezed straight over as if he'd sent an embossed invitation. By then, I was in a quiet panic. The days had flown and still I had nothing but bits and scraps.

He was talking about ground rules as soon as I sat down. I will speak to you about culture, he said. No security. No terrorism. No politics. Only culture, and only on *deep background.* A second diplomat joined us for reasons nobody explained. Just sitting, and listening.

"Okay," I said slowly, running my eyes over the questions I'd jotted, scanning for something that fit his demands. This was unusual. In other Arab capitals, you could have tea with the ambassador, or at least a political counselor. The quasi-interviews were never on the record and often disingenuous, but a trip to the embassy was helpful. You couldn't expect any hard information, or let yourself think that they were on your side because you were all American. But if you paid attention to what they didn't say, to questions that made them testy, the tone they used to talk about the locals, the mistakes they made—all of this gave a glimpse of what the U.S. government wanted, and how it hoped to be perceived.

In Yemen, America had nothing to say.

I sat with the diplomat and chatted about tribes. He told me guardedly, haltingly, about water wells. If a question veered into the perilous territory of the newsworthy, he'd cut me off. "Sorry," he'd say archly. "I can only talk about culture." I'd sigh. He'd shrug. The minute hand dragged itself in a ring around the clock.

One of my last nights in Yemen, Mohammed and I drove out of Sanaa to hear a poetry recitation in the countryside. At the edge of the capital, thin mountain air was blown with fine dust and rank with rotten perfumes of garbage and sewage. We passed trucks sagging under the weight of broken basalt; fruit stands heaped with rusty grapes, oranges, pomegranates; mountains of piping and tile to build or adorn a home. The road sank, rose, and rolled behind the rocks, wrapping a black cord up the mountain. "You whose beauty is killing me, you still live in my eyes," wailed the radio. "I am suffering but I have no other choice." The mountains were slumped and rounded shoulders, worn by the seasons, skimmed by the shadows of clouds. We were far from the city now. Wild dogs roamed the roads. Mud houses crouched in the scabby clearings of qat orchards.

They don't grow anything except qat, Mohammed said. Qat is killing our country, deadening our soil, squeezing out other crops. People here, they live only to grow and chew qat. Drums throbbed dryly from the radio. Mohammed's own plastic sack of qat lay at his side.

We were meeting a poet named Amin Mashrigi, who penned verses scornful of terrorism. The government paid him to roam around the hardscrabble, qat-addled countryside, reciting his poems and encouraging the villagers to come up with their own rhymes.

Outside the capital, the rule of the tribe, the power of Islam, and the communal balm of poetry trumped the authority of the central government. Out here, spoken verse was enough to wed or divorce; protect or condemn. Poetry was practical. When tribesmen headed into negotiations over water or grazing rights, boundaries or vengeance, they came chanting verse to advertise their grievances. Negotiations might stretch for days.

The villagers of Jerif pressed tight against the truck—men staring stolidly, children yanking on my jeans, women hanging shyly back, eyes locked on my face. "They've been waiting for us." Mohammed grinned. "They say you are the first foreigner who's ever visited their village."

The town was just a handful of mud huts in the meager shade of spindly qat trees. Only one structure qualified vaguely as a municipal building, and that was the qat-chewing hall where the men passed long afternoon hours. They led us through the slanting sunset, and I entered with the men while the women lingered outside.

Cheap sports coats covered the men's thobes; pistols bristled from their hips, and curved, carved daggers lay against their guts. They had apparently laid waste to orchards for miles around, and we lolled in a bower of qat. Mashrigi stood before us and his voice rang out, proud and acrobatic, gliding up and falling low to perch on a single, long-stretched syllable.

*Shame on you, kidnapper*
*Take your clothes and leave from here*
*Don't be mad or extreme*
*You've gone too far and there's no honor there.*

His audience sat rapt.

*Now the ships can't come to Yemen and the country is suffering*
*The World Bank is paying the debt*
*Neither New York nor Texas banks paid the price*
*Your victim is not the right one.*

Then he called out: "Who is writing poetry?"

"I am!" the voices rose around the room.

"Is anybody writing about terror and security?" he asked. "About carrying a gun?"

A wiry villager stood, an enormous ball of qat jammed into his teeth and a cigarette poised in hand. As he chanted the green showed between his teeth:

*I hope the sky is clear for me*
*And all the universe is like a shield*
*And the sun is my light*
*And if I wish the stars in the sky become bullets*
*To fight the Russians*
*Bush be under my shoes*
*And I free Jerusalem and sentence the Jews to death.*

The men clapped and hollered.

Another man rose to recite. He stood, long and thin before the crowd, brushing flies from his face. There was no sound but quiet chomping. He began:

*The more we try to be Muslim, the more American they try to make us.*
*Our literary teaching and great heritage have been invaded by the West.*
*They drove us crazy talking about the freedom of women.*
*They want to drive her to evil.*
*They ask the women to remove the hijab and replace it with trousers to show their bodies.*

*Now people who do their village rituals are accused of being extremists.*
*Even the music is now brought in instead of listening to good, traditional music.*
*Now people are kissing each other on television.*

All the faces turned upward. Mohammed was whispering the translation. The poet was carrying on now, sinking into a groove that was anti-American, anti-Semitic, and antigovernment.

*The Arab army is just to protect the leaders.*
*They build their leadership on the suffering of the people.*
*Democracy is for people who have money.*
*If the poor man becomes democratic, they accuse him of dishonesty.*
*In 1990 we gave clubs to Saddam and advised Bush to go fight him.*
*He waited nine years for the son to come,*
*And if the father is a donkey, the son is an ass.*
*They said in Iraq there is WMD.*
*As they beat the drum, we play the pipe.*

*For money's sake we sell our brothers to the States.*
*We used to love Saddam but now we step on his picture.*

The poetry dried up, and we climbed to our feet. On the way back to town, headlights probed the dark earth like sliding eyes, Yemen and terrorism and the rest of it slipping back into the murk, into the unseen.

"You're never gonna believe this."

Here was Faris, with a huge grin.

"I already don't believe it."

"Houthi's dead."

"What?"

"Houthi's dead. They killed him in a cave last night."

"Who did?"

"The Yemeni army. There was a big shootout. He's dead."

"Are you serious?"

"Yeah! I just heard about it from some contacts. Top officials."

"COME ON!" I shouted at him. "Are you kidding? You expect me to believe that?"

Since our afternoon of qat and Snoop, formalities had fallen away.

"It's true." He spread his hands. "I swear to God. It's true."

"I can't believe you. Do you think I'm an idiot?"

"I swear."

"This is insulting, Faris."

"All right, fine. But it's true. You'll find out soon enough on your own. I'm trying to give you a tip."

"I don't want to talk about this anymore."

"Suit yourself."

"Well, wait. Can you get somebody else to talk about it with me? Somebody from the military, intelligence . . . ?"

"They're all in meetings. About Houthi."

"Later?"

"We'll see."

Faris's story was true. Or at least, it became recorded history. The defense and interior ministries released a joint statement. The wires picked it up. I wrote 612 words that appeared on page A-3 of the *Los Angeles Times* on September 11, 2004. Everybody pretended this was the end of the war we'd never seen. But Houthi had a father who took over for him, and the guerrillas raged on. He had brothers, too. And so it went, and so it goes. The unseen war is pounding along still. Last time I flew out of Sanaa, in 2007, I sat with a friend on the plane back to Cairo. Just before takeoff, we watched fighter jets roar off into the sky, one after the next, loaded up with bombs.

"Jesus," he said. "They're pounding the hell out of something."

"Yes," I agreed, "it looks that way."

## TWELVE

# A CITY BUILT ON GARBAGE

On Valentine's Day in 2005, hundreds of pounds of explosives roared in the heart of Beirut. Death had been dispatched for Rafik Hariri. The blast was strong enough to tear a hole in the city, and to expose Lebanon as a country divided.

A few words about Hariri: He was a sixty-year-old Sunni Muslim, and he was rich beyond all dreaming. He had grown up poor in the southern city of Sidon. When he came of age he set off for Saudi Arabia, ingratiated himself to the royal family, and earned billions in construction. He waited out Lebanon's civil war there, rubbing robed elbows with sandalwood-scented Saudi princes and gathering bottomless stores of money. When peace came at last to Lebanon, so did a reinvented Hariri, flesh packed into fancy suits, throwing cash to orphans and scholarships and mosques like a Muslim Rockefeller, to build his mansion and let them whisper about the source of his wealth. He came home fresh and rich to a cowering nation with the audacity to imagine that he could reinvent his country just as he had reinvented himself. He became the prime minister and, stone by stone, he rebuilt downtown. He lured tourists back. He flew Pavarotti on his private 727 to sing at Beirut's rebuilt sports stadium, the one Israel had bombed at the start of the 1982 invasion.

Hariri was not universally adored. His manic reconstruction had helped saddle the country with $30 billion in debt and, moreover, he colluded with the Syrian government, which had been invited under a

1989 peace deal to linger in Lebanon after the civil war as a de facto occupying power. But then, in those years, no important leader in Beirut spurned the road to Damascus; they all cut deals with Syria's Assad dynasty. But recently, Hariri's loyalties had shifted. He was trying to get Syria out of Lebanon; he was conspiring with Washington and Paris for a UN resolution. He told his friends that Syrian president Bashar al-Assad threatened him: *I would rather break the country over your head than lose it.* And then the bomb struck his motorcade. He had left Parliament that morning and finished his coffee at a café on Beirut's resurrected Place de l'Étoile. The explosion killed his bodyguards and his former economy minister; it killed twenty-one people along with Hariri.

Hariri's mansion loomed over the apartment blocks and tightly packed shops of a crowded quarter that sprawls uphill from the lip of the Mediterranean. Even on bright days, the urban tangle throws shadow over the streets. Most people would set a house like that on a mountaintop or seaside cliff, but Hariri's house told of his wealth and of his populist pretenses. I am self-made and I walk among you, the house announced, but please don't forget that I am royalty.

The day of the funeral, I made my way to that house through the streets of West Beirut. The capital was in shock that day. Overnight, Hariri had become the martyr of a new Lebanese mythology; his image was washed clean and his critics fell silent. Hariri's death had been the obliteration of an idea, an improbable promise. He had told the Lebanese that it was all right to leave the civil war behind, divorcing them day by day from guilt and blood. Hariri had bestowed sweet forgetfulness on a stripped and silent place, a country withering under the weight of memory. In the end they could overlook the suspicion that he had cheated them—and which Lebanese leader had truly clean hands?—because he had restored a national faith, and Lebanon had discovered that faith was something it needed more than money. These ideas were embedded in the image of Hariri, and that was part of the shock. The assassination told the Lebanese that violence would suck them back down. People believed Hariri had been killed for turning against Syria, and his assassination became a focus for all resentment amassed in the fifteen years since the end of the war—for the sense that Syria had hijacked the country into a military occupation, thick with corruption and heavy with political repression. Sunnis, Christians, and Druze vowed a revolution, an intifada, to drive Syria out of the country.

Now mourners poured into the Hariri home, jammed the metal detectors and thronged the steel elevators that slid silently between immaculate floors. I was carried along by anxious bodies, through marble hallways and reception rooms as big as bowling alleys, laid with Persian carpets and cornered with Phoenician artifacts. Hariri's wife, sister, and daughter waited in the women's sitting room, their red faces and black dresses and blown-out hair draped in scarves. Women filed in to kiss their cheeks and squeeze their hands, then stood whispering through painted lips. Waiters circled with thimbles of bitter yellow coffee and teacups fragile as skin. It was almost time to take the bodies out, to start the slow parade down into the city center and sink Hariri into the dirt. The women were nervous and sick with it; they didn't want to see the bodies go. His coffin was in the hall, smothered in a Lebanese flag and flanked by the coffins of his dead bodyguards. Everybody drifted and milled, wringing hands, dabbing eyes.

"God raise them," somebody called, and all the grief tamped down under polished skin and polite faces suddenly throbbed in the hall. Women wailed and bent, bodies wilting over the coffin. Men with steely hair and tailored suits thrashed the air with strings of prayer beads, dropped heads into hands, and keened. "If you love him, let us lift him." Pallbearers tried to peel the women off the box that held whatever pieces remained of Hariri.

Marwan Harmadeh limped through the crowd to the edge of the coffin, swaying heavily between a walking stick and a young nurse in a white coat. Harmadeh had been an early, outspoken critic of Syria and he had been targeted first; that was four months earlier and he still couldn't walk properly. The bomb killed his driver but he survived. Now another man stepped briskly to Harmadeh's side, and a look of understanding slid between them. It was Talal Salman, the editor of *As-Safir* newspaper, whose cheek had been trenched by a bullet during the civil war. *We are scarred, just like our city*, Salman had told me a year earlier. All the lions are here, I thought. The two men stood straight and haughty, and stared at Hariri's coffin. They looked and looked until tears spilled down their faces, these proud and body-broken men. Then they stood together and cried.

Somebody was reading prayers; the voices rang off the walls:

*God is strength.*
*Nothing exists or was born or is created that is stronger.*
*There is no God but God.*

The people in these rooms had the power to take the country someplace, but they had to decide where. We stood in a dwindling circle of time. Somewhere a cleric prayed; his voice piped through the rooms. The voices turned panicked as private grief swelled into something public and general. Soon they would move into the street, they would put Hariri in the ground and turn to face this new Lebanon.

"May God grant us victory over our enemies and avenge the crimes of the killers," the cleric said. "The enemies give us no methods to make up for this loss."

A middle-aged woman turned to her friends and spread her hands. "We're not going to remain silent anymore," she wept. "He wouldn't speak, but we're going to speak for him now. Speak, and don't be afraid."

We were moving then, past the green lawns and the boxwood hedges, into streets that seethed with souls. Steel paddles of news helicopters pounded the day. They waited for miles, in lines that stretched all the way down to the center of town, and everybody was yelling now, spitting out their slogans.

*They've killed progress by killing Hariri!*

*May God break the heads of those who've broken our backs!*

*Bashar, what do you want from us? Just leave us alone!*

We waded down in the trail of the coffin, pushing against strangers' skin and breath, and all along the road people cried, people screamed about Syria and Hariri and God, people waved flags, people stepped on one another and collapsed in the arms of strangers. Down at Martyrs'

Square they flooded the pavement, blanketed rooftops, dangled like spiders from the construction crane at the side of Hariri's mosque. Because, yes, Hariri had been building a mosque, the biggest and most sumptuous Sunni mosque Beirut had ever seen. He died before the mosque was finished, but they laid him to rest in its shadow all the same, with thousands of flowers and candles and drugged white doves blinking dazedly into flashing cameras. Lebanon is stuffed with martyrs, but Hariri would be the most resplendent martyr of all time. They wedged him right into the heart of Beirut. Whatever he did in life would be nothing compared to what his death could achieve. There was nothing Hariri's followers wouldn't do in the name of his blood.

There is a chunk of Beirut that stands on a foundation of garbage. Like many of Lebanon's curiosities, the explanation for it traces back to the civil war. The city cleaved into two during the fighting, split by a no-man's-land that cut through the middle of town, from the shore past the prime minister's office and back toward the airport, and everything wound up on one side or the other. The municipal garbage dump was east of the divide. So people in west Beirut threw their trash into the sea, and the toilet paper and broken plastic things and rusting hubcaps piled and fermented and packed and gelled into solid ground. The dump became earth and the size of Beirut grew. Things like that happen during a war; they happen to people and to cities, too. The landscape changes; the ground shifts forever. And then afterward you've got a city built on garbage, a place smooth and cured on the surface, but rotten at its roots.

I thought a lot about that garbage the first time I visited Beirut. It was back in 2003, and I came to write about the city's architectural rebirth. Hariri had razed the shell-chewed skeletons and put in a Tower Records and sidewalk bistros and Häagen-Dazs. New limestone was quarried down out of the mountains and all the destroyed buildings were put back together, pane by pane, stone by stone. The apple smoke of water pipes hung in the streets; Gucci and Rolex opened boutiques where gold watches and alligator shoes never went on sale because the Saudis and Kuwaitis poured in with their bottomless purses. Few honest Lebanese could afford to shop or eat there, it was true, but the tourists came flocking back and, anyway, there were enough dishonest Lebanese to make up the difference.

The downtown was perfect except that it was a lie, a shiny facade slapped over a war that had evaporated but never ended, questions that nobody asked, a history too contentious to be taught in school. A new generation was coming of age in a segregated country, in neighborhoods cleansed by their parents' religious slaughters. The warlords, militia leaders, engineers of kidnappings and torture—those men still ran the country. The armies of Shiites, Christians, and Druze had tucked away their guns and shrunk themselves down to political parties. None of the reasons for fighting had been discussed or resolved or excised. Lebanon had decided to live as if it were all a bad dream, a false thing that could never happen again, as if they had not torn themselves into a thousand pieces, as if they had not spent fifteen years slaughtering one another. Syria had sent in soldiers and intelligence agents after the war, passed out power among the different communities, and squelched dissent. The blank architecture was the face of collective amnesia. Lebanese moved through that city and the war breathed on their necks but nobody talked about it.

I'd ask: Aren't you afraid you will have more violence? Because it doesn't seem like anything is resolved.

They all said no. Oh no, never! The Lebanese have learned their lesson. The war was not really our war, not of us. It was America and Israel and Syria and Iran, meddling from outside. Wars take money, and we can't afford another war. We are too tired to fight. This new generation will be better. War is impossible.

Those were the stories they told themselves in the city built on garbage.

Hariri's death spun the city like a top, through days that melted into night and then day again, dizzy and sleepless with fever. Rich housewives and students cutting classes and old hardened fighters marched down into the streets by the thousands, the tens of thousands, and on big demonstration days, the hundreds of thousands. They hid away their militia flags and bought Lebanese flags instead. Suddenly patriotism was fashionable and party politics were gauche—or so the party leaders quietly instructed their flocks.

They took over Martyrs' Square, the one downtown spot left battle scarred, where bullet holes still showed on the central statue of triumphant gods and fallen fighters. Around the statue stretched vacant lots where large, unanswered questions lurked. It was into that awkward, gaping space that demonstrators surged. The shrine to the civil war would be the rallying ground for a new Lebanon. They pitched tents, threw up a stage and a booming sound system, and announced that they would stay until the Syrians were out of the country.

*Syria out*
*We hate you*
*Fuck Syria*

The crowd melted, the crowd morphed. It was a picnic, a rave, a campfire, a rock concert, a party of Christians, Sunni Muslims, and Druze that rolled through days and nights. A man dressed as a grim reaper carried a coffin through the crowd. Turn around and you saw college girls with the Lebanese flag painted on their faces. The old snipers and guerrillas who had become taxi drivers and shop owners stood quietly with hands in their pockets and unknowable expressions on their faces, roaming the encampments with guns in their pants. The darkness came down from the hills and skimmed over the sea to the sky, and footlights shone from the grass. The girls wore skin-tight jeans and knee-high boots. Babies crawled at their feet. Somebody blew a harmonica. Music throbbed from the speakers, big and sweeping, as if some bygone army were marching off to war. The flag wavers worked in shifts. There was a joke that floated around Lebanon that year, as winter made its long descent into spring. It started as a cartoon, I think: A Filipina maid stands alongside the diamond-draped housewife who imported her as slave labor. The housemaid carries a sign: "Madame says, 'Syria out!' "

The young people were giddy with it all. The mingling of Christians and Muslims gave them the idea that their generation would lift the country away from the bloodstained claws of their parents. I met a string of earnest young activists like Marwan Hayed, a twenty-six-year-old lawyer I came across one night among the tents.

"I was born before the war," he said. "I never got the chance to meet the other Lebanese. I was a Christian and I never knew the Muslims.

"For thirty years they have been lying about the war in Lebanon," he told me grandly. "They said it was a war among the Lebanese people. That was a lie. That's what you're discovering right now, what all Lebanese are discovering now. That we love each other. That we know each other better than ever."

"Now we have a new face. We are looking to our children and we don't want them to suffer like we suffered. Both sides paid too much blood. During the war, we were the same age as the people you see here." That was Sami Abu Gaodi, a Christian militiaman who struck up a conversation one night. His eyes moved fondly over the crowd. "The young generation, they are making us change."

Those interviews made me nervous, like listening to drunk people gush. It felt wobbly and dangerous, too slick and too easy. The protestors talked all day and all night about how Lebanon was finally united. Sectarianism is dead, they hollered. We are all one.

But—the Shiites weren't there. And nobody wanted to talk about it.

There were a lot of reasons for their absence, and the first was Hezbollah, the popular Shiite party and militia that held sway over most of Lebanon's largest sect. Hezbollah depended upon Syria for weapon-smuggling routes and political cover, so the prospect of a Syrian withdrawal scratched nerves. And there was a vaguer, deeper truth: the Shiites, historically shunted aside, impoverished, pushed out into the provinces, were wary of Lebanon without Syria. They had gained prestige and political clout under the tutelage of Damascus, and they were leery of being left alone with the Christians, Sunnis, and Druze. At first they closed their mouths and faded into the background. Hariri's blood was fresh and there was nothing they could say. Incredibly, nobody paid much attention to their conspicuous absence. Not the politicians, not the journalists, and certainly not the Lebanese themselves. It was treated as an irrelevant aside. But at least a third—as much as half—of the country was Shiite. In the end their distrust—of Israel, of America, of the Christians and Sunnis—was the most devastating corrosion of all.

One morning during those early protests, I visited a Shiite cabinet minister in his office. Syria had kept Lebanon stable for years, he argued over coffee. "The opposition is assuming they have the upper ground and they represent the majority, and this is dangerous. You have to have a dialogue with the majority party in Lebanon." He meant Hezbollah and the Shiites. "To liberate Lebanon, you don't want to destroy it."

In the streets, you could feel the danger, not in spoken words, but in silences. The anti-Syria crowds either pretended the Shiites didn't exist, or denied their absence. "There are Shiites here!" they said defensively.

"Where?"

"Here among us. I have met many Shiites. The Lebanese are all united."

"But where?"

"They are here!"

Two weeks of protests passed before Omar Karami, the Syria-backed prime minister, announced that he wouldn't rule against the wishes of the people. He resigned. The government fell.

The tent city dug in deeper. It wasn't enough. Faces were fixed toward one slogan: Syria out. Those words had been burning a hole in their tongues for fifteen years of silence, and now they screamed them. They protested and struck and marched. What did it mean, what came after, was it enough—nobody knew and, for the moment, nobody cared.

Washington was there all the while. Faces and neckties glowed on big screens spread behind the crowds, speeches boomed over the vacant lots. President Bush climbed behind podiums and said enormous things about Lebanon. No longer was this a small, forgotten place, a hopeless nest of killers passed off to Syria in desperation. Now, Bush proclaimed, Lebanon was the soul of the war on terror:

"All the world is witnessing your great movement of conscience. Lebanon's future belongs in your hands and, by your courage, Lebanon's future will be in your hands. The American people are on your side. Millions across the earth are on your side. The momentum of freedom is on your side, and freedom will prevail in Lebanon."

His enthusiasm was understandable. It was a hard winter, and getting harder. Close to 1,500 U.S. soldiers were dead in Iraq; insurgents beheaded their hostages on television and the United States had recently acknowledged losing track of almost $9 billion intended for the Iraqi government. There was no hope of peace talks in Jerusalem. The Taliban was rearing back to life in Afghanistan.

And then came sleepy little Lebanon, like manna from some neoconservative heaven. There were beautiful Muslims and Christians who lived in cosmopolitan seaside towns and spoke plausible English, so committed to their independence, to *democracy*, that they slept out under the stars. Here was the villain: Syria, irascible outlaw among a field of compliant Arab dictators. The American ambassador in Damascus went stomping back to Washington in protest the day after Hariri died. Democracy was on the march.

"Any who doubt the appeal of freedom in the Middle East can look to Lebanon, where the Lebanese people are demanding a free and independent nation," Bush said. "Democracy is knocking at the door of this country and, if it's successful in Lebanon, it is going to ring the doors of every Arab regime."

Lebanese basked eagerly in the attention. "All the world is now worried about Lebanon," marveled a middle-aged Christian lawyer. "President Bush, every day he talks about us."

One night in early March, the other shoe came clattering to earth, dropped from on high by the Party of God. Hezbollah chief Sayed Hassan Nasrallah stared from television screens and ordered his followers into the streets. These anti-Syria demonstrators were the handiwork of Israel and America, he said. All the talk of international law was a thin disguise; they'd come to meddle in Lebanese affairs, to disarm Hezbollah on behalf of the Zionists. When Nasrallah talks on television, bustling Beirut streets freeze—hotel lobbies, cafés, and electronics shops fall silent as people clump together and watch. When Nasrallah issued his order, the Shiites obeyed.

The day of Hezbollah's rally dawned gritty and gray. The Mediterranean stretched like steel, breathing a stinging wind over town. Hiking down the hill from the Hamra district, I turned a corner and stood staring at a livid, teeming human blanket. I thought the other crowds had been tremendously big. I thought I'd never see so many people packed into the streets and plazas of Beirut. But Hezbollah's crowd dwarfed all that had come before, smothering gardens, overpasses, and tunnels. The other Lebanon had arrived, ready to declare itself to the world in a show of loyalty to Syria. The original demonstrators, the ones who hollered for Syria to get out, stood just down the hill, holding their ground at Martyrs' Square. Lines of Lebanese soldiers kept the groups separated. Once again, the city was split in two.

The Hezbollah demonstrators were mostly farmers and workers from the south and the Bekaa Valley, people who'd suffered the Israeli occupation. They came in rattletrap buses, with dirt under their fingernails, and walked the streets with the weary patience of people accustomed to waiting at the back of the line: men in work clothes and sensible boots; women swathed in head scarves, moving silently along behind their husbands. They didn't have Hummers and Pierre Cardin and Sri Lankan housemaids. They didn't jump around or snap photos of themselves or sway to patriotic music. They stood grimly, carrying posters that said, "Bush, we hate you," "All our disasters come from America," and "America is the source of all our terrorism."

A passing woman grabbed my arm. "Are you a journalist?"

"Yes," I said.

"Well." She squared her thin shoulders and poked her chin forward. "I am a Shiite."

"Okay."

"All the Shiites are not poor," she pressed on indignantly. "All the Shiites are not from the south. Look at me. I am a Shiite, too."

She was a small, lithe woman in her thirties. She looked quintessentially Lebanese, meaning she looked beautiful in a contrived and doll-like way—a beauty concocted from hair dyes and foundation creams and expensive clothes. She wore spike heels, tight jeans, and a sequined Daisy Duck T-shirt under a stylishly distressed leather jacket. A diamond pendant dangled from her neck; her fingers tapered into manicure; glossy hair swished to her shoulders. She was roaming with three shiny-haired, perfumed girlfriends carting signs that said "No to foreign intervention."

"So what are you saying?" I asked her.

"I'm a Shia. I go to the beaches in my swimsuit. I studied with the nuns. I went to the American University of Beirut. My kids don't know whether they are Christian or Muslim. Last time somebody asked my son, 'Are you Christian or Muslim?' he didn't know."

"So," I said, "do you feel like these demonstrations are creating sectarian trouble?"

"We are with the people over there," she replied, pointing down the hill to the anti-Syria camp. "But some of them are racist, they've been dealing with Israel. They want to divide the country. I have four kids, and sometimes at night I can't sleep because I'm so worried that my kids will live what I lived during the war."

"You really think it will come to that?"

"I don't know. I am very, very worried."

She was gone, swallowed by the crowd.

The announcer bellowed surprise news: *Sayed Hassan Nasrallah is here.*

That name! It stirred the bodies and lit the faces. Nasrallah, hunted by Israel, a famous ghost who flitted through underground chambers and hidden offices in the warrens of the southern suburbs, would show his face in the heart of Beirut for the first time in years. "Thank you to Syria," the announcer cried, heating up the crowd. "Thank you to President Assad." The men leapt up and down, fists pumping. The women's faces tipped skyward, saintly and pale, eyes swelling to take him in.

And there he stood, impossible as a hallucination, on a balcony over the Buddha Bar and the Casa del Habano cigar shop. Silence grabbed the crowd by the tongue. But Nasrallah wasn't talking to them; they were merely his context. Nasrallah was talking to the world.

"If you really want to defend freedom in Lebanon and democracy in Lebanon, then you must look with your two eyes," he said. "Are we not the people of the Lebanon you love? We tell you we want to maintain and protect our historic ties with Syria and we believe in the resistance."

"Now let me turn to America," he said.

Fists drove to heaven. "Death to America!"

"You've made a mistake with your calculations. Lebanon will not change its name or its history or its politics," Nasrallah informed America. "Do you think the Lebanese are afraid of American fools? Don't interfere with our internal affairs. Get your fingers off our country."

As darkness settled over the streets, there was grogginess in the air; the alarm had shrilled and the dream was gone. This was real. This was the danger that nobody wanted to write or talk about: The "popular revolution" existed only in one half of the country. The dancing in the streets, the fast push for toppled governments and new days, was tearing the country in two. In the tent city on Martyrs' Square, the activists shivered and stood their ground.

"Those weren't Lebanese," they said irritably. "They bused in Syrians. They bused in Palestinians."

"Maybe," I said. "But there were Lebanese, too. A lot of Lebanese."

"Those people are not Lebanese."

That's the essence of it, I thought. They see only their sectarian mythology, the stories they tell themselves. They are wrapped in dreams, believing only the narratives of their own creation.

"If they represent half, then we're the other half," a student spat out. His tone was almost desperate.

"We can't get rid of them," said another student, "and they can't get rid of us."

The clash wasn't country against city; poor versus rich; Shiites squaring off against the rest. It was all of that, a little bit, and none of that. It was deeper and darker, harder to say, and impossible to fix. Lebanon was pushing blindly toward change, and it had to decide what kind of country it was going to be: a protectorate of Syria, tied to Iran through Hezbollah, verging on pariah status, battling endlessly with Israel, or this new country that Hariri and the others were trying to forge—free from Syrian influence, oriented toward France and America, liberal and warless, luring tourists and making nice with the neighbors. Each side saw its own extinction in the alternate vision. They weren't living in the same country anymore; they had become divided until they couldn't even recognize one another. I was haunted most of all by the Christians who looked at the Shiites and said simply, "Those people are not Lebanese." Because they believed it.

*If they represent half, then we're the other half.*
*We can't get rid of them, and they can't get rid of us.*

In the end, the Americans managed to pry Lebanon out of Syria's hands. They sent the Russians, the Saudis, and everybody else to lean on Damascus until they didn't have a friend left in the world, aside from Iran. The demonstrations helped, of course. The protests, tent city, and anthems gave America an irrefutable screen to lean over the Atlantic and smack Syria across the jowls.

I watched the last Syrian soldiers pull out of Lebanon on an April day when the sun dripped like hot honey through the straight, fresh pines of the Bekaa Valley. The crust of words had flaked away. The politicians had raged; the kings and presidents had slathered on their threats. The Lebanese had called the Syrians dogs and bastards and sons of whores, hollered their heads off, beaten luckless Syrian construction workers. Now it was time to swallow the acid long enough to say good-bye.

A lot of questions massed under the surface that day: Can you undo long years of domination by emptying out a few army bases? What about proxies and undercover intelligence? What about Hezbollah? How will this country, which is really two countries, find its way forward? The day Syria left, nobody asked.

At a military base near the border, the Syrian and Lebanese army commanders strolled side by side through beds of roses and daisies, saluting the troops. The two national anthems wheezed from brass horns. Mountains loomed splendidly against the sky.

"Lebanon will endure. Its rocks, its mountains, its waters will stay. And that's thanks to the Syrian military presence, which ensured the unity of Lebanon," Syrian commander Ali Habib told the soldiers. "The civil war is over and Lebanon, once weak, is strong through its people, its army, and its resistance. Our relationship is bound by the pure blood spilled by our forces."

Wordless, blank, the soldiers stood in straight lines under their berets—red for the Syrians, green for the Lebanese. Bugles blared, songbirds trilled, cell phones chirped.

The Lebanese commander embedded in the soil a square of marble commemorating twelve thousand Syrian soldiers killed in the civil war. Then he stood there, this Christian general, and thanked Syria for arming Hezbollah and protecting the country from Israel. It was a reminder of the truth that lurked under the resentments: at the invitation of the world, Syria had taken on broken, impossible Lebanon, with its dagger-in-teeth warlords and its slick, shiny liars and its endless capacity for blood and more blood. Syria had waded into a mess and pacified Lebanon.

"Dear brothers, in our hearts we feel love and great thanks and we want to tell brotherly Syria, its army, and its people, thank you," the Lebanese commander said.

The drums cracked, and hundreds of boots hacked crisply at the blacktop. The Syrians turned their backs to Beirut and their faces to the ramshackle buses that would carry them home. I bumped into Adib Farha in a pale, fancy suit, and was immediately hurtled back to the nasty realities of Beirut. He was a Lebanese American, one of the countless well-groomed, white-teethed analysts you could count on to flay Syria in tidy English. Today, he stood sputtering.

"So what do you think?" I said.

"It's ludicrous, surreal," he yelped, swallowing a laugh and then leaning in a little. "It's hard to imagine a country that feels occupied for thirty years is thanking its occupiers as they leave. This really shows the huge schism between the Lebanese president and government and people.

"Here," he said, interrupting himself, "take my number and call me later. I'm going to be on CNN." And he was gone, rushing off like the White Rabbit in shiny shoes.

The buses of Syrian soldiers rumbled east, through vineyards reconstructed from the wreckage of battle and fields greening with the first breaths of spring. They rolled past fading roadside pictures of Ayatollah Khomeini; kiosks where fresh fruit dangled on strings; tractors and orchards. The buses wept paint chips as they belched over the hills. Beneath the plastered portraits of Bashar al-Assad, the windows were cracked. The Syrian army is desperately poor; it was hard for anybody to hate the skinny young soldiers too much, simply because they lived so badly, moping around with the faces of kicked dogs.

Housewives and old men and schoolchildren lined the road and stood there silently, waiting for the Syrians to pass. They crowded the doorways of banks and gritty vegetable shops and clothing stores. I pulled over in the village of Riyaq, and stood with some women who had abandoned their mirrors at a beauty shop to watch history groan past. "The Syrians suffered a lot here," a Christian woman told me. "At the time they entered, sectarianism was rife. Many people left here, and there was a lot of violence. The Syrian presence helped keep the Christians here. Without a doubt, a lot of mistakes were made, but we will remain friends."

When the Lebanese saw the Syrians, they smiled and waved their arms and honked horns, as if they were watching relatives pull away. The Lebanese smiled up, and the Syrians smiled down, and they held up two fingers in the sign of peace and victory.

The pinched faces of the young soldiers hung in those busted windows, and their hands waved good-bye, good-bye. "To Damascus," one of the guards chanted through his open window, his smile spread all over his face. Syria leaving and good-bye. A new day coming, and good-bye.

They disappeared over the borderline, off through the tanks and pine-shaded hills. All along the road back to Beirut, the people were returning to houses that had been seized by the Syrians. They were counting the things that were stolen, the fruit trees crushed, asking each other whether the townspeople who fled for America and Europe and Australia might finally come home.

I kept stopping to ask people how they felt. They all said the same thing.

I feel scared, they said. We don't know what's coming next.

These months of revolution would all come back like a bad dream. There was a promise embedded in all those Bush administration speeches: that if the Lebanese fought against Syria and formed a new government, Washington would back it up. Confident and strident, Lebanon pushed Syria away. Washington applauded, and said some nice things. But nobody addressed the tangle of Hezbollah's power and Shiite fears—not the Lebanese, who could hardly admit the other half of the country existed, and not the Americans, who talked about Hezbollah as if it were an alien force, a fringe enemy, and not a grassroots movement woven into the fabric of Lebanese politics and society.

A year later, when Israel pounded Lebanon with bombs, broke the roads and bridges, and crushed the economy, when the country's Washington-backed leaders wept and begged the Bush administration to call off the attack, Washington sat back and let Israel ravage this fledgling country in the name of crippling Hezbollah.

Lebanon found itself on the wrong end of the war on terror, after all.

## THIRTEEN

# THE EARTHQUAKE NOBODY FELT

The knowledge gathered in Cairo, the things you assumed about Egypt, fell away on the long, gritty road out of town, along the Nile banks through bawling vendors and groaning minivans, over bridges wilting under the weight of steel and flesh. Cairo collapsed into fields of swamp grass and clover, resurrected itself again in spits of tenements, and finally faded behind. The road to Damanhour pressed north toward the sea, through the thick of the Nile Delta. Brilliant rice fields nourished the lumbering water buffalo, whose fleas in turn fed the white birds plucking at their hides. The road was wild, crammed with darting creatures and half-broken machines. Rolling mountains of cheap clothing rose from flatbed trucks, and workers slept, their bodies wedged into cliffs on those wobbling textile hills. Vast families crammed into the beds of pickups, punched by wind. Even the edges of the road were jammed with donkeys, goats, and camels, mopeds spitting black smoke, schoolgirls who peered owlishly from beneath the brims of head scarves. This route was unfathomably old when Napoleon limped along it, and today it still courses with traffic, with families who have ridden this road for generations, from the fabled fields of the delta to the dented, overgrown splendor of Cairo; between schools and factories, farms and slatternly inner-city markets.

There was a place where the Jeep spat out of the farmlands and into a little town too poor to pave its stretch of roadway. They'd pressed stones into the sand instead, and as we bounced and jolted our way over the rocks, fingers splayed on the ceiling, Hossam said through chattering teeth, "Welcome to the Latin Quarter." He said it every time, and every time, it made us laugh.

I'd hired Hossam, a bohemian city kid who moved among the intellectuals and expatriates of the Egyptian capital, as a reporter and translator. He was a stalwart socialist with a shamefaced penchant for lattes from Starbucks, music by Moby, and Scandinavian death metal bands. Sucking a ceaseless string of Marlboros, he waved his arms and rambled about how the left would eventually join ranks with the popular Muslim Brotherhood and form an overpowering opposition bloc.

I'd snort. "If the Muslim Brotherhood take over they'll put you against the wall," I'd tell him, only half joking. "You know what happened in Iran."

"I'll be the commissar of information." His face lit with bravado. "You'll have all the interviews you need."

By 2005, American enthusiasm for Arab democracy was sinking back into silence. Every time Arabs voted—in Beirut, in Gaza City, in Karbala—Islamists grew more powerful. Hezbollah and Hamas were gaining sway. Egypt, the most populous Arab country and the psychological core of the region, rippled with tension between Islam and democracy. There was only one source of serious political opposition to the Egyptian autocracy, a single party potentially strong enough to unseat the government—and that was the Muslim Brotherhood, a nonviolent Islamist movement with deep roots across Egypt. Officially, the Muslim Brotherhood was outlawed, but the reality was nuanced. The government would pass through bouts of tolerance, then abruptly round up activists and raid party offices in crackdowns. Nobody stood to gain more from democratic reform than the Brotherhood, because no other force in Egypt had its legitimate popularity, the grassroots credentials, the air of moral authority. And yet the United States refused to speak with the Muslim Brotherhood. It was an unlikely stance, especially given the pro-democracy rhetoric ringing through Washington in those days. The Brotherhood is illegal, U.S. policy went, and therefore we will not recognize it. Now there would be parliamentary elections, and I would watch the race from the battleground of Damanhour.

The first night we rode the grinding road to Damanhour, I met

Muslim Brotherhood candidate Gamal Heshmat. On that sharp night, the Muslim Brotherhood had called a political rally, and Heshmat would speak to his hometown. The silt of autumn dark thickened on the square. From the front row, we had a good view of a towering Koran and a podium under pictures of crossed swords. Hossam and I stood and gawked. There were hundreds of people. No, thousands. You couldn't see the vanishing point where the faithful tapered into the night; their bodies faded down every side street and alleyway.

Hossam's eyes swelled huge enough to reflect the moon. His swagger had melted away. "I can't believe it," he muttered. "It makes the left look like shit."

"How many people do you think this is? It must be every man in town."

"Yeah," Hossam said. "Shit."

I knew what he was thinking. I was thinking it, too: The secular, pro-democracy demonstrations we'd covered back in Cairo were nothing by comparison. A ragtag army of aging labor leaders, embattled human rights workers, scruffy bloggers, and rheumy professors would rally on a tiny scrap of stained pavement. Layers of security lined up on all sides and pressed in, plainclothes thugs bused in from the slums and uniformed conscripts in riot gear, clubs hanging from their hands. Maybe they would glower and snap photographs for bottomless security files, or maybe they would smash the demonstrators' limbs with clubs, kick their ribs, and haul them off to prison for genital electrification and sodomy. It could go either way, any way, depending on their mood.

Now we were far from Cairo's hallucinatory concrete forests; stars gleamed in a black sky and there unfolded a subversive force on a scale we'd never see in the capital. These men were factory workers, farmers, and fathers, not political activists. They turned up because the Muslim Brotherhood had invited them, and stood quietly, filling the streets and listening to their leaders. There were women, too, veiled, robed, and arranged in careful rows. Men and boys linked hands to form a human screen of segregation between the sexes.

They had come because, like the rest of Egypt, and like the other Arab countries beyond, these people sensed some vague change, a long-awaited political opening. That was the mood: guarded, incredulous hope that had seeped, somehow, out of Iraq. They had heard the radical promises of American leaders—the vows to support democracy over dictatorship in the Arab world; the acknowledgments that propping up tyrants and torturers might have bred terrorism. This was brand-new rhetoric, and it made Arab potentates nervous. President Hosni Mubarak, Egypt's modern-day pharaoh, had gone through the charade of running for "reelection." (He was never elected to begin with.) Before the parliamentary elections, Condoleezza Rica came to Cairo and embarrassed the Egyptian regime with an unusually sharp speech. "People will watch what happens in Egypt," she warned. Egyptians started talking about the Americans as parents who'd just stepped out of the room, as if they might come back and give Mubarak a spanking if he didn't behave. The Muslim Brotherhood boldly fielded dozens of candidates across the country.

A few lines from the Koran, and the speeches got started. Hossam translated, breathing the words into my ear. The men glared down; we were outsiders, whispering while the clerics spoke. Hossam sucked sharply at air and groaned. He stopped translating, raised his eyes sheepishly, and hoisted himself to his feet. Even the big shots on the stage were looking down, smiling. Hossam turned to the crowd, flashed a smile that looked more like a grimace, and raised a reluctant hand. Applause swelled. Suddenly, the same men who'd been glowering over our shoulders were smiling, reaching big paws to pump Hossam's hand in the air, giving me approving little nods.

"What the hell was that?" I hissed.

"Don't freak out, but they said they wanted to thank the *Los Angeles Times* for being here and for our support," he muttered.

"Great."

He shrugged. "They don't understand."

A half moon dangled from the desert sky. Women and children jostled on balconies spangled with flimsy Ramadan lanterns. A sea of faces glimmered in light from the podium. Far from the dingy Cairo offices of slick-talking Brotherhood leaders trained to say the right things to Western reporters, out of reach of the U.S. embassy, Egypt seemed to open itself. This was the Muslim Brotherhood where they had evolved organically, where it thrived unself-consciously.

Some people argue that the popularity of political Islam is exaggerated. Others say that groups like the Brotherhood are only powerful because repressive rulers have shut down every single public platform except the mosque. But that night showed a simpler truth: These people were profoundly religious. Poor and abused, they passed faith from one generation to the next because it was the only precious thing they could bequeath. They didn't trust the greedy, potbellied suits in the capital—those people meant corruption and sin. They rallied to the Islamists who came from their towns and mosques because they felt at home with them and recognized in their piety a reflection of their own moral values. The people weren't stupid; they knew these Brothers represented problems, too. But this was their life, the devil they knew. I thought about the powerful Christian movements back home. Could Americans see nothing of ourselves here?

A sheikh from the ancient Al Azhar university warmed up the crowd, his voice rising and dropping in evangelical waves. He preached politics, preached Islam, preached divine intervention. He was calling down God, calling out the vote. He was magnetic.

"Corruption is a disease that has destroyed our country. Those who accept life without religion have accepted annihilation."

"We will not compromise, we will not bow down. We've come to hate low voices. Every minute that passes is too much time."

He steered his talk from heaven to earth and back again. The townspeople were instructed to bring twenty other voters to the polling stations. If the government stole the election, he pledged, the Brotherhood would go to court.

"They might mock us for it, but we'll pray to God to send his wrath," the cleric said. "We will shout, 'God is on our side,' and he will compensate us for what's happening."

When the candidate took the stage, a murmur passed through the crowd. Heshmat peered down through spectacles, a lone tuft of hair clinging to his shining scalp and a shabby wool blazer drooping from his shoulders.

"Who are they, and who are we?" he demanded of the crowd. "They are the princes, the sultans, they have the money. They make shows with music. They play politics but all they're really good at is putting more brass on their shoulders."

"The youth of this nation are just sitting in coffee shops, jumping into boats, trying to get to Italy," he said. "Are we a country without natural resources?"

"Yes," I muttered to Hossam.

"Are we a country without a professional class?"

"Pretty much."

"Are we a country of politically immature people?"

We laughed quietly.

"Are we going to take that talk from the government?" Heshmat thundered on. "How dare they say that?"

A single voice rose like a wisp of smoke from the crowd.

"*Inshallah . . .*" God willing.

The night exploded into voices. The men sprayed fake snow into the darkness, poked fingers to the sky, and hollered, "Victory is for Islam!" They spread out and marched aimlessly, as if it didn't matter where they went—as if they owned the whole town, as if the vast stretches of country beyond had already fallen into their laps, a rich gift from God.

The banners passed. "Islam, we are for you." "May you make a staircase of our skulls and go high to glory." "If your banner gets thirsty, our youth will give their blood."

Such a thing seemed possible in this strange witching hour, that their skulls could pile one atop the other, that they could clamor to the sky. I tried to imagine what they imagined; tried to feel the fire of faith when you had nothing else to hold.

The rally was over soon. A man from the stage gave a gentle reminder to the silent women:

"Now the sisters have to wait a bit aside until the people leave," he said. "Then, they can leave after."

*People first*, I wrote, *women second.*

Like so many other Egyptians, Heshmat had fallen under the rapture of the Brotherhood in college. He became a doctor, and eventually wormed his way into Parliament the way everybody in the banned Brotherhood sneaks in: by running as an independent, with a wink and a nudge. Once in Parliament, he rabble-roused, holy-rolled, and generally made a nuisance of himself. He griped about corruption. He was a driving force behind the riots over *Banquet of Seaweed*, a popular Syrian novel the Brotherhood deemed too lewd and blasphemous for Egyptian bookstores. By 2003, the government was fed up. They kicked Heshmat out of Parliament and threw him into jail for six months. Damanhour, his hometown, went crazy. Riots erupted. The army was dispatched. Young men were beaten and carted off to jail. And then, for years, bitterness festered.

This election was to be Heshmat's comeback. The townspeople were still angry; they wanted revenge as badly as Heshmat did, maybe even more. Every man and woman I met in the streets vowed to vote for Heshmat. If the government plays any of its old tricks, they said through tight jaws, they'll have a fight on their hands.

"They humiliated the people." Heshmat was perched in a thinly stuffed armchair. "But now I'm even stronger. I may have lost a parliamentary seat, but I won another seat in the heart of the people."

In his ill-lit walkup office, plastic flowers erupted from the walls and aides bent in prayer, foreheads pressed to the floor. Sitting before Heshmat, I asked the question I always asked Islamists: A lot of Egyptians worry that if the Brotherhood gets more power, you will impose *hijab* on women. This is the fear of secular and Christian Egyptians. Is it true?

Heshmat didn't like the question, not coming from a young American woman. He frowned and launched into a lecture on the feminist values of Islam. Muslim women keep their names after marriage, own property, and choose their husbands, he argued. "Islam grants so much liberty, but only in a moral framework," he said. "This moral framework benefits us a lot. It gives us a lower HIV rate, makes sure there are no children out of wedlock."

You didn't answer the question about head scarves, I said.

"We get asked all the time to respect others, but others should also respect us and our privacy and our specifications," he said, shooting me a sharp look. "Globalization shouldn't be a globalization of morals, of interfering in affairs of every stripe."

It didn't go much better with the other candidate, Mubarak's man. His name was Moustafa Fiqi. He had been educated in London and sent around the world as an Egyptian diplomat. He hadn't won the election yet, and theoretically the odds were against him. But powerful people in Cairo were already whispering that he would rise to a prominent role within Parliament.

Fiqi hardly bothered to campaign in Damanhour. Instead, he borrowed a computer shop to serve as headquarters and dispatched his "campaign manager," who turned out to be a mid-ranking intelligence officer.

When I met Fiqi, he flashed Dior cufflinks and spoke careful English. The Muslim Brotherhood, he argued, was trying to take over the country. The national anthem scratched, over and over, from a cassette player.

"Our Brothers on the other side should know, and I've announced from the beginning, I'll quit if there's any rigging," he pledged in a campaign rally that night. "I believe in my freedom and the freedom of others."

That was the last I saw of Fiqi.

The diplomats lounged in a teahouse off the main square, sipping thimbles of Lipton and looking pleased with themselves. They were two men, both on the young side, an American and a Frenchman. It was election day, and they'd trekked from Cairo to observe the balloting. We hauled chairs over to join them.

Everything's quiet here, they said, draining their teacups, postures slack. We're going to move on.

We've heard they've been fighting since morning, we said.

We don't see anything, they said. They were bored. They were headed by car for Alexandria.

Hossam and I wandered around the corner to the closest polling station—and into the heart of a standoff. Bearing helmets, clubs, and riot shields, the Egyptian soldiers had surrounded and sealed off a school where the voting was supposed to take place. The men clustered as close as they dared, packed the alleys and side streets, pressed themselves against the worn shops. They wanted to vote but instead they cowered, glaring at the soldiers. A skinny young man peeled himself out of the crowd, straightened his spine, and marched toward the polling station. The soldiers pounced: shoes and fists flying in the dirt, they beat and kicked him to the ground and dragged him off toward the paddy wagons. The rest of the men glared some more.

On the eerily empty bit of road between the two sides, I stood awkwardly with Hossam. We made the security forces uncomfortable, I guess. They ran hostile eyes over us, muttering to one another. I stared back, wary. When I covered demonstrations in Cairo, the police and soldiers had pushed me around, slapped me, groped at my breasts and backside, ripped at my clothes. One glaring summer day, a pack of government thugs had pinned my female translator to the ground, kicked her, and sexually molested her. Working as a journalist in Egypt had taught me what it was like to fight, physically—to thrash instinctively, to pound at flesh until the air opened around my own body, until I was clear.

Hossam tugged a camera from his pocket and quietly snapped a few pictures of the riot police.

Before we saw them coming, lumpy thugs swarmed. Hammy fingers snatched Hossam's camera away. Hossam bellowed, scrawny arms clawing after his prized possession.

"*Sahafiyeh*!" I yelled, digging around in my jeans pocket for a press credential. "Journalists! Give us the camera back!"

They separated us, and thick male bodies closed around me. Hossam's voice came from a place I could not see, behind a wall of flesh, still hollering about his camera. No time to think or feel; there was only a wash of white rage, the accumulated anger of all the fights with the henchmen of Mubarak's ruling party. A sharp awareness and a deadening at the same time, I felt it flooding through my veins like chemicals. This time, I was sure they would beat Hossam. They would beat him because he was Egyptian, because he was a man, and because he had come with a foreigner. And it would be my fault, because I hired him and brought him here. I forced my hands into the light between two of the thugs and tried to drive their bodies apart, to get to Hossam. One of them, a man with bulbous muscles and hair pomaded into place, shoved me backward. I pushed him back, as hard as I could, cursing him in English. He showed his teeth. We grappled; he hit me in the face.

"God DAMN you!" I shouted miserably, and pushed him again.

I wanted to cover an election, and instead I had to fight in the street.

I thought about the teahouse diplomats who came to see but didn't bother to look; about how my own government pumped Egypt full of a billion dollars and then some, asking nothing in return but the maintenance of a frosty peace with Israel. I remembered the American human rights official who told me that Egypt, of all the Arab states, came closest to having a modern-day gulag, and the U.S. officials who stayed mostly silent in the face of torture and arrest and misery. The pictures swam through my mind: soldiers beating people bloody to keep them from voting; four-course lunches with necktie-clad Americans at the embassy in Cairo; the knowledge that my own government lurked in the background, propping up this machine of greasy, perverted men, not seeing this because it was convenient not to see.

The men turned their backs and left, sneering over their shoulders, taking Hossam's camera with them. I stood with heart hammering on the muddy street slick with the shit of water buffalo, blown with fading trash. I touched my stinging face. Hossam's eyes were bulging with anger. "Okay," I told him stupidly. "Okay."

I tried to tell myself that the best revenge would be to document all of it, every little piece, write it all down and commit the story to the public record. This is how you are supposed to think, but it doesn't always make sense. I was struggling to channel the anger. I wanted to share this strategy with Hossam, but I mangled the words.

"We just have to keep going now. Forget about your camera. Forget it. We'll think about it later. This is not about us, okay? We're not the story here."

"Bastards," he said. I patted his back awkwardly; it felt stiff as stone under my fingers. He didn't want my consolation; he was seething. This was his fight, his future, his broken promises. It was his country, not mine.

We were joined on the streets by our friend, an American analyst with the International Crisis Group, shaking his head from side to side. When he finally spoke, the words came out slow and matter of fact:

"I'm not convinced that if the Muslim Brotherhood took over, imposed sharia, and started chopping off heads in Tahrir Square, it would be worse. If there were some justice to how they were chopping heads, it might be better."

---

Dusk smeared the steely sky. APCs loomed on the streets; the army had deployed artillery to keep the people out of the polling stations. Darkness injected the crowd with new recklessness. The promised day of justice and retribution had been wasted; the hours burned off like fog, and people were crazy with rage.

Men snatched up chunks of broken lumber. Little boys lobbed rocks at the steel swell of armored vehicles. "I can't believe we're in *Egypt*," I told Hossam. He shook his head, eyes darting around. The pop of tear gas canisters rang in alleys, then a dull hiss as chemical clouds swallowed the butcher shops, cigarette stands, and teahouses. Children squeezed themselves flat against the buildings and wept. We buried our noses in the crooks of our arms, eyes streaming, throats clenched. Out of the haze stumbled Sayed, our driver, hacking and choking. I couldn't tell if he was coming to fetch us, or looking for shelter from the gas. He didn't seem to know either; he just wept and coughed. People were shredding rags, soaking them in water, pressing them to their mouths. Egyptian hospitality unflagged, they kept offering me their rags because I was a foreigner.

"May God avenge me!" screamed a nearby man, tripping down the street with tears coursing down his face. "Take a picture of me while I'm crying," he sniffled.

"I can't," Hossam snapped.

The tanks loomed like dinosaurs through the haze. Forms stumbled forth, scattered words at our feet, and lurched onward. Rubber bullets slammed through the air.

"We are determined to vote in spite of this," said Reda Shamma, a twenty-three-year-old engineering student who washed up at our side like something tossed from the sea. He raked his hands through his hair. He didn't seem to realize he was screaming.

"We won't elect somebody with liquor at his place," he ranted on. "He's against God's choice and we can't elect this guy, we just can't."

In the square the men chanted: "Fiqi, you fucking pimp; Fiqi, you fucking pimp . . ."

"Look at this!" another man shouted. He handed over one of the spent tear gas canisters. He pointed to the block lettering. MADE IN THE USA, it said. He looked at me, waiting for an answer.

I had none to give.

Cold darkness fell over the town. The polls closed. A drizzle began. A long winter sat ready to swallow the countryside. Boys wheeled on bikes; women wandered along the edges of the canals. When you passed people in the street, they muttered his name: Gamal Heshmat. But they didn't look at you, and they kept walking.

Judges packed the padlocked ballot boxes into taxicabs and drove them to the military academy, where they would be counted by hand. The street in front of the counting station writhed with bodies. It was the kind of crowd so big and mad that it forces you to cede control; it will bear you along, but if you resist it can crush you. The Brotherhood representatives who worked for Heshmat tried to follow the taxis toward the school. They had a right to monitor the vote count. But the police turned them away and hauled out metal barriers.

A chant rose from the crowd: *With our blood and our souls we will sacrifice for you, Islam*. If they fake our votes, we will die here, they said, eyes snapping and flashing. The officials marching past bore duffel bags, backpacks, and bulky brown paper packages. The crowd attacked one of the officials and ripped the sack from beneath his arm.

The package was crammed with blank ballots, each one marked with the official eagle stamp of the Interior Ministry. "We're being raped!" the people howled. "It's fraud! It's fraud!" Hundreds, thousands of blank ballots piled in the street like snowdrifts, shredded under a scuffle of sandals. Men pounced on the paper like children snatching at candy from a piñata, scooped the ballots up, yelling all the while. They were righteous; they had proof! But they looked around and realized there was nobody to show. A man stopped and stared in my eyes. "Please tell everything you see here today to the international organizations with great frankness," he said. I nodded. I didn't bother to answer. People in these places always cling to that hope—that somewhere in the world, something stronger than their government is watching. Against all evidence, they still believe in referees. They see me, a foreigner, and think I represent the referee. They don't know that this story has been written before, over and over again, and still the status quo sits stolid.

A slight man in a sweater vest and necktie lingered at the edge of the crowd, watching with weary eyes. He did not scream or wave the ballots. He was a forty-seven-year-old engineer. "I am not a Muslim Brother," he told me pointedly. But watching his hometown vote get rigged, he was melancholy.

"I did my best to be a good man in this society," he said, carefully pronouncing the English words. "But I feel too much small. I cannot find myself in my own country."

He waved an arm at the ballots. "I am feeling that I am nothing," he said. "I want to feel that I am a man, that I am a member of this society." He shook his head, and stopped talking.

Boots clattered on the sidewalk; police conscripts had come to control the mob. They ringed the school and probed the crowd with anxious eyes. Some of the Brothers slipped near and spoke to them quietly over their shields. "All of this is just for you," one of the Brothers said. "We're doing this just for you, so you shouldn't beat us."

The conscripts nodded and smiled blankly at the Brothers. They looked young, underfed, and nervous. "What a black night," one of the conscripts muttered to his neighbor. And then he said it again: "What a black night."

The rain came slowly at first, but then the skies opened. The streetlights with their cheap wiring sizzled and snapped overhead. The dust turned to mud in the road and then disappeared under gleaming puddles.

The men of the Brotherhood stood straight and said a prayer for the rain. They prayed that the rain would fall all around them but would leave them dry. They prayed that the water would go straight down to the roots of the plants. They prayed as if the rain were a promise from God, and after each line the men said, "*Ya Allah.*" O God.

Their voices rang like metal through the wet streets, carrying to the high walls ringing the school where the ballots were being counted, over the heads of the police generals who cowered beneath the dripping trees with their shoulders full of stars.

The night wore on and on. In the end, we drove back to Cairo. The men were still locked up in the ballot station. There would be no word until morning.

In the morning, it came. Moustafa Fiqi had won the seat in Damanhour.

Things like this happen, and you wait for the world to explode. You have heard all the words and threats, the vows of vengeance. I woke up the gray morning after the vote with a hangover from teargas, adrenaline, and other people's rage. A bruise had come out on my face. Terse and silent, Hossam and I jolted back over those long, rutted roads to Damanhour, expecting to find a riot in the street, the town closed by tanks, fires in the sky.

There was nothing. Violence came to Egypt, raged up from the earth, strong and stripped of warning. It did what it had come to do. And then it vanished as if it had never existed at all, and you couldn't tell anything had passed.

A bedraggled brown sheep plodded through a winter drizzle in the main square. The shops were closed, the shutters yanked to the ground. The streets were empty, the balconies deserted. We drove to the Brotherhood's walkup offices, and found a padlock on the door.

A little boy wheeled by on a bicycle. "They arrested two of the big guys," he said. "That's all we know." He pedaled quickly off.

We asked blank-faced men, punched numbers into cell phones, and finally we found a Brotherhood lawyer who took us to Heshmat's home. He looked frail, folded into a low armchair in his button-down cardigan. Reedy ankles poked from his pants. He told us what had happened the night before.

He had been ahead at 1:30 in the morning. The judges had started to wander over and shake his hand. Then a security director arrived and asked Heshmat to leave. He called some judges he knew in Alexandria. Was the supervising judge trustworthy? Word came back: Yes, he's clean. Go ahead. Heshmat left the building in high spirits. Only a matter of time, he thought. But dawn broke. Security forces were being trucked in from neighboring provinces. The government, it seemed, was bracing for unrest. At seven, the judge and security director finally emerged. They didn't make eye contact with Heshmat. Their announcement was plain: Fiqi by a landslide.

Now Heshmat's bravado was gone. You could see defeat in every curve of his posture.

"I don't know how he'll feel, being Parliament speaker, knowing he won by forgery. As an intellectual, he's finished," he half whined. "I'm planning to appeal and planning to go global to expose what's happened." But his voice was listless.

He dropped his head.

"This is such a stupid regime. Stupid, stupid, stupid."

A neighbor burst into his apartment. He had come angry; he wanted Heshmat to put the men out to fight in the streets.

"I really disagree with you," he told Heshmat, white beard dancing jerkily to his words. "The people are ready to die."

"So many people were arrested . . ." Heshmat trailed off.

"So what? So what? Even if they arrest a thousand, so what? We were all willing to die for the ballot boxes yesterday. What they did was unbelievable."

But Heshmat was unmoved. His son, an art student, had been carted off to jail overnight, along with dozens of other young men. He didn't have any push left.

"I'm concerned about the people's safety," he said. "At the end of the day, this is a crazy regime. They walked all over the people's will. They can do whatever they want."

This is called compromise in Egypt: giving the regime what it wants, and what it always knew it would get, one way or the other. Egypt is a study in endurance.

Heshmat finally popped up in Cairo, but it was too late. He made some angry speeches. He said he'd been robbed. He wasn't the only one: other Brotherhood candidates risked arrest to tell the world they'd been cheated in their precincts. Some judges came forward, too, and testified to the vote rigging.

But their moment had already passed. Ancient, implacable Egypt was creaking forward, crushing the things that had to be crushed.

Fiqi became head of the foreign affairs committee, just like everybody had predicted. He never made any excuses for what happened in

Damanhour; he didn't discuss it at all. He knew, I think, that it didn't really matter.

Even with all the dirty tricks, the Brotherhood still did better than anybody expected them to do. They wound up with a fifth of the Parliament. It was their strongest showing in history. The Bush administration saw that, too. They saw the Brotherhood, and Hamas, and Hezbollah all cashing in on elections. After that, we stopped hearing so much about democracy for Arabs. As it turned out, it didn't look the way they had expected.

I was asleep early one morning when I felt an earthquake roll through the house, as if Cairo were a spread of water and my bed a raft; it rippled and rolled beneath my body. I knew, even half asleep, that it could only be an earthquake. But when I asked around, the driver hadn't noticed, or the supermarket clerk, or even Hossam. You would think an earthquake would be enough to break something, to shred an old idea, that the shifting of tectonic plates couldn't help but express itself tangibly in our constructed world. You forget that most earthquakes simply aren't very powerful. Not compared with all the concrete, bricks, pillars, braces, rocks—the architecture of structure, the foundations of inertia. Something has shifted below the earth, and maybe it will keep moving until it means something, but that day may only come when we are no longer here to see. The earthquake came to Egypt, rattled things about, and rolled off again. Nobody noticed. In the end, I found a wire story on the Internet—a marginal clump of paragraphs, flickering through half-life in cyberspace. An earthquake came to Egypt at dawn, the wire story said. No damage was reported.

At least I knew I hadn't dreamed the whole thing.

## FOURTEEN

# ALL THINGS LIGHT, AND ALL THINGS DARK

I stared at the name, and from the sterile text of wire reports, the name stared back. *Atwar Bahjat.* I screwed my eyes into a long blink and opened them. The name was still there. *The bodies of Atwar Bahjat and her cameraman and soundman were found early Thursday . . .*

Winter light struggled through the windows. Outside Iraq clenched tight as a muscle, the streets of Baghdad hollow and silent. I had been writing all night, overcooked coffee chewing my stomach. I was alone in a silent room in a drab hotel, staring at a computer.

The day before, an enormous thing had happened. Sunni militants crept through the streets and set off bombs in the gold-domed shrine at Samarra, revered place of pilgrimage and worship devoted to the tenth and eleventh Shiite imams. Sunnis and Shiites had been murdering each other all day and all night, taking their revenge. Civil war had never felt so manifest. The translators and drivers who worked for the various news bureaus in our building had sorted themselves into separate rooms: Sunnis here, Shiites there. Just like that, all at once. Tight-jawed and tense, they clumped around television sets listening to their respective clerics, getting angrier by the hour. Everybody in the building was nervous.

Staring at Atwar's name, all I could think about was color: green and orange, blue and red. Instead of memory, that's what came—the idea of bright color. I hadn't seen Atwar in a long time, and it felt even longer. Time moved slower in Iraq, weighed down by life and death.

When we met in the summer of 2004, the city rotted and sagged with hues: the wicked sheen of sunlight on new cars; wilting red flowers taped clumsily to car windows in blaring wedding processions; the soft, green haze of date palm groves. In the few seasons since, Iraq had blurred itself into dry-eyed black and white.

Atwar had worked at Al-Jazeera that summer, covering the world's biggest story for the world's most controversial news organization, struggling to prove herself in the crucible of Iraq. Those were the days when homemade beheading videos were delivered to Al-Jazeera and broadcast to the world. U.S. officials openly loathed Al-Jazeera, complaining that the cameramen cropped up conveniently whenever a car bomb went off and accusing the reporters of alliances with insurgents. For their part, the journalists had little to model themselves after: the Arab world didn't offer many examples of responsible journalism. The network made an interesting story. I asked to shadow a Baghdad correspondent, and they sent me to Atwar.

"Atwar Bahjat!" The Iraqi men in my office had admired her full cheeks and carbonated eyes ever since Saddam's days, when she'd dished up propaganda on Iraqi state television. "She's a poet, you know," Salar told me. It was true: she was a poet, a feminist, and a novelist. She was just twenty-eight that summer, and already emerging as one of the Arab world's most respected war correspondents.

We met in July, when trees sagged with heat and the landscape blurred into a shimmer by noon. The sun had teeth and a hard glare; every blade of grass glowed like a stalk of ice. An Egyptian diplomat had been freed by kidnappers that day, and Atwar would cover the story. By the time I reached the Egyptian embassy in Baghdad, she was inside. Dozens of sweating, jostling, cranky journalists, mostly Arabs looking for a scoop, pressed together in the framed gaze of Hosni Mubarak and the clammy embrace of broken air-conditioning.

Adorned with lipstick, eye shadow, blue head scarf, and huge turquoise ring, Atwar barely grazed a seat before bobbing to her feet again. She laughed from her stomach, looked men in the eye, and dropped whispers in ears.

The diplomat had been freed overnight. He stepped into the room and cameras snapped in a rain of shouted questions.

*Who paid for your release? How much?*
*Do you think Arabs should leave Iraq?*
*Will this kidnapping be the last?*
*Was your family aware of what was going on?*
*Did they threaten to kill you?*

A smug smile played on Atwar's plump baby face.

"Don't you have a producer?" I asked.

"I'm from Iraq," she said coolly. "I don't need a producer for this."

The press conference was over, and Atwar hadn't asked a single question. I looked at her, wary. She winked and pulled me into a back room. While the other journalists elbowed for camera positions outside, she had arranged a private interview with the ambassador. She sat with him at leisure, and he answered all of her questions.

Later that night, in the swampy darkness of the Al-Jazeera editing room, we talked about the corrosion of war reporting. I liked Atwar, I realized, and it surprised me a little. I had expected a musty, middle-aged man or a sallow-faced, veiled nationalist. But here was a woman my own age, tugged by ambition and emotion, trying to keep intact. Atwar had never taken a break, and the months were piling up on her. Now she had peeled herself out of her reporting persona and sat there pale and contemplative in the half dark.

"There are a lot of complaints about Al-Jazeera's reporting," I said. "The Americans criticize you, and so do the Iraqis. How do you respond?"

"I would like to say one thing." Her voice was soft. "My generation has been in war ever since we were born. Before this war, we always felt left in the dark. The government would say one thing and we'd see something else. During that time, we got used to that kind of pressure. During this war, it is the same. The Iraqis say one thing, the Americans say something else. Since the war there is more freedom. It's better since the war."

Atwar's job hadn't come easy. Her bosses didn't want to send a woman into combat, but she pestered and pleaded, took on the political beat and covered it relentlessly to prove herself. In the end, her bosses relented.

"She was very strong. People in Al-Jazeera always told her, 'If you ever feel uncomfortable, come back,' " Ali Taleb, Atwar's cousin and bodyguard, told me after she died. "But she never did."

Darkness had begun to nudge against her that summer of 2004. She had driven over a roadside bomb on her way to work one day. Her car was ruined, but she stepped out in one piece. She had been arrested and questioned by American soldiers. She had covered combat in the holy city of Najaf, reporting with bullets and mortar rounds flying overhead. A corner of her character had been dipped in blood—its tinge was on her, but she still seemed whole. Glimpses of death had given her a new reverence before God, she said, and had inspired her to adopt the Muslim head scarf.

"When I go to hospitals and see children dying, I fight myself to be objective," she admitted. "I've been affected mentally and psychologically, but if you're not neutral around here, you can lose your job."

She couldn't afford to cry at work, and so she pushed through the hours, drove home, and collapsed in tears.

"I have seen death now." But she said it lightly, by way of explanation. "I have been touched by it."

When we said good-bye, she looked at me with her warm eyes and apple-cheeked face and asked me to keep in touch. To call her if I needed anything in Iraq, any contacts, any help. And I said yes, I would call, but I never did. One story melts into another, an assignment becomes a plane ride, a new hotel room, a different country. I kept moving forward, and so did Atwar, and I guess neither of us had the luxury of time or retrospection.

After she died, I sat with her sister, her aunts, her cousin, and her colleagues. They were the ones who told me the rest of her story: That Atwar had been the head of the family since her father died, and had resisted pressure to get married even though at thirty she was an old maid. She was too caught up in history, too busy building her own career, to start cooking dinner for a husband. She published a book tracing her adventures as a war reporter and had begun writing a second, examining the role of women in Iraq.

"During the battle of Najaf, the correspondents wouldn't go out in the streets. The Shia felt Al-Jazeera was against them," recalled Amna Dhabi, her colleague. "But Atwar was very neutral. She'd say, 'I'm for

Iraq, not for a specific sect.' She got in her car and went to Najaf and went live on TV."

The death threats pelted her for years. First she moved her widowed mother and younger sister to a new house in a safer neighborhood; a few months before she was killed, she took them to live in Amman. But it didn't feel right. She couldn't stay out of Iraq. She came home again.

"She believed fate had decided for her to stay in Iraq," Atwar's twenty-five-year-old sister, Itha, told me. "She would always say, 'It's better to stay in one's country.' "

It was a deliberate choice. Atwar, unlike most of her stranded countrymen, had the talent and connections to get out of Iraq. But she wouldn't go. She turned down jobs abroad, determined to tough out the violence. When Al-Jazeera was expelled by the Iraqi government, she went to work for the rival station, Al-Arabiya.

All the while, the threats kept coming.

This is not only the story of Atwar, but the story of Iraq. Her aspirations were the finest hopes of a broken country; her murder reeked of the hopelessness of a lost cause. Here is one woman, one soul among some 100,000 Iraqis who have been sacrificed, fed to appease the nihilistic blood thirst of a slow-motion national collapse. She was no more than the doctors, children, professors, street sweepers, goat vendors, soccer players, and other Iraqis who were snuffed in this war. But she lived on television when television was the national security blanket—the only glimmer of the outside world still allowed to penetrate an Iraqi home; a flashing, talking companion; an addictive succor. She had kept company with the country all down the darkest days. Her death matters because all of the deaths mattered, but most of them were anonymous, and she lived as a symbol of mad hope for an impossible, alternative Iraq: a place of liberated men and women, and the free exchange of ideas; a society that had moved beyond its sectarian differences. She died because that hope was indeed insane, a bold and audacious rejection of visible evil.

Life under Saddam meant existing in a very tight space, a land without horizon, discouraged from dreams. Then war comes and absolute change washes in on tides of killing. Iraqis, who had pined for everything in the world, were glutted with everything, all at once. Every imagined possibility, the ones that were hidden in the shadows, suddenly shimmered and breathed in the air. Saddam was gone, the country would reinvent itself, anything could happen. But . . . every possibility was chained to its own weight in danger and death. The claustrophobic closets of dictatorship gave way to the wild and wide-open and deadly plains of war and foreign invaders. The people found themselves stranded with no constraints except rusty imagination and the violence that stalked the land. There came to them all things light, and all things dark.

So it was confusing, talking to Atwar. She kept saying it was better since the war—more freedoms. But under her words welled decay and downfall.

"My country is collapsing, and it's my job to watch this collapse," she told me. "The Iraqi people are waiting for their dream, and now they find it's only a nightmare. People find out that nothing has been done. Many people who hated Saddam Hussein now wish he'd come back. They're feeling they were fooled."

Islamists gathered up power, and set about reestablishing the domination of men over women. They prowled the streets, threatening to kill women who bared their heads, encouraging men in the mosques to do the same. So that was one thing: Atwar was a woman on television at a time when rabid armies were trying to stuff women back into unseen rooms. Behind her elaborate and vague explanation of taking the *hijab* because she had seen death, I felt the big, unspoken truth of her fear, and believed she did not speak of this fear because she was too proud.

Then there was the ancient and relentless question of sect, tearing apart the Muslim people ever since Muhammad's earliest descendents tried to shape the religion and move it forward. Like so many lingering tensions, this had been squashed by Saddam and his endless armies of spies, policemen, and torturers. The Sunnis were in charge under Saddam, and the Shiites and Kurds kept quiet. And then Saddam was gone, power and oil and money were all up for grabs, and Iran came rushing into Baghdad and the south—and the sectarian war began.

Atwar was a theological half-breed; she didn't fit anywhere. Her mother was Shiite, her father Sunni. She told people she didn't believe in sect. Her country kept on breaking down, and Atwar kept on refusing to acknowledge it. She wore a gold pendant in the shape of Iraq to indicate her disdain for splitting people into categories: Shiite, Sunni, Kurd. That pendant was famous. Anonymous callers threatened to kill her for wearing it. She battled her editors about whether people in the stories should be identified as Sunni or Shiite. Atwar thought the sectarian identifications were immoral. The hatred was hot enough already, she told her bosses. She wanted to calm things down, not stoke the anger.

There was no place in Iraq for a woman like that.

At a time when Iraq was so blood-jaded and numb it seemed as if shock had abandoned the country for good, the bombing of the gold-domed shrine gripped the nation. Atwar must have been shocked, too, because she didn't stop to ask permission. She rounded up the camera crew, piled into a van, and raced homeward. She thought she was safe in Samarra, surrounded by her own people. She called her younger sister and told her not to worry. "I'm among family," she said. The crew found the roads into the city choked shut. Soldiers had surrounded and sealed the town, desperate to contain the violence. The entire country was clapped under curfew. Shiite gangs roved the streets, mad for vengeance, slaughtering Sunnis.

In the farmlands outside town, Atwar's crew set up a shot with the rooftops of Samarra in the distance. Curious villagers gathered around. As the light faded from the wintry sky, Atwar picked up the microphone. She arranged her haggard features into a television face and spoke straight into millions of Arab living rooms, to the far corners of Iraq, the other Muslim countries, and the wide world beyond. She must have known that civil war was at hand. Her words were defiant, and scared.

"Whether you are Sunni or Shia, Arab or Kurd, there is no difference between Iraqis," she said. "[We are] united in fear for this nation."

When the live shot was over, Atwar called the Baghdad bureau. She talked with her colleague, Amna.

"Iraq is swinging on your chest," Amna teased Atwar. She meant the pendant.

"Yes, Iraq is swinging between insurgents and these Iraqi politicians," Bahjat said wryly. "It needs a warm chest to lie upon."

By now the gunmen were coming for her. They had seen her on television, and they were hunting her down, peeling up the country road in their pickup truck. "Where's the announcer?" they bellowed. They leapt to the ground and seized Atwar, along with the cameraman and engineer, and fired into the sky. Atwar screamed to the crowd for help, but the villagers backed away. Somebody called the police, but it was morning before anybody came to help. By then the bodies were laced with bullets, and dumped in the dirt.

In the days after Atwar's death, we all watched her last standup dozens of times. The Iraqi channels looped the clip over and over for viewers who were caged indoors with nothing but television to stave off the anxiety of curfew. Death squads stole through the streets, the Shiite "black shirts" sacked Sunni mosques—and all the while, the image of Atwar flickered in corners. She wore a turtleneck and tied her head scarf in the jaunty sideways knot that had become her trademark. The face on the television screen was etched with the story of her homeland's degeneration. Her skin had grayed, her eyes grown heavy, her face puffed with fatigue. She looked exhausted.

The decay I saw in Atwar's face had eaten into the city, too. Baghdad faded and sank; Baghdad was lost. The swollen and thrumming streets where we'd met, dripping in heat and life and gaudy shouts of color, had vanished. The clatter of city life gave way to the scrape of machine-gun fire, the roar of car bombs, and the dull thud of mortars. Baghdad, with its tightly packed neighborhoods, sleepy gardens, and lazy river vistas, was swallowed by infinite reels of razor wire and blank-faced cement barriers.

Atwar looked sick, and so did Iraq. Atwar died, but Iraq just kept bleeding.

The day after the shrine bombing, we held a staff meeting. "The violence is getting worse," Borzou, the bureau chief, told the Iraqi staff. "We need to prepare for what's coming. We need to be ready for the fighting to get much heavier. We need to figure out how to work under curfew. I'm asking for any suggestions you have."

"A bicycle," said Suheil.

Everybody laughed like it was the funniest joke they'd ever heard. Nervous grumblings, too-quick jokes.

"No, really, I am thinking about getting a bicycle!" he protested. "Because I think we will face many more times like these."

Everybody talked at once.

"I can't believe we're preparing for another war here."

"Some of us can work from home."

"Not all the time. In the mornings and afternoons we don't have electricity."

"Some of you are close enough to walk."

"But the problem is, if there's a curfew in your neighborhood and you leave, even by foot, everybody's going to wonder, 'Where's this guy going?' Even your family panics when there's a curfew."

"If something like this happens, we can't freeze," Borzou told them. "This is our calling. We can't shut down. You deal with the shock later."

I looked around me, at Raheem, Suheil, Salar, Caesar—at the drawn faces of Iraqis who risked their lives working for us. They have been here the entire time, I thought. When does later come?

It was just a short walk to the Arabiya offices, cutting back around the hotel where we lived, crossing a small gate, and traversing some parking lots.

"We will send somebody with you," Salar said.

He means a bodyguard. With a gun. Like the one he sent to follow me through the supermarket.

"No, I don't want it."

"This is a bad time," he said.

"Please, Salar, I really don't want it. It's just across the parking lot."

"I'm sorry, but this is my responsibility. Today is a difficult day."

So I shut up and walked along silently with my own private gunman, out into the wintry afternoon. In the Arabiya offices I found some of Atwar's family members forgetting to drink their coffee on stiff couches. Raw silence stretched between their words. They spent a lot of time staring at the floor. On the walls gleamed pictures of prettier places: palm trees and beaches, golden sunlight brimming in leaves.

The aunt had hard eyes: "She's an honor to her tribe, she's a martyr, she's better than ten men. She's a martyr for Iraq."

"How did this happen?" wailed Atwar's sister, collapsing onto the aunt's shoulder. "What did she see? She didn't see anything."

With curfew in place, they hadn't been able to bring her broken body back from Samarra. All the roads were closed, the checkpoints tight. Nobody could move; nobody could get to work. Only militiamen, gun-toting gangs, and soldiers moved like spirits on the roads. It took days to get the bodies through the routine tests at a forensics laboratory. There would be no sunset burial.

"They were not treated like martyrs," the Arabiya bureau chief, Jawad Hattab, told me in quiet indignation.

Somebody had already printed makeshift posters of Atwar's face; she stared down from the walls, portrayed in cheap blurs of color, tacked up with Scotch tape. I ran my eyes over her features, thinking of the yellowing faces of suicide bombers that peeled from the walls of the West Bank and Beirut. They had made Atwar into a martyr.

Hattab related all the eyewitness details of the deaths, and he told me about the other deaths—eleven Arabiya employees had died in Iraq since the invasion. At that time, sixty-six journalists had been slaughtered. Of those, forty-seven were Iraqi. By now, those numbers have more than doubled. They have been shot by U.S. forces, gunned down by their countrymen, crushed by bombs. They were liberated to tell the story of their lifetime, to write their own national history, but only if they flirted with death. All things light, and all things dark.

"If I give up my position, if I am weak, who will be the substitute, who will carry this message?" Hattab said. His voice was oddly flat. "Every day we are exposed to many, many threats, killing or bombing or threats against our families. But Iraq deserves this from us, this sacrifice. If we are defeated, and we consider ourselves the educated segment of this country, what will the people in the street do? What will happen to our country?"

Looking at him, a fifty-year-old man, I wrote in my notebook: *Journalists in Iraq are hardened. They have scars and heavy eyes.* They believed more in journalism than any American reporter I knew. Clinging to it as if it would save them in the end.

We stood.

"We're not telling the truth when we say we're still strong," he blurted. "Inside we are broken. Our aim was to give the message of truth and the only thing we got back was bullets."

Even her burial had a death toll.

They laid Atwar's body in a plain wooden box, and strapped it onto a flatbed truck. The men gathered around the casket, and the wind pushed back their hair as the truck began to roll. They had fastened a black banner to the grille—a promise from other reporters to continue Atwar's work. *We will finish the message she was carrying.* Atwar, too, had spoken of her message. As if they traveled a one-way road, as if they would finally get to Athens from Marathon and then collapse. It sounded strange, perhaps because I thought of news not as something you could carry, but as a force that defined its own terms. I was still a part of the world that was not Iraq, and these journalists were marooned in the land that was Iraq, and they wanted desperately to be heard. American reporters of my generation vied to write the story of the wars—it was something we strove for, competed for fiercely, a privilege. And when we were done with it we simply went away again. Iraqis covered the war because it had landed on top of them, and they would have to keep on covering it until it killed them or went away altogether. It was their fate and their destiny and in many, many cases, the death of them.

The truck cut through empty streets, between ragged palm trees. Mourners straggled behind in a rough column. They were headed into the badlands west of Baghdad, to the Sunni cemetery in Abu Ghraib.

The funeral procession was passing through the town of Hassuwa when cracks of gunfire erupted: sniping between followers of one of Iraq's most important Sunni clerics and the Shiite policemen who were escorting Bahjat's funeral convoy. Those first bullets drew more bullets, and soon the air was crackling.

The mourners abandoned the coffin on the side of the road to hide behind the walls of an old cement factory, but the cameramen kept on documenting. This account is drawn from their footage; I was working the day Atwar was buried. The photographers crouched like cats, moving silent through the rubble, under sagging telephone wires and tired trees. Dogs yelped in fear. From the minarets of the mosques, the town muezzins called for jihad. A convoy of U.S. Humvees rolled by and kept going, leaving the Iraqis to fight among themselves.

"Please call the interior minister and tell him that our convoy with Atwar Bahjat has been attacked," Iraqi journalist Fatah Sheik barked into his cell phone, crouching close to the ground. "Can't you hear the shooting? Please tell the minister."

Commandos raced through the courtyard. Somewhere, a rooster crowed.

"Send us Americans and national guard," Sheik begged. "Among us are correspondents, there are almost fifty of us."

The gunfight lasted more than two hours, until the police escorts ran out of ammunition and the shooting slowed, then stopped. At least two men had been shot dead. The Sunni cleric who presided over the neighborhood sent along a message of apology. It was a misunderstanding, he said. He invited the mourners to stop by his house for coffee. It was just another working day in Iraq. No hard feelings, just two more souls.

At the graveyard the men hoisted the coffin down. Atwar's friends had covered it with the Iraqi flag and placed orange flowers on top. Because she died a single woman, her family had draped a bride's veil over the head of the coffin.

They prayed over her body, repeated that there is no god but God, and hurried her coffin along a dirt path through the cemetery. At the lip of her grave, the men began to argue. Nobody should see her body, they said, not even the gravediggers who lowered it into the earth. They shoved and yelled. At last, somebody produced a bedsheet to stretch over the body, to protect it from view. The cloth was blue and yellow and green, its patchwork pattern childish and light.

Atwar's mother tossed fistfuls of candy into the grave.

"Atwar, my love!" she cried before the cameras. "Can you hear me?"

But Atwar was gone.

As the cars turned back toward Baghdad, a plume of black smoke arched into the sky. It was a homemade bomb that had been laid along the road, planted to strike the mourners as they left the cemetery.

Sometimes you are lucky, and turn the other way.

## FIFTEEN

# THERE WOULD BE CONSEQUENCES

After Atwar died, the months spun out fast, hotter and bloodier, until another summer caught Baghdad in its claws. Ariel Sharon fell into a coma and was stripped of his job as Israeli prime minister. Iran announced the successful enrichment of uranium. In Iraq, it was dying and more dying, death getting stuck in the glue of itself. You didn't know how to tell the story anymore. When I returned to Baghdad in the summer of 2006 I went looking for a young Shiite, somebody whose life and aspirations and circumstances could serve as an emblem for a tortured land.

At Baghdad University heat beat the air stiff as egg whites. Dust flew loose from the dying grasses, shaking like pepper into the lungs, and the trees struggled to hold up their branches. Students trickled down the scorched paths and shaded lanes to the parking lot and the street beyond, eyes low and books clutched over their hearts. They moved away when we tried to talk to them. The university had gone to war with the rest of the country. Professors had been murdered and driven into exile. Militiamen moved among the students. You couldn't just blurt it out: Are you Shiite? We had to finesse, talk about politics and The Situation, listen for dropped hints. Iraq was fractured enough that people tipped their hand when they talked politics. We stopped a young man, but he was shy and inarticulate. We stopped a girl with a Winnie the Pooh lunchbox, but she turned out to be a Sunni.

Then there was Ahmed, stretching in the shade of a spreading tree, jouncing on worn running shoes. When I approached he stood his ground and cast judging eyes over my face, my clothes, my notebook. Then, satisfied, he gazed at the horizon and answered the questions in nearly perfect English. Caesar, the translator, faded back and finally sprawled on shaded grass as Ahmed's flawless sentences rolled out.

Ahmed was twenty-three years old, a Shiite living in the urban killing fields of Baghdad's Hay al-Amal neighborhood. He had the kind of pinched face you see all over the world, and never on a wealthy man: the kite corner jut of cheekbones over wasted dents; eyes deep and suspicious and darting, too dark to tell the pupil from the iris. It was the hardness of his face that was familiar, the anger that glimmered deep behind his eyes like a piece of light at the bottom of a deep well: the face of a man who is learning, bit by bit, the limitations of empty pockets and lowly family stature.

He ran all the time, ran until the flesh burned off his bones. He was running that day, in a T-shirt and old jeans and sneakers he'd bought secondhand. When Saddam was still around, Ahmed had run the half marathon on Iraq's national team. Now he came to the university campus every day to train, though he couldn't afford to attend classes. The college kids bustled past to brighter futures as he worked on his body, the only part of him that had ever proven profitable. He'd picked up his girlfriend on campus; she was a college girl drifting forward while he ran circles around the grounds.

"Why do you run so much?" I asked him.

"To forget," he blurted, and then he shrugged a little, as if to say, I know this sounds melodramatic but it's also true. "I do this to forget the problems, the situation outside. I can't stay in the house all day. My father's afraid. He says, 'I'll give you anything to stay home,' but I can't, and that makes a problem between me and my father. Even my girlfriend, we had a fight yesterday. In my neighborhood now we live one afraid from the other, because we don't know who anybody is. When I drive to my house and come home at night, they think I work with the government or with the terrorists. They don't know. They're afraid. Each one is afraid now."

He was a Shiite, though, so maybe he was pleased with the newfound political power his people had picked up since the war. Maybe he viewed these hard times as transitory. He frowned.

"They took the power place, but it's too bad," he said. "The problem in the past was just Sunni rule. Now it's just Shia rule. It's stupid. We have to find a balance between Sunni and Shia. I just follow my mind. I think that's the right thing. God gave us a brain to think, not to follow. Most Iraqis are ignorant, they don't understand that. If you say Ali al Sistani is bad, they want to kill you. But if you ask, 'Why do you follow him?' they can't answer."

He didn't want to talk anymore. His body was turning away, his face fixed in expectation of good-bye. But he took my notebook and copied down his mobile telephone number before bounding off into the stifling gold of day.

"This Ahmed, he's—he's *noble*," Caesar said as we walked back to the car. "The way he answered the questions. It's great. You know what I mean?"

I did.

I wanted to go to Ahmed's house, to see the street and rooms, to meet his family. But I couldn't go to Hay al-Amal without signing their death warrants. Nor could he visit our place—we couldn't invite a stranger off the street to see the checkpoints and the layout, to glimpse the faces of the Iraqis who lied to their families and neighbors about working with foreigners. Everybody had too much to lose.

So I called Ahmed and arranged to meet neither here nor there, but in the brick-sheathed purgatory of the Babylon Hotel. I had been encouraged by colleagues to think of the Babylon Hotel as a refreshing liberation from our claustrophobic offices, a small, accessible slice of a deadly country. But like everything else in Iraq, the hotel had turned weird and sad. It had been, before, a popular place for posh weddings, but it had gone derelict and sinister, full of tight, hot air and hard glances. Sitting in the sticky cave of the lobby was like squatting in a dried husk of beehive, all industry and motion and joy drained away, abandoned rooms rising into the sky overhead. Thin natural light filtered through streaked windows; dusty stairways rose to dead ends at locked doors; darkened corridors disappeared into shadows. I passed the security guards at the front doors, tugged open my bag to show the contents and stayed silent, wondering who they were, who their friends were. The footsteps of the armed gunman echoed behind mine in the great halls. He talked quietly to the guards and they didn't take his gun away. The bodyguard was skinny and owl-eyed, and every time I looked at him I had a queasy urge to run until I lost him. I hated having him there and so I pretended he had nothing to do with me, this poor man who'd been paid to kill people for my protection. Still the knowing itched at the back of my thoughts.

The Babylon Hotel had a lobby café where nobody ever came to take your order, a men's barber shop, and a women's beauty salon. The beauty parlor was a gaudy grotto stuffed with cloth flowers and cans of cheap hairspray the size of rocket launchers. Upstairs there was a grubby, smoky restaurant cut from a 1970s disco hall, with deep round pod seats and low tables. There was also a sad little gift shop where I bought, that summer, a baseball cap embroidered with the Iraqi flag and this promise: TOMORROW WILL BETTER.

I didn't really expect Ahmed to show up. Somebody would talk him out of it. Something would go wrong. The meeting was a risk for both of us, based on ill-advised mutual trust. He could get spotted and tarred a traitor. As for me, I had to trust he hadn't sold me off to somebody in the neighborhood: *I know where you can find an American. She will be waiting for me at two on Friday*. But there he was, grinning a shy grin and loping my way, the same jeans and T-shirt hanging off his skinny frame. His girlfriend swished behind in skirts, tinkling in costume jewelry and ramped up on high heels, polite smile under her makeup.

"I'm so happy you came," I cried in relief.

"Me too."

"Let's have some tea."

We climbed up to the disco restaurant, and I began to extract, piece by piece, the story of Ahmed.

What did Ahmed think when he heard the war was coming? He didn't know what to make of it. A dust storm tinted the air blood red for two days straight. Ahmed's family thought it was an omen. The neighbors said it was the end of the world. His family had fled Baghdad for Karbala when the invasion began. They got so scared they dug pits in the yard, planning to hide underground if the fighting grew too intense. Ahmed dug for twelve hours without stopping, hollowing out useless craters, working just to feel his muscles ache, to create the illusion of action and control. "Everyone was afraid. The women, the children. You had to do something to make them less afraid, even if it's a lie. You have to do something.

"I was entirely sure they'd kick Saddam Hussein out, and I was glad. I was sure it would make a difference in five or ten years. Maybe our kids will face a different life, not like our life."

Ahmed had sailed through high school on smarts and taught himself perfect English by listening to BBC radio, but there was no money for college. He had to find work and prop up his family. His father, he told me that first afternoon in the Babylon Hotel, had "political problems." In Iraq, political problems can mean anything. Politics are power, machismo, tribal pull, *wasta*. Even a casual squabble with the wrong person can swell ominously into a political problem. Ahmed's father had a disagreement in the 1960s with a man Ahmed called, capital letters in his voice, "a Tikrit Guy"—a man from Saddam's hometown and tribe. Ahmed's father had shot the Tikrit Guy in the leg, and the grudge had never faded because grudges were a national sport. The Tikrit Guy had hounded Ahmed's father for years, pulling strings to punish him at every turn. Ahmed's father was arrested, imprisoned, and tortured three times under the old regime.

The second time, Ahmed's mother had sold everything they owned to raise $25,000. She'd given the cash to a corrupt official who, in turn, wrote a report claiming Ahmed's father had been executed in the desert, closed his file, and set him free. That was back in 1981, before Ahmed was born. His father, after stopping home long enough to conceive Ahmed, had escaped to Kuwait and found work with a British oil company. When he finally made it home six years later, he'd stuck around long enough to get his wife pregnant again before vanishing back into the government's clutches. This time his arrest was secret, and the family couldn't track him down.

"All those twenty months we were looking for my father," Ahmed stared down into his teacup, memories dark and jumbled. "My mother was pregnant, her abdomen was getting big. We didn't have a place to live so we were living in rental houses, we moved seven, eight times. We asked everyone. In the end we found a way to get him out of jail."

The family fled to Karbala, hoping to get off the Tikrit Guy's radar.

They stayed there until 1994, then moved to Najaf for a few years before finally, warily, creeping back to Baghdad.

Those were long, grinding sanctions years, when Iraq lay frozen under Saddam and Ahmed plunged blindly into his youth. On languid summer days he'd sleep until afternoon, find his friends, look for pretty girls in the market, and thrust his telephone number into their fingers in a fit of hormones and hope. Buy a sweet, cold ice-cream cone, maybe see a movie. The hours clicked out in pool halls. "I'm a professor of billiards," he says.

At midnight he met the other runners for training, and they bounded like antelopes through the darkened streets, feet ponging off the blacktop, night hot as an oven's breath. It was all in his voice: the boys moving like animals, the quiet intensity of the night, music slipping from parties, closed gates and silent windows and dark cars all sliding past the running boys. The possibility, and the youngness.

Ahmed ran until he was one of the best endurance runners in the country. They paid him four dollars a month on the national team, but he didn't run for the money; he ran because he loved it, because it cut his world into a simple, Manichean place, neatly divided between good and evil. It was combat as much as a race.

"When you fight somebody you're the good one and he's the bad one. And if you defeat him, I can't describe it when you live this moment. They say you're the best."

Since the war, he had begun to lose his taste for running. He couldn't run anymore in open spaces. The students at the university taunted him as he bounded past: "Hey crazy, what are you doing?" Gunfire cracked his concentration.

"There is no emotion now."

His thoughts spun in circles, swallowed their tails, and his feet pounded to earth, over and over again. The students were ignorant, he thought. Many came from the south, same as his family. "They've been in darkness for the 1980s and 1990s, so what can you expect?"

Why was there nowhere better for running?

First, because there was a war. And second, because he was poor.

He dreamed of being a rich man. Then he could buy himself a treadmill and train at home. He could stay inside the four walls of his house all day long; he would never have to leave. He could buy the luxury of his own prison, one he designed himself and loved.

Instead he works a poor man's job in a pharmacy. He hates it, and the pay is thin. His perfect English, the tongue he pieced together one word at a time during long, dark hours hunched over a transistor radio, is languishing. The words are slipping away. Sometimes he strikes up a quick conversation with the American soldiers, just for the practice, but they don't say much. *Hey*, they say to Ahmed, *what's up?* And then they move on. If Ahmed's father sees him approach the soldiers, he's in for a fierce fight. His father doesn't want him speaking English on the streets; the neighbors might suspect Ahmed of working with the Americans. That's where the money is. Ahmed knows it—doesn't he know it? His friend came to him and offered him a job as a translator with the Americans. He won't do it. Too dangerous, he says, and then his face twists up and he puts his teacup down and sets in to explain that he's not afraid, per se, it's just that his family can't afford his death. This is the manly choice, he explains.

"I don't mind dying because I'm faithful. I have an idea that you'll die on your day. But if I die, who will support my family? We don't even have a house now."

Now he is talking quietly, glancing over his shoulder.

"They killed one of my friends. He was working as a translator for the U.S. army. They took him from his home. His mother was worried. She called me and said, 'I don't know where he's gone.' I said, 'Don't worry.' The next day they found him. They had cut his throat and wrote on a piece of paper, 'Don't work with foreigners or you will die,' and they put it on his head. That made me cry for a week. He was twenty-six. He'd been working after the fall [of Saddam], but they threatened him and he left the job. I told him, 'Don't go back.' I think he told his mother, 'I'm going to sleep with my friends,' but he was working. He didn't want her to worry. Now his mother is completely destroyed."

Everybody is getting killed these days. You could be sitting out on the stoop, like Ahmed's neighbor was a week ago, and wind up dead. Four militia thugs had rolled past, threatening people on the street. We'll kill you, they said, we swear we'll kill you. The neighbor punched their license plate into his cell phone. The gunmen saw. They made a

U-turn, drove back to his house, and shot him cold. Just another disposable Iraqi soul, lifeless on a whim.

"My neighbor was twenty-eight, with green eyes." Ahmed has a habit of dragging his long, skinny hands down his face, as if tracing the shape of a mask. "So handsome."

That was why Ahmed's father didn't want his son to leave the house. That was why the two screamed and fought like cats, day after dreary day. Mostly, they fought out the classic struggle—a restless Ahmed demanding independence, his father steeped in worry for his safety. But it cut deeper in Baghdad. The war wasn't everything; it's just that it never went away. Ahmed was fighting the timeless battles of being twenty-three years old: for adulthood, for a path through a hard world, for love. But the war was tangled up in everything, not wholly responsible for his woes but tainting them, seeping into them, coloring everything.

Another friend kept coming by the house. "I'm going to sneak into Europe," he told Ahmed. "I'm going to get a fake passport. I know a guy. You speak English. We can find work. It will cost you $6,000." "Give me a break," Ahmed said. His friend went home, and then his mother started in. "Why don't you go?" she demanded. "This could be good for us." Ahmed stared at the ceiling all night. "I was thinking, if I go, what will they do? My father is sixty, what if he can't work, who will support them? Even if I get there, maybe I'll get caught."

He heard about a way to get to America, too, but it cost $12,000 and you didn't even know if the passport was real or counterfeit. "Now just Chinese can go to America, by containers," Ahmed said, and it was one of the many moments I realized that Ahmed paid a lot of attention, not only to the world around him, but to everything. All that information was loaded up behind those dark, angry eyes, and sometimes a crumb floated to the surface.

Ahmed has some relatives in Seattle, and others in Minneapolis. His cousin came from America to spend a month, but he ended up taking off after five days. "He came and saw and said, 'What's this? It's hell, it's dead here.' He got really upset."

One of his relatives has a company in America. He invited Ahmed to stay with him, work under the table for eight dollars an hour, and woo a woman into marriage before his ninety-day visa ran out. But how would he get a visa to begin with? His relative told him he needed to put $100,000 in a U.S. bank account. He might as well have told Ahmed to lasso the moon and water-ski over the Atlantic.

Baghdad shifted like a kaleidoscope, the tortured fragments of the streets rearranging themselves into bloody walls, panicked faces, rubble piles, then scattering again. For a while, Ahmed's feverish face looked to me like the face of a city.

The trial of Saddam ground along that summer, but few people paid attention anymore. The Americans dropped two 500-pound bombs on Abu Musab al-Zarqawi one morning, but the insurgency was diffuse and powerful and protected by the tribes and, at any rate, the violence in those days had more to do with civil war than an anti-American insurgency. They'd stop buses of laborers, round up all the Sunnis, and slaughter them. The bodies turned up constantly—tortured, executed, handcuffed, blindfolded. A country in the throes of a nervous breakdown; every day was a long limp.

I asked Suheil, one of the translators, how he could stand it. How Iraqis could bear to go on living like this. We were standing together in a room stuffed with computers and televisions, puzzling over another day of mass murder. Suheil fixed his thick glasses on his nose and answered immediately, precisely, as if he had been giving this very question a good deal of thought, just waiting for somebody to ask.

"You can put a frog in boiling water and it will die immediately," he said. "But if you put the frog in a pot of water and raise the temperature gradually, then the frog will survive even when the water is boiling. The frog survives because it's not receiving the heat in a lump sum. There is something called adaptation. Iraqis have been prepared for this. They receive this gradually, gradually. When the regime fell the horrors increased, gradually and slowly."

Ahmed almost never dreamed. He couldn't dream when he was depressed, only when he was happy, and since the war began, that was almost never. His family lived in a cramped rental house. Ahmed slept on a cushion on the hallway floor, lulled to sleep by the flash and croon of television. Sad songs, that's what he liked, Turkish songs. Mickey Mouse, Popeye, and Sindbad until sleep swallowed him sweetly down. When he was lucky enough to dream, it was always about her. He dreamed she was driving a convertible in the summertime, no head scarf, hair streaming loose and free behind her. In the dream he stood on the side of the road and watched, yearning, as she passed him by. This was his girlfriend, Birak, a twenty-three-year-old temptress who tormented his days. Another night, after we had started to meet at the Babylon Hotel, he dreamed that she married him in an enormous hotel, four hundred floors arching into heaven like a layer cake of money and security, a sturdy tower of possibility and pleasant expectations. Ahmed, who could describe everything, had no words for the beauty of that dream.

But that was a dream; daytime was different. In the morning his father came home from work as a night watchman and screamed at Ahmed for making too much noise, keeping him awake. Daylight meant the endless hunt for gasoline, which they needed for the generator. Ahmed and his father fought epic battles about that generator, driven half mad by the constant, ancient male pressure to keep it filled. In waking hours, his father fell into debt and decided to sell the refrigerator. Ahmed couldn't bear it. "Next time, he'll sell the cushion I sleep on. You wake up one day and you can't find anything to sell."

So he gave his father all the money he had, sold his fancy mobile telephone and took a cheaper model. He wore his old clothes. Students at the university, other men, taunted his girlfriend, told her she shouldn't waste time on a man whose prospects were so visibly shabby. "They tell her, why do you go with this guy? He always comes in the same clothes."

While I talk with Ahmed, she pouts and rolls her eyes and wiggles her feet, watching her shoes flash while he talks in English.

"What do you think I should do about this?" Ahmed says one day in anguish.

"About work?"

"No," he says, as if it's a foolish guess. "About this girl. My friends said you have to love her for a while, maybe she'll begin to think of you seriously. She makes me suspicious. She makes fun of me. I know why she does this. She don't want to tell me the truth. She pretends most of the time, actually."

Ahmed was fighting to keep her. He was besotted, obsessed. Maybe he needed that to get through the days, the illusion of working for something, the promise of payoff, pretty and good. Ahmed scraped together spare money to take her to restaurants, sometimes. He took her to Internet cafés. But not too much, he added quickly. "There's a lot of curious guys. She's a very beautiful girl. And she's not helping me with this. She says, 'Why are you getting angry? There's no reason to get angry.' She says, 'I can't fall in love. Don't talk to me about this subject.' I said, 'No problem.' She's faced a lot of bad things in the past."

She was torturing him; anybody could see that. Earlier in the war they'd dated for ten months. "The first sixty days we flew to the stars together," he says, "so she got inside my heart." But they squabbled and split. She started dating another student, a man Ahmed knew.

"We don't like each other, but we smile, face each other, say hello, how are you," he muttered darkly.

Seven months after they'd broken up, they bumped into each other on campus. All the feelings came back to Ahmed, all in a wash. He began to spend a little time with her, just friends, they agreed. She needed to go to the doctor to check on a skin rash, and he gave her a lift. Afterward Ahmed bared his soul. I'm starting to love you, he said. I can't call you my friend. Now they were together every day, and Ahmed was living a sweet torment.

"I can't reach anything with her!" he told me woefully. "She always gives you a different opinion. I don't know how I should do, what I should think. It's strange for me, because I'm always thinking the right thing, doing the right thing. Not with her. Sometimes she's trying to trick me. I'm sure of something, but she says, 'No, it's not like that.' "

She knew when she was being discussed; she'd sit up straighter, bat her hazel eyes, and rub against her chair like a cat, in an awkward, exaggerated imitation of wiles she'd seen on television. She was all dressed up in a skirt cut from tulle like a ballerina's tutu, woven with sequins of silver and gold, tottering forth on high heels, chubby fingers heavy with rings, eyes weighted down under thick, runny makeup.

Ahmed and I both looked at her.

"The one thing I dreamed in my life was to make her love me," he said balefully. "But it's too hard."

With Ahmed, I couldn't make it clean. Why did he keep coming, risking his life? Was he bored, curious, did he hope I'd give him money or help him get a visa? Maybe he just wanted to impress his girlfriend, to show her that an American woman found him so fascinating she bought him tea and spent hours copying his words into lined notebooks. Maybe he himself didn't know, perhaps he just said yes because I asked and he wanted to see what would happen. And there I was, sopping at puddles of spilled words, sponging it all onto paper. He was a character and a type. Even as he spoke I was seeing him as a soul built of black letters on a bright electronic backdrop, a spine and legs and arms constructed of short newspaper paragraphs, representing a generation, representing a sect. Imagining how his words would reconstruct themselves for the reader, hoping these quotations I snatched up would transport Americans into this boy's world, into this filthy, exhausted war. I wanted that badly from Ahmed—the impression he left. I was trying to steal—not his soul, but his shadow.

I was pushing my luck, asking for too many meetings. I wanted Ahmed's story to be good. I knew I'd never be able to visit his home, but I sketched diagrams as he described the rooms—the kitchen, the family tree and Koranic verses framed on the wall, the nylon bag where he kept his few pieces of clothing. Then I had a better idea: I'd give him a camera, and he could shoot pictures of his home, his world.

We never got around to it.

One day I met Ahmed, as usual, at the restaurant in the Babylon Hotel. And, as usual, Birak came along. But something was askew. They were quarreling, lapsing into Arabic in front of me. Her features were knit; she held her tongue. She gazed at the table. Ahmed stared her down, defiant.

"Is everything okay?" I asked.

"Yes," Ahmed snapped.

Then some men moved into the restaurant, and she tugged on his sleeve.

"Well," Ahmed said, "actually, there is a problem. She has been recognized."

Recognized. Cold fear shot through my veins, pushing from my heart all the way down to my toes.

"What happened?" My pulse bulged in my throat.

"As we were coming in downstairs, at the door, she saw somebody she knows from university. This guy. He's strong, he's somebody . . . you know what I mean?"

"Yes." He was involved with one of the armed groups.

"So this guy, he says to her, what are you doing here? And she says, nothing, just coming to spend a little time. And he says, you're not going to meet with that American upstairs, are you? She said, no, of course not, what do I want with an American? And he says, good. Because you know, if you were meeting with an American, there would be consequences."

*Consequences. That American upstairs.*

But Ahmed is still talking.

"Well," he says, "we thought he was leaving. But now he has just come into the restaurant. He has seen us, and he has seen you, and he knows we are together."

I sit perfectly still, frozen, understanding what it means. I know, we all know, that this could be as good as a death sentence for Ahmed and Birak. And there is absolutely nothing I can do about it. *There would be consequences.* Nobody will touch them here. It wouldn't happen like that. If it comes, it will come to them later. Nobody will believe I am a journalist. They will think these two are collaborators. The best they can hope for is an empty threat. But people will remember. This label will stay on their heads for years. Secret meetings with an American.

"What do you want to do?" I ask Ahmed. "Do you want to leave?"

"No," he says.

Suddenly I can't think of a single question to ask. The blood won't get out of my face. Birak fusses. She's barely touching her tea. She whispers to Ahmed.

"Are you sure you don't want to leave?"

"She wants."

"Maybe it's a good idea. Why don't you two go first?" We never walk out to the parking lot together.

"Okay," he says.

"I'll call you."

They are gone. I pay the bill and walk out into Baghdad's sordid steam.

Back at the bureau, my Iraqi colleagues tried to make me feel better. "You know, maybe it was a joke," they said. "Iraqis say anything and you can't tell if it means something." There was worry in their eyes.

It's true—the problem with Iraq is that you just can't tell. What begins as a notion hardens into truth. Threats and jokes turn into suggestions, take on plausibility and then achieve reality. Impossible things happen every day. The blood of the Iraqis has gotten cheap. All of that is the problem with Iraq.

Ahmed's telephone never rang again; it was permanently switched off. He might have gotten scared and changed it, but I don't think so. His determination was too fierce to cower; his sense of courtesy too deep-rooted for him to vanish without an explanation. Unless, perhaps, he was embarrassed. Unless Birak threatened to leave him. Unless he got so rattled he told his father the truth, and his father locked him up in the house. I have invented one hundred scenarios to explain his disappearance. They lie like a flimsy mat over a tiger trap of sorrow and guilt.

The truth is, I don't even know if they made it home from the Babylon Hotel that day. I don't know if they lived through that summer, or the summer after. Maybe he is alive somewhere. Maybe he made it out to Europe, or to America. I want to believe that he is unscathed, not just breathing in body but whole in spirit too, that the woman he worshipped was not hurt, that his heart was not broken.

Either way, I know that I am guilty. I took a chance with their lives, walked up to the table and gambled. I came to Iraq in a cloud of violence, part of an American plague. I lured him in with the seductive promise that he was interesting to American readers, that his life had meaning beyond his daily world and that his experiences mattered enough to document. For a young man like Ahmed, shunted aside and mocked, it must have been like a drug.

All of that, for a story I never wrote. Newspaper stories ought to have endings, and Ahmed's tale didn't—it just stopped.

# SIXTEEN

# KILLING THE DEAD

The operation didn't even take ten minutes. On a fine and cloudless July morning, Hezbollah guerrillas in southern Lebanon scrambled south over the Israeli border and attacked a pair of Israeli Humvees. Three Israeli soldiers were killed and two others spirited back into Lebanon. And with that, another war erupted. Most likely, thirty-two-year-old graduate student Ehud Goldwasser and twenty-seven-year-old law student Eldad Regev were already dead when Hezbollah dragged them over the border to use as bargaining chips. More than one thousand dead Lebanese people and billions of dollars of crushed Lebanese infrastructure later, Hezbollah's leader, Hassan Nasrallah, acknowledged that if he had anticipated Israel's wrath, "we would definitely not have done it." It wasn't an apology, exactly, but it was as close as the Party of God has come, at least in public.

The two Mediterranean neighbors had been clawing back and forth for decades. Israel invaded Lebanon in 1978 and 1982, attacked again in 1993 and 1996, and had occupied southern Lebanon until 2000, when attacks from Hezbollah guerrillas finally drove Israeli soldiers out of all but a small corner of the country. Hezbollah brags that it is the only Arab army that has driven Israel off a piece of land, and in a sense, it's true. After the withdrawal, Hezbollah continued firing weak rocket salvos into northern Israel. Just enough to say, we are still here. Israel, in turn, barged its jets into Lebanese airspace. Just enough to say, we are still here, too. Escalation was always a possibility, but until the day Hezbollah guerrillas grabbed those two soldiers, it seemed improbable.

The morning after the raid, I watched the first flush of light creep over the desert airfields of Cairo. I was burrowed into a hard chair at the gate, head wrapped in the wool of sleeplessness. The suitcase had been handed over, the boarding pass clutched, the passport stamped. Every limb throbbed for want of sleep. The cell phone rang. It was the desk in Los Angeles.

"Israel just bombed the Beirut airport," the dry, calm Los Angeles voice said.

"What airport? The civilian airport? In Beirut?"

"That's what the wires are reporting."

"No." I was impervious, half dreaming. "That's impossible. Because I am sitting here at the gate and they gave me a boarding pass to Beirut and nobody has said a word."

"It just happened."

The beacon of Jazeera glowed from a mounted television. A jabber of confused breaking-news voices; scratchy pictures of fire and smoke. No, it couldn't be—Israel wouldn't bomb the newly renamed Rafik Hariri International Airport, with its cappuccino bars and sunburned tourists and duty-free Cuban cigars. It was one thing to jab back and forth with acts of war; it was another to actually have a war, to bomb the civilian airport.

"Hello?"

"I'm here."

Sunrise spilled on the dirt, flecked the wings of planes.

"I have to go figure this out."

The steady, dry Los Angeles voice was correct: there was no flight to Beirut, and there wouldn't be another flight for more than a month. That night, a haggard, chain-smoking taxi driver and I stood on the Syrian border, at the lip of Lebanon. Darkness had slammed down. The war had begun.

"They're bombing the road into Beirut. It's very dangerous," the driver said accusatively.

"I have to go, anyway." Soldiers and workmen clustered stone-faced around the immigration offices. Is there another driver reckless enough to breach the dark mountains with bombs coming down? No, I see no such fool. Desperate, half-ashamed, I pulled the one trump card that is truly fail-safe in the Arab world: I stuck a pin into his masculine pride.

"Are you scared?" I bluffed. "If you're too scared to go, I'll look for another driver."

He looked at me sharply. He sighed. "This is crazy. It's not worth the money to get killed."

"I'll give you another hundred dollars."

"For a hundred dollars?"

"What do you want? One fifty."

He sighed again. He shrugged. He nodded toward the car and we trudged over, climbed inside, and shuddered off into war. Bombs and burning spiced the summer darkness. The road twisted and dipped; we wrenched the car through villages to evade bombed-out bridges and fresh, gaping craters. A checkpoint reared from the darkness and a Lebanese soldier filled the windshield, face twisting, screaming at us to get off the road. "There are Israeli jets overhead!" But we kept driving, hearing and smelling the bombs. News flashed on my cell phone: *Heavy bombing cuts road from Beirut to the border*. I turned it over on my thigh. "We're almost there now, right?" He ignored me. Long, cold minutes passed. They destroyed the road around us as we drove.

At last the car dropped out of the hills, spun down to the rim of the Mediterranean Sea, out of the dark countryside and onto the empty roads of a city hushed. The driver's body eased; he chattered and joked. At the curb in front of the hotel, I gave him the money and some guilty words of thanks. Of course, he said as he counted the bills, it was no problem.

I am at the desk of the Commodore Hotel and a huge bellow of sound shakes everything. "What was that?" I snap. The clerk is young and thin and serious. He is running my credit card. He freezes and looks at me. I see him cast for something false to say, but then he simply says, "It's a bomb."

"Oh." I laugh. He does, too. It sounds like we are strangling. I had known anyway. I just wanted somebody else to say it.

Most of the bombs in the capital are falling in the Dahiyeh, the district of sprawling, poor Shiite neighborhoods run by Hezbollah in the southern suburbs. I couldn't get Hezbollah on the phone so I took a taxi to their offices. I expected to find them, like always, in their shabby rooms, sipping tea under morose portraits of Iranian ayatollahs. Instead I found everything scattered and broken, the Dahiyeh tensed in the unnatural urban silence that means you have come to the wrong place. Israeli planes had started the bombing that would crush the neighborhood to a fairy-tale forest of smashed apartment blocks and yawning craters. Dolls dangled in fallen wires in the shell of a baby clothes shop; cars were twisted to rubble; highway overpasses snapped and collapsed. Hezbollah security recruits buzzed their scooters along cratered streets that reeked of cordite and garbage. They shook their heads: *What are you doing here, you'd better get out of here—look at that.* They pointed at an unexploded missile; it lay in the gutter in front of Hezbollah's media office. *The Israelis are up there*, they said and pointed to the sky.

"The only thing that will scratch your skin is your own nail." That was the taxi driver on the way out of the Dahiyeh. He meant that Hezbollah did well to kidnap those soldiers. We have Lebanese detainees over there, he said, and what does our government do to get them back? Nothing. At least now we have something to trade. At least now we can bargain. We know we can always depend on our own leaders, on Sayed Hassan Nasrallah.

Refugees pour into Beirut in ragged caravans, abandoning the Shiite places where the bombing is the worst—the southern suburbs, and the entire southern third of the country. They wash into scabby parks and fading schools and distant relatives' apartments. They wilt in molten July, hungry and thirsty and dirty. Nearly one million people have been displaced, and many of them are poor. It's a disaster. The Americans can't get their citizens out fast enough. There are about twenty-five thousand U.S. citizens in Lebanon when Israel begins to attack the country with American bombs. They are shocked, in that American manner of people who are used to liability insurance and 911 and the Better Business Bureau and all the other safety nets that don't exist in the rest of the world.

I jog the packed streets of Hamra, around the American University, down to the sea and along the corniche as a dying sun bleeds into the salt waters. The streets are intimate and hushed. Fingers of trees lace overhead, casting shadows so cool and quiet they remind me of childhood woods, the secrecy of weeping willows, summer dusk, and the pock, pock of a tennis ball. But it is awful. Men and women wander lead-footed with their children. Their bodies and clothes are dirty; their faces hang slack as they drift homeless in their capital. They watch me, listless and resentful, as I jog past.

One night there was a middle-aged man. He looked worried and decent. His hair was thinning and he had the quiet posture of an engineer, or maybe a schoolteacher. His daughter's frilly dress was streaked and rumpled, and he was walking her down a quiet street, holding her hand, as darkness thickened under the twined fingers of the trees. I saw them coming from a long way off, and knew from their slow, heavy steps that they had nowhere to go. I had been to the shelters, where old men slept on filthy pads on school playgrounds, where the toilets overflowed and babies screamed and the smells of food and sweat and heat could knock you down. Even the worst shelters were full, and refugees slept skin to skin in city parks, under bushes, on sidewalks. I met the father's eyes as I jogged past and felt sure they had been sleeping in such a place, and that he wanted to distract his little girl, to walk with her in the fresh air and tell stories under the trees. Their feet fell like steel onto the concrete. He looked back at me, wooden and humble, and I saw myself through his eyes, my clean cotton clothes and running shoes springing light off the sidewalk. Saw myself there and not there, slogging untouched through the murk of desperation, moving past, and I had to keep on running because I was drowning in shame.

We jounce over the dirt trenches and wrecked roads. Refugees trickle toward us, roll past, and push on, Beirut beckoning them north. You never know what people will bring at a time like this. A cow skids and stumbles in a flatbed truck. Sofas are lashed with clothesline to station wagons. Children turn their faces to us, wary and pinched. I keep my notebook in my lap and write everything down. The notes are a filter; I am watching but not really here. I am on the other side of writing. The car windows are open and there is the sweet breath of honeysuckle, the hum of bees.

There is nothing left for me to do except go south. Nobody is telling Israel to stop the bombs. The Americans say this is the war on terror, part of the New Middle East. There is no end to the war in sight, and nothing to do but go south.

You lie to yourself when you decide to accept more danger. *We will drive to the Litani River, see how it looks, and interview some fleeing refugees. Then, if it feels okay, maybe we'll keep going.* Israel says there are no civilians left south of the Litani, and so the river is the line where the war loses all mercy. Maybe we'll keep going: That's a lie. Of course you will keep going, you will go all the way to the south, to a little bed and breakfast in Tyre. You are traveling with other reporters. You are bringing supplies for people who are already there. You sort of know. But it's easier to get out of Beirut if you tell yourself that maybe you'll be back that evening, ordering an omelet and a big cold bottle of water from room service. Just in case, you bring your flak jacket and helmet and satellite phones. Just in case.

We twist up into the mountains. The driver is nervous. He pulls the car over in a village and disappears into a warren of dark, shabby shops where you might find anything at all but nothing of use, like sponges and caged parakeets and old dusty crackers. There are great crowds on the street, everybody pushing around, looking for black-market gasoline, talking about the war, fleeing the war, tasting the war. He comes back with bright orange tape and spells "TV" in big letters on the roof of the car. I am not sure whether it makes us safer or more vulnerable. On we ride.

We can't avoid the coast road anymore. As soon as cars hit that road they are naked in the crackling heat. They gun it fast, as fast as rusting parts can crank. This is a road of targets. This is a road that is being bombed actually. *Actually* is a word that has been degraded to adornment and punctuation, but it has a meaning too: it means right now, while we are on it. The smoke of fresh strikes snakes up from scorched ground. The sea pokes the horizon like the tongue of a parched man, blue corroded by salt. There are Israeli gunships out in the water, firing in toward us. We are exposed on this road, there is nothing but air between us and the long flat tongue of the sea. We drive in the wrong direction, deeper down into the war. So why shouldn't they shoot us? I realize that I am forgetting to breathe and swallow down some air. *You can't be lucky forever*. My mother has said that to me lately, more than once. She has run out of tolerance. And me, have I? I am conscious of being afraid. In other wars I felt numb, but now some internal Novocain has worn away. Sky, sea, cracked day. Myheartmyheartmyheart won't stop beating, a dry, sore little hammer pounding at me from within. I breathe deep and it feels like the bones of my chest will crack apart. My jaw is hard and tight. *Don't think, don't say a word, not one fucking word, just keep your mouth shut.* I sit and watch and write everything down.

Now the refugees are going fast as hell, flapping undershirts out the windows, bleached rags knotted around their antennas in crude imitation of white flags, begging wordlessly to be spared. Broken-down cars litter the road like forgotten toys; filling stations stand deserted, army checkpoints vacant. We are off the coast road now, following a dirt track through orchards to the river. It is a landscape empty of people, and the soft white powder of the road coats everything. Fruit flashes in the car windows, the green, hard bananas in the trees, dates and oranges, branches pushing in and scraping at my cheeks. Shutters of village houses pulled tight and streets still as plague. We cross the Litani on a sagging makeshift bridge of old wood. We are over the river now and I think of Dante fainting when he crossed the Acheron into hell. I don't faint, I just sit there thinking about breathing and sensing the planes skimming the sky with dismemberment and death in roaring bellies.

We pass more orchards and green waves smashing in off the sea and somebody says, we are here, we are in Tyre. And like the war itself it came up too fast; even those frozen minutes under bombardment have evaporated. We have come this far and there's no question of going back now.

When you are too close to the bombing, you can't hear the jets or see them. The explosions erupt upward like ejaculations of smoke, as if they came from the earth and not down from the clear sky. The spy drones click and whine, softly. When you hear them you know the jets won't be far behind; you'd better go, and you'd better go fast.

The truth is, you don't know whether any of that is true. Once you arrive you can't remember anything you learned to prepare yourself for war. I went to war school for a few days on a snowy mountainside in Virginia. Former British soldiers taught us all sorts of useful things: how to hide in underbrush without being seen, how to administer emergency first aid, how to poke a stick in the dirt, looking for mines. I can't remember any of it. All I remember are the scraps of folk knowledge passed around war zones like sticky pieces of candy. You sock them in your cheek and suck, try to sweeten your days.

I believe that bombing is the worst dangerous thing. I would rather get shot at, risk getting kidnapped, or walk across a field knowing there might be mines. When you move loose over the ground under bombardment, death drops down gracefully from the heavens, from an atmosphere you cannot see or hear. Maybe you will get hit, and maybe you won't. It feels like God himself is doling out the bombs, and down they come from that clear, empty, infinite sky. Every minute you live or you don't. Maybe the bombs will come to you and maybe they won't. No matter what happens, you will be shell-shocked. A few days under bombardment teach you everything about your nerves—where they live in your body, how they can vibrate and ache and make you shake, make you want to bite right through your finger or peel your skin off your body just to get free of them. All around you is the crashing sound of the bombs, the smell of the bombs, the bodies and buildings that have been hit by the bombs. And still you stand, for now. You think all the time about shelter. They tell you it's best to be in the basement, but why? I don't want the building to come down on top of me; I don't want to be crushed and trapped and die a slow death. I imagine myself on the top floor, coasting down gently, afloat on collapsing structure.

I was in Chechnya once, in a time of peace, and an old man looked at me and said, have you ever been where they are bombing from planes? And I said, yes. He said, then you know. That was all we said; it was everything.

The sun is shining like every mad morning in this garish war. I wake up to the crash of bombs and tell myself, just do it for one more day. Anyway you are trapped. If you try to get out of here they will kill you on the road. So do it for one more day. You know you wouldn't leave, even if you could.

The car skims fast through the empty boatyard, mangy cats poking in overflowing fishy dumpsters, the smell of garbage and fear in a frozen city. They are gathering the dead in the Palestinian refugee camp. There are too many bodies crushed by bombs, people bombed in their homes or on the road trying to escape, and nowhere to put them. The hospital has some old coolers, but they leak and the corpses are rotting. So they'll dig a mass grave in a vacant lot. Just for now, they say, just to be decent.

The Palestinian camp is not really a camp; the transitory has hardened into permanence. There are paved streets, old buildings, generations of family born and died in suspended exile. Even the refugee camp has been destroyed and built anew in cycles of fighting that span over decades. Now Lebanese refugees hide here from the bombs because they believe the camps are safer than the rest of the south.

The men stayed up all night hammering together the plain pine coffins and stacking them in the hospital yard. Some of the boxes are short for the dead children; no use wasting the wood. Under the pine trees they strung a tarp for families to sit in the shade, but the shaded chairs are empty. Most of the dead have no family in attendance, and nobody who is not a family member feels entitled to a chair.

The refrigerated trailer lurks in the grass, obscene and unmentionable. Nurses in blue scrubs pass surgical masks among the crowd. The permanent refugees and the new Lebanese refugees jam together nervously, pressed against the hospital walls, spilling into the streets beyond.

Soubiha Abdullah rocks back on forth on her feet, hugging herself. She will identify and bury twenty-four people from her family of tobacco and wheat farmers, including her sister and her sister's nine children. They died trying to escape their village; Israeli planes attacked the road as they drove. Soubiha has been waiting for more than an hour, surgical mask knotted over her *hijab*, heel-toe, heel-toe, eyes smoldering.

"I'm saying, 'God give me the strength to see them.' We just want to see them, even if they're pieces of meat.

"May God curse those who killed them."

Clouds of formaldehyde catch in the hot sea breeze and carry over the crowd, and the people cough and rub tears from their eyes. The hospital workers haul open the back doors of the moldering trailer, spilling the stench of death. The smell is perverted and cold, like a creeping creature of mist, clamping clammy hands over the flowering shrubs. Somebody shouts, "God is great!" and then others echo—God is great. The crowd is angry. The crowd is not crying. The crowd is hard. Children stand there too, eyes swollen, soaking in their destiny.

Hospital workers holler out the names as they deliver down the remains: stiff long things mummified in sheets of clear plastic or old blankets, bound with duct tape. Some are broken into pieces, loose in black garbage bags. They nail down the pine lids, spray-paint the names on top, and set the coffins out on the sun-baked clay of the camp road. The street fills slowly with coffins, and people stand around and stare.

The masked man in the trailer door holds up a cake box. He pulls out a baby, purple and mottled, so tiny you can't tell whether it had been born yet when it died. "Look at this!" he shouts.

"Oh no no no," a man at my side mutters. "God is great!" shout the others.

I pull myself out of the crowd and pace on the grass, where the nailed coffins wait. A doctor looks down at the dead, shaking with anger.

"They can't fight Hezbollah because Hezbollah is not an army," he spits the words. "They kill the people because they think it's the only way to stop Hezbollah."

This is funeral as indoctrination, and rage is fiercer than grief. The sadness is just a pale shadow on a burning day. The cheap spectacle of rotting bodies and a purple baby is more than a society can tolerate without hardening into hatred. You could stare into the enormous eyes of little boys and watch them turning to rock. You could feel it all taking hold, driving forward, another generation crushed, another generation rising. One war breeds another war. We create what we try to kill. Gaze too long into an abyss and the abyss also gazes into you, Nietzsche said. The Americans, the Israelis, say they want to destroy Hezbollah, but what does it mean? Hezbollah is rooted inside these people, in their houses and neighborhoods and bellies. The more people you kill, unless you kill all of them, the stronger Hezbollah will live in the ones who remain. They would do anything for Hezbollah, yes, and it was naive to expect anything different from Shiites in the south. It is a matter of fact that Hezbollah formed up as a guerrilla force to fight back against an Israeli invasion. These people have it fixed in their minds that Israel finds some reason to invade their land every generation. That is a one-sided view, yes of course, but it's the one they have, the one all victims will always have. There is a reason we can't depend upon victims to mete out justice in courts. "Every time there's an Israeli war, we have a massacre in my family," one of the women tells me. Now the Lebanese army watches, mute, as a foreign invasion unfolds. The president swims laps in his crystal swimming pool; he can see Beirut burning from his manicured lawns. The prime minister cries on TV and flies to Rome to beg the West to make it stop. Hezbollah snatches up Iranian-bought guns and fights back. This is not romantic lore; it is cold fact.

"Where are the young men?" An old woman moans a mourning song. "Where are the young men?" She puts her head into an empty coffin.

The dead bake in the sun. The men turn their palms to heaven and pray. The Lebanese army has sent trucks and soldiers to move the bodies. This is the first time I've seen the army deploy since the war began. Silence congeals thick as pudding when the coffins pass on the shoulders of soldiers. They load the coffins into green army trucks and drive to a vacant lot littered with telephone poles and bulldozers. They have dug a long trench into the sandy, salty earth. The earth is ready to swallow the bones. The shadows are thin and elongated now. The crowd from the refugee camp stands and watches.

A man with white hair scrambles to the edge of the trench. "Hey Americans!" he bellows. "This is what Bush wants! This is what this dog wants! It's full of children!"

An elderly woman in black perches like a crooked crow at the edge of the grave. "My darling Mariam, my only daughter," she moans. "Twenty-seven years old, my darling, twenty-seven years old."

Somewhere close by, a muezzin sings the call to prayer, gentle as blown cotton over the fields. The shadows grow longer still on the quaking dirt. Somewhere close by, bombs are falling.

*Allah hu akbar. God is great.*

Noses tip up into the sky. What will they do, somebody asks, bomb us here? Maybe they will, says somebody else. Maybe they will even kill the dead.

Somebody will stop it. They must, because it can't continue. The United States will call for a ceasefire. "We are urging restraint," Bush says. The bombs keep falling. A ceasefire would be "a false promise if it returns us to the status quo," Rice says. These words sound like rusted tin, scraping at skin, breeding infection. Anonymous Washington officials tell reporters that they won't even try until next week. Hezbollah needs to be defanged, they say. How many will die before next week? The two soldiers are no longer the point; it's turned into something bigger, about defeating terrorism and this interminable fight for something intangible.

A dead body rots in an old sedan. The car was hit on a dirt road that dips through the shadows and green leaves of a banana grove. The Mediterranean rolls nearby. The car is blown open on one side. Somebody keeps saying, "That's a body? I can't see it." Maybe that was me. All I hear now is the voice, high and weird against the dead silence of war. And somebody else says, "There. There. See the head? See the arm?" I am not a photographer and I feel dirty, like we've paid to peek at something pornographic. The body is a dark gelatin mold, melting, spreading, vanishing into the fabric of the car seat, into the shirt he wore the day he died. In a nest of man-made things, the flesh is the first to go. We, the people, are the most delicate of all. The stranger rots as the war goes on. Finally, somebody comes and cleans everything away. We drive by one day, and the car is gone.

One day there is a tiny baby girl. She washed into the Tyre emergency room in a wave of bloodied families who'd been bombed trying to drive north. Nobody knows which family is hers. She is dressed in little overalls with rainbows and bears—six to eight months, the nurse says. *I don't know whose baby it is, I just found it here.* I stand and look at her and she looks back at me from the nurse's shoulder. Her body smells of burned meat. Her baby hair is scorched to her scalp, each strand shocked straight out, the end dipped in charcoal. Her sausage arm is bleeding. Her face is bruised.

The baby doesn't make a sound. She lays limp and passive, sucks on a pink pacifier, and stares at the wailing, bleeding emergency room through brown eyes, one frozen pinpoint in a swirling storm. The baby is in shock. I didn't know that babies could go into shock—shock without language, without reason. They will take her to see a doctor, so the nurse lays her down on the cold plastic sheet of a big adult stretcher. The baby shatters back to emotion, she writhes and screams, and they put a hand on her belly to keep her still and wheel her away, parentless and burned. I look at my cell phone. It's only noon and the whole day is still to come.

Then a bomb crashes to earth just outside the door, and I run to see.

Another day, I am in a tiny hillside hospital in Tibnin. The grass is on fire from Israeli shells, heaving up smoke and confusion. The hospital is packed with 1,500 refugees and Israeli shells slam to earth outside. There is nothing but fear here, no doctors or food. More hungry, thirsty, crazy people pour in every hour to curl together in hunger and shiver in the heat. They have no clean water and they are wracked by diarrhea.

I climb down the stairs, into the deep caverns of the hospital basement. People lurk like medieval things in their grotto. Quivering light leaks from a few broken candles. Babies cry in the darkness. The elderly and the sick are strewn like crumpled scrap paper on the floor. I am walking through another age, a medieval prison, something that can't exist now. I turn a corner and the air is a sheet of black, embroidered with voices.

*There's no water.*

*The road is closed.*

*There's no water, no water.*

*We're tired, we're tired. Our kids' nerves are shot. They are terrified.*

A throat rich with decades of cigarettes. A voice without a face.

*I was at home and a missile struck the house but we weren't killed. We could have been chopped to pieces.*

*Look how people are living. Our children are going to die of thirst.*

*We want a ceasefire, we want peace. I was born in war and I am forty years old and I live in war. We build our homes and they destroy them.*

*Don't leave us here! Send airplanes for us, please . . .*

*There is no water.*

In the dark I write as fast as I can, and upstairs voices are screaming that it's time to *go*, we have to *go*. I don't understand why we have to go, the shells are coming thicker, but there is only one coherent idea in my mind: if I get abandoned in this dark, rich whale belly overnight I will lose my sanity. So I clamber up into daylight, into the thick crowds of weakened humans who crawl into the sunshine because they can't bear the hospital bowels anymore. "A chain is broken in the ambulance," a Red Cross volunteer yells. They climb under the ambulance, shake their sweaty heads, and talk fast. We followed the ambulance here, clinging to its wake for thin protection. Israel is bombing ambulances now, too, but still it seems like a shield. The shells are crashing, smoking, chewing the dirt. Soon it will be dark. The Red Cross men tell us to go away. They think the Israelis are shelling around the hospital because we are here, because the ambulances gave cover to the journalists. They want us to leave on our own because maybe once we are gone the shelling will stop. So we creak back through ghostly towns and bomb-scorched valleys, past the sign reminding us that RESISTANCE IS A NATIONAL DUTY. My heart is in my mouth. I know what this phrase means now. The heart swells, slicing off breath, sending beats in echoes through your skull. My heart is in my mouth and we drive as fast as we can.

Adrenaline is the strongest drug. When it floods your veins the world smears around you in a carousel spin, except that each detail is crisp and hard, the colors are not negotiable, the hardness of shadow and sunlight cut you but they feel good and real and you keep on standing. Words drift for hours and days on the surface of your thoughts, gathering like algae. Ever since the mass funeral I have had these words in my head: killing the dead, killing the dead. People look like ancient animals, lurching over some primordial land. A single bird's cry is clean and hard enough to carve your skin. This is why people get addicted. When adrenaline really gets going you can't get sick, you don't need sleep, and you feel you can do anything. I know when this is over it will be like dying.

It is the last day of July and the land has no mercy, it dries out and flakes off, bearded by yellow grasses. The whine of the cicadas rings in my ears like the voice of heat itself, higher and faster until you think the vibrating song will lay you flat in the dust. There is no other life left in the hills, only the space left over, the empty dent where the noise of drones, jets, and explosions used to be. Suddenly they have stopped and there is only the space they left.

Israel has stopped bombing for forty-eight hours. They just killed a lot of civilians at Qana, and the world is angry, and Israel says it will investigate. I was in Qana yesterday and now I am going to Bint Jbeil. That is where the fighting has been the worst and nobody has managed to get there. You know there is a war going all over the south but you can only know what you can reach. By now they have wrecked all the roads and everybody knows they aren't kidding: they will kill us if we get in their way.

The refugees are coming out of Bint Jbeil and we are going in. They look like hell, or as if they have recently been there. Coated in dust, faces cut sharp by hunger, dry as the yellow grasses. They are packed into cars or staggering on foot. They put their dead eyes on our faces and beg us for help.

*Can you take us to the hospital? We can't walk anymore.*

No, we are going forward.

*There's nobody there. Nobody at all.*

*They won't take us.*

*We haven't been able to get out of the house for twenty days.*

The car rolls by slowly, rocking and rising over the dents in the road. Little boys sit crammed in the trunk. Everybody looks. Nobody speaks. Their eyes are empty and dead. When we try to interview the refugees, they interrupt to beg.

*There's nobody there. Nobody there. Take us to Tibnin. We've been in the shelter two weeks, they've been hitting us, they hit the house. When we heard there was a ceasefire we left. We are just eating apples we can find, drinking water from the wells.*

*I found a pack of cigarettes in a store. I will give you some. All of them. Please.*

The cicadas sing in the dying grasses. The cicadas will sing on the bones.

*They won't take us.*

We drive on, through the dying grass, leaving the refugees to fend for themselves. I tell myself we will find them on the way back. I remind myself this is the right thing to do. I am sick with myself.

On the edge of town there is a hospital on a traffic circle. A lone doctor stumbles from the shadows, blinks his green eyes, and says, "It's been like hell." There is no power and no light. He has hauled a dusty cot over to the open doorway where the sun is smacking the pavement outside.

"We're trying to work over here where there is light."

Blood crusts the cot and the floor and hangs in the air. He has no staff left, only a bottle of iodine and this cot hauled over into filtered sunlight.

"You see there is not much we can do except first aid and CPR."

They bombed the hospital. Light pours through the hole in the roof.

"The other day we were sitting here counting shells and in half an hour we counted 350 bombs. All the people here are supporting Hezbollah—if you live here and see your people being killed and tortured. There are times we sit and cry because children are in pieces. You have to have somebody to fight for you to protect you. It makes you sick because you see what is happening to you and all the world is talking about you, but it doesn't stop."

Shafts of sunlight fall through the ceiling onto mattresses coated with dust. The doctor is fleeing. He says: "Not much you can do anymore."

We head deeper into town. You have to keep going. Not because it is your job but because it is inevitable. Because you got onto this road and it goes only forward, not back, and you can't change it.

Bint Jbeil was a small, hilly town with buildings and streets, but now the center of town has vanished. The buildings were crushed and crumbled into great dunes of wreckage, mighty and unmovable, as if they were swept into place by centuries of wind. The streets have disappeared underneath the dunes. Consider this word, *wreckage*. It means every thing in town, mangled and mixed. The buildings smashed into chunks of concrete, tangles of rebar, broken doors and windows and screws and nails and framed pictures and stoves and refrigerators and beds and closets. It is toys and lamps and bowls and potted plants. Mostly it is the broken buildings themselves. When you melt it all down, the structures are greater than their content. You can't drive into town because there are no more roads. You can only look down at the awesome tides and dunes of a broken city and surmise where the roads once ran. The silence is enormous and relentless. The sky is full of God and sun and Israeli warplanes, looking down from one vast, blank eye.

We park and I can see there was a road leading down the hill, and so I walk along it over the wrecked buildings, the frames and thresholds of shops gaping on either side, vomiting their dirty guts of toys and soda pop and dresses and medicine. *I found a pack of cigarettes in a store. I will give you some. All of them.* Those refugees on the road, where did they come from? There can be no life here.

There is a noise over to the right, the mewing of a wounded cat. But I look and it is worse; it is an old woman.

"Take me to the hospital," she calls. "I want a drink."

There are some other reporters walking near me and we draw close to her and she gazes up. She is filthy and sprawled in a sea of broken things. Flies crawl all over her blackened face but she smiles a dreamy smile.

*God brought you. God brought you. I didn't want to die alone.*

Somebody has gone into a broken store and found a small bottle of yellow juice, and she sits up and drinks. Her blue bathrobe is slick with dust.

"Don't leave me. Six days without food. Please take me to the hospital. I can't walk, I walk a little and I fall down. I've spent six nights sleeping down here, there was a little water left in the puddles and I was drinking. I am a widow. I have a daughter in Beirut. I fell on my hand. I can't hear I can't hear, there were so many bombs I can't hear. I'm an old woman. I got tangled up in the electrical lines and tangled up in the stones."

Other reporters are ministering to her, taking notes and foraging for bottles of water, and I slip away from them. This was a pharmacy once and now it spills its contents, bars of soap, boxes of flu medicine, aspirin—the archaeology of that exquisitely organized time commonly referred to as a few weeks ago. Somehow this is still a summer afternoon and a dragonfly lights on the rebar. The blasted fixtures of a chandelier shop poke at crooked angles. Somebody's lingerie drawer hangs open, bras dripping down like vines. I hear music and look down to see a singing birthday card open on the ground, chiming "Happy birthday to you," over and over again.

At the water reservoir at the bottom of the hill, a middle-aged man wanders abstractedly. He wears an old plaid shirt and a baseball cap advertising a tire shop.

"If you write a thousand words it's not worth one bullet in the head of an Israeli. Thank God there are some tomatoes left in the ground. What's the benefit? I am asking why. Because I am Muslim? The whole world is crying for Israel to stop and they don't care. Why do I fight? Why did God create me? Not to be a fighter but it's an emergency. You think I like it? I hate it. All the time, fighting, fighting, fighting. They occupied Lebanon for twenty years."

When he talks about Israel he turns and points over the hill. I hear the walkie-talkie scratch from his pocket and understand that he is with Hezbollah. But he is not like the disciplined others. He has been driven a little crazy.

"I can't tell you my name. What does it matter? I am one person. The only thing that matters is after the war is over we gather money and buy rockets and buy missiles and buy guns. Because nobody in this earth loves us. I can't believe it. Just because we are Muslims. We won, so what? We won on our land, so what? It is our land, we will win in the end."

The bombs drive everybody crazy, and there isn't much you can do about it. He says he is a forty-three-year-old schoolteacher and a fighter.

"There is some resistance, they are seeing you but you can't see them. It began since fifteen days. Every night, shelling. I saw the tanks burning with my bare eyes. Excuse me for a second."

He walks across the dirt and snatches a yellow Hezbollah flag from the dirt.

"You know it's our flag. It can't be down."

He stuffs it down his pants. "My friend has been martyred in battle," he says. Then he starts to cry.

"I wish I were in his place and martyred instead of living this dog's life. People think we like to fight. They don't think we want to live with our children and raise them. If you live without your dignity it's a dog's life. I swear to God two days ago I had a can of tuna and a dog went by and I couldn't eat without giving it to the dog. I wonder how God will judge people. Why did God create the earth, why? There is a bright side and a dark side. You stay with one or another. There is no gray side. The gray side is the dark side. Tomorrow they will come and give us a few dollars and say, okay, let's forget everything, let it pass. But I've lost friends, I've lost family. You cry for people you lost. You cry for the town. You cry for history. You cry for the Jews too because I know very well they will be in hell. Those who remain quiet and don't speak the truth, they are silent devils."

I leave the crazy shell-shocked shell of a Hezbollah fighter and climb into the rubble. It's dirty work and hard climbing over the crushed buildings and broken glass, and I am wearing the same shoes I have had all this time, black leather loafers I brought with me from Cairo, and how long ago was that, anyway? Unblown missiles glint evilly in the sun. There are no walls left standing and so there is no shade, only the enormous sky, pitiless sun, and silence.

A miracle is stirring. The broken, vanished town is full of Lazaruses and they are staggering now into the light. They crawl out on cut legs and bleeding feet, half-dead, half-mad impossibilities, old and fat and weak. They have heard that somebody has come for them. They have crazy eyes and a few things crammed into plastic grocery sacks or cheap duffels. They fall in the rubble and cut themselves. The journalists begin to help. Nobody can bear anymore to stand around taking photographs. They lift the old people and stagger far up the hill where the Red Cross ambulances are stuck, unable to drive into the town that no longer exists on roads that vanished under dunes of wreckage.

A wrinkled woman sits against the lost frame of a shop. Her fingers are coated with clay, as if she has been digging.

*We were under the rubble. When I hear that plane it scares me my nerves are shot God help me. Let them come and take me. My brother is ill.*

She pours water into his mouth. He is mentally handicapped. He sits cross-legged at her side, giggling and weeping. His tongue lolls out of his mouth.

*Are they going to hit us again today?*

This is who gets left behind when war comes: poor people, old people, and handicapped people. This is who they are bombing now. In this moment I am numb and still, but I am aware that I deeply hate everybody for letting this happen. I hate the Lebanese families for leaving them here. I hate Hezbollah for not evacuating them, for ensuring civilian deaths that will bolster their cause. I hate Israel for wasting this place on the heads of the feeble. I hate all of us for participating in this great fiction of the war on terror, for pretending there is a framework, a purpose, for this torment. I sit in hatred and write everything down with filthy fingers. An old man perches on the hood of a car that rises from this sea of rubble. His feet dangle bare and swollen from the cuffs of his pajamas. His sister, an old woman, babbles and squints like she is trying to remember something, apologetic and amazed.

*Our house fell on top of us. No food no water I'm talking now and I don't know what I'm saying. He can't walk at all. I'm talking I don't know what I'm saying. I can't even walk. We found muddy water to drink. I'll never come back to this village I don't care what they say.*

Another old woman is talking to me when I realize I've had a rock in my shoe for a long time. This recognition breaks through the glaze of shock—pain has pulsed unrealized. I take off my shoe and it's full of blood. A thick spike of glass punched through the sole; I've been walking on somebody's shattered window all this while. Well. Oh well. I will tiptoe on that foot. The woman is still talking so I write down what she says. Everybody is cut; neither of us bothers over my bloody foot.

*My brother who is blind was living underneath me. He's still there. I knocked on his door and he said yes I'm still here. I am an old woman staying in my house nobody came for me I can't walk. I couldn't take him with me he's still there every minute I think we are going to die.*

Yes, I say. No. You will be all right now. The Red Cross is here now.

The sun is sinking low into the hills. Soon the lull will end and the Israeli bombs will fall again.

## SEVENTEEN

# I THOUGHT I WAS A SALAMANDER

The war no longer feels temporary. Now there is a hardening, an acceptance of this condition. Roads are death and sky is fear and people scurry down into the scorched earth like moles. The country creaks to freezing under blockade. Nothing comes in or out. Hospitals are empty of medicine. There isn't enough food or clean water. The worst thing is you get used to it. If the bombs would just stop for one minute, I could calm down, organize my thoughts, breathe. But quiet brings no peace. When the bombs stop, all you hear is the possibility, the promise, of another bomb. The quiet is pregnant with contained fire, about to fall.

The car lurches and tears along empty, sun-blasted roads, through the popping yellow silence of a summer afternoon. I can't remember what day it is anymore. Daylight rolls into darkness and then blasts back again. Schedules, school buses, markets: none of these things have any meaning left. They are empty. The way the body senses the physical presence of another person in a dark room, by magnetic field or gravity or the secret stirring of air—with that same instinctive, physical knowing, I feel the steel bombing machines above us, circling like great mute sharks in the cloudless blue. I am too nervous to talk. I am jumping out of my skin. Except for interviews, I can hardly stand to interact with people anymore. Conversation demands a calm I have lost. I can summon the manic focus of journalism, or I am adrift on nerves. I put headphones in my ears and stare out the window, breathing in and out. We have no illusion of safety. We keep quiet and follow the road map. *Deaf and lost are the children*, Radiohead whispers in my ears.

Heat shimmers around the man at the psychiatric hospital gate, and the steady, urgent stream of Hezbollah's wartime news pours out from a transistor radio at his feet. His plastic chair is nested in a flame of hibiscus and rose. He holds a rope in his hands that pulls the gate down or slackens to let it up. As we approach, he snaps off a taut salute.

We are journalists, we say. We would like to visit some of the patients.

"I'm a patient," he says in a strange, high voice. "I've got family problems."

He smiles up at us, rubs at his thinning crew cut, and fidgets his fingers. "I am a schizophrenic," he says.

So what are you doing with your days? we ask.

"I wake up, have some breakfast. Then I sit down and listen to the radio. What can I do?" he says. "I'm in charge of the gate."

Where are the doctors?

They ran away.

The other staff?

"Because of the war," he sighs. "Nobody comes."

"It's because of the grass," he adds.

Aren't you afraid?

"There's no human that isn't afraid. Everyone is afraid."

He looks at us, and pronounces the next two words blissfully:

"It's normal."

On an ordinary day, in regular life, I would be anxious, walking into a mental institution. A place like that cuts too close to the nerve: its medicine smells and white rooms and trees hang in imagination as the collapse of time and logic, the ultimate swoon of surrender, the end of trying. It is said that people are afraid of heights because they secretly fear they might jump. That is the feeling I get when I think of psychiatric hospitals.

But every place is horrible now, and so it doesn't matter anymore. A morgue or a mental institution is better, in a way. There is no engrained expectation that it will be pleasant—abnormality feels normal, and normal feels good. Thick, spicy pine groves huddle around the buildings. Orange butterflies flicker in the flower beds. Bars slice the windows, but a clean breeze breathes through, cooling the quiet corridors.

Only two members of the medical staff remain. This nurse's name is Hossam Moustapha. He is twenty-six years old and dipping into the anxiety medications. "We get depressed, man."

The pills are running low and the patients are now on half doses, which may or may not be enough to keep them in control of themselves. There isn't enough food left. And every night, the bombs come.

The men's ward is dim and vast and barred off like a jail cell. Patients loom over picnic tables and smoke cigarettes into the gray air. We look at them through the bars. A few of them stride over and stare back at us, mouths hanging open, grinning or puckering their faces in scowls.

A haggard, pale man speaks to me in English. "I lived in Michigan."

"What were you doing in Michigan?"

"I worked at a gas station. When they hear the bombs," he confides, wiggling his brows toward the other patients, "they *do* get frightened. I've been here twenty days. I'm new here. Matter of fact, I *almost* don't belong here. My father is old-fashioned. He brought me in here. He tricked me because I stopped taking my medicine. I felt more normal without it."

He doesn't believe he's seen a doctor since June 12. Today is August 4.

The other patients' wariness melts, and they begin to shout.

"Why are you here?" one of them demands. "Go to your own country!"

"We are with Hezbollah!" another yells.

"Who's crazy?" somebody hollers. "Us or them?"

The former gas station attendant breathes through the bars, "Write this down, write this down." He whispers a telephone number in Beirut and watches me write the digits. "Call my mother," he says intensely. "Tell her to get me out of here."

"Hush," calls Hossam.

"They're getting too excited," he tells me.

We walk into the waiting room, where a mounted television blasts and flashes in the stillness like a tiny contained storm. Like everybody else in south Lebanon, the staff is watching al Manar. This is Hezbollah's station and they have constant war coverage, even a reporter who is embedded with the guerrillas. I look out the window into the afternoon of bombs and yellow, yellow sunlight. Here we are a small island of people. The rest of the day is empty of people. They have gone into hiding.

Everything is moving too fast. I stand there on the white floor and try to think for just one minute. You are in the middle of an insane asylum. You are in the middle of a war. You are under bombardment. You can get killed driving out of here. Maybe you will. Don't think it can't happen, because it can. Take some of that realness, and ingest it.

We are walking back out, through the pines and butterflies. One foot before the next, down to the main building, but all the time the words won't stop. This war around me now doesn't feel like a dream. That's the problem: I have been dreaming ever since Afghanistan. I let myself get tougher and smaller, pulled myself back, back, back, behind my face, behind the interviews, behind the stories. The uglier it got, the harder it got, the more I drew myself in, the more I distracted myself with colorful myths. I am a foreign correspondent. I am covering the story of our times. I am covering the wars. It all matters. It is worth everything. You turn yourself into something separate, something absent. There and not there. It works, putting thick glass between you and the world. You can be anywhere if you're not really there. You can walk into any room, drive down any road, ask any question, write about anybody's pain. You tell yourself you are unscathed. You stand smooth and count yourself unaffected. And basically, it's true—compared with the people around you, the civilians and soldiers, you are unscathed and unaffected. That works fine until all of a sudden it doesn't work at all. It occurs to me now that maybe this is the most American trait of all, the trademark of these wars. To be there and be gone all at once, to tell ourselves it just happened, we did what we did but we had no control over the consequences.

Now, on this day in Lebanon, it doesn't work: there is no divider, no case around me, no audience and no costumes. I am just me, and I am wholly here. I feel like I sleepwalked out onto the interstate and opened my eyes just in time to see the trucks blocking out the sky, groaning down. I said yes, yes, yes. I went along every time. If you want to succeed in journalism, you should say yes, yes, yes. Yes, I'll go. Yes, I'll stay. Yes, I'll write it. Yes, I'll rewrite it. Yes, of course I'd like to go back. You should never say no.

There is an ancient belief that salamanders can live in fire without getting burned. Zelda Fitzgerald, languishing in an asylum, drew a picture of a salamander and wrote: "I believed I was a salamander, and it seems I am nothing but an impediment." We have all tried to be salamanders, but nobody really survives the fire. The mystery is that some get burned worse than others; some get burned in ways that are livable, and some do not.

The Palestinian owner is made of sterner stuff than the doctors. Her name is Adela Dajani Labban, a great sprawling lady of unspoken age and iron-colored hair. "I am the wife of the late Dr. Labban, who made this hospital," by way of introduction. Swathed in black, roped with jewelry, she lounges under chandeliers in a vast drawing room. Her dead husband smiles beatifically down from the wall, enshrined in black and white. She smokes one slim cigarette after another. Her phone lines have been cut for days, and the crash of bombs kept her awake all last night, but she stays. She has lived her life as a refugee, and she is too implacable to keep running.

"I went down yesterday to see them and it was 'I want my mother, I want my father,' " she sneers a little at the patients' fragility. "Where am I going to go with 250 people? We can't go anywhere." She painted a big red cross on the hospital roof, fashioned white flags from bedsheets, and goes about her business.

"The Israelis are my enemies until the day I die," she says. "I was born in Jerusalem. My parents died in Jerusalem, and I still have a hospital in Jerusalem. In my class there were seven Jews. Four of them were my friends."

Labban doesn't smolder with fury; she doesn't howl with grief; she doesn't even seem particularly frightened. It's as if she can't be bothered to be impressed by Israel. She has seen all of this before; she was ensconced in this same hospital when Israel occupied south Lebanon in 1982. The soldiers had swarmed over the asylum grounds. "I was very rude to them. Mind you, they did not answer. *Ahlan wah sahlan.* Welcome. Let them come. I will free the patients and maybe one of them will make a problem," she cackles.

I stare at her, at her knickknacks and the owlish face of her husband, and think hard. I know everything that I am supposed to know. How she came to be here, and the other facts that shaped the biographies of the Middle East. I see all of it in one glance, how the borders were drawn, religion swept over deserts and through empires, colonialism came and went and came again. I've read the books and considered the arguments. I signed up for the listservs of professors and writers who argue over Islam's perpetual promises and America's eternal interests. Everybody lying; everybody failing a little, then failing some more. The powerful tripping along, blinded by their own mythology, led astray by their morals. I can see all of it. I am bogged in facts. But here I stand among the mad and maybe that's all it's ever been. The Middle East goes crazy and we go along with it. So many of my generation have trooped here for these latest wars—the soldiers, the sailors, the UN workers, the State Department enfants terribles, Mad Max contractors with guns strapped to beefy thighs, the writers and volunteers and freelancers and adventure-hungry travelers. We chased it all down into the Middle East and we came up dry, coughing on other people's blood.

And now, in the depths of this war, I believe that nobody will ever see this, that Israel will never really look, and America will never really look, either. This is real to nobody. This would never be real to me if I were not here. Oh God just make it stop. Make the bombs stop. There was this policy, and that policy. One war and then another, all of it clumped together. It must have meant something—it seemed to mean a great deal—back when we all went into Afghanistan. Somewhere between Afghanistan and Iraq, we lost our way. The carnage of it and the disorder, all to create a new Middle East. But naturally there would be no new Middle East because the old Middle East is still here, and where should it go? Only a country as quixotic, as history-free, as America could come up with this notion: that you can make the old one go away. Maybe you can debate until it makes sense from a distance, as an abstraction. But up close the war on terror isn't anything but the sick and feeble cringing in an asylum, babies in shock, structure smashed. Baghdad broken. Afghanistan broken, Egypt broken. The line between heaven and earth, broken. Lebanon broken. Broken peace and broken roads and broken bridges. The broken faith and years of broken promises. Children inheriting their parents' broken hearts, growing up with a taste for vengeance. And all along, America dreaming its deep sweet dream, there and not there. America chasing phantoms, running uphill to nowhere in pursuit of a receding mirage of absolute safety.

Voices murmur as we pass from room to room in the women's section, and patients perch like drooping birds in their barred space, human ornaments against white walls.

"Do you know my brother? He's in Riyadh," says a woman named Mariam Khalil. She is curled onto a cot, eyes chasing shadows around the walls. "I'm trying to fly to London. I want to go out of here but I don't know how to go with the war. I don't know how to go, how to do." She asks me to call her children. She wheedles and bosses until I write down her husband's name and telephone number. Tell him to come and get me, she says.

I move toward her neighbor, but Mariam doesn't want me to go. "She don't understand anything," she shouts. "I tell her there's a war . . ."

"I don't know," echoes the other woman. "There's a war. The airplanes." She hauls her knees into her soft chest, and begins to rock back and forth. "They are just hitting and hitting." And then she giggles.

I wade deeper, and feel the excitement in the room rise. The women are thrilled by the diversion of a visitor. They touch my clothes, my hair, peer anxiously into my notebook, eyes gobbling up words they don't understand. The frenzy grows, blurring the cascade of awful thought. A woman with dark, matted hair bats madly at her own head, driving away invisible insects; another laughs hysterically.

There is a fifty-five-year-old woman who has colored her fingernails blue and purple with a magic marker. Somebody has shorn her hair unevenly; it spits out at odd angles, thinned to her scalp. A woman in teal hides her face in the corner. A woman pulls on her hair and looks out the window. A woman sits with her mouth frozen downward, as if she will frown for the rest of her life, through war and peace, just sit and frown.

Does everybody here know there's a war? I ask.

"We all know there's a war," one of the women says. Her face cracks and she begins to cry. The other women see her and they start, too. Everybody around her sits and weeps like children, with the purity of contagious emotion.

I move along to another room, leaving the weepers behind, and a woman grabs at my hand. There is fever in her brown eyes, in her flushed cheeks. "Make a party for me this evening!" she breathes. "I will fall in love with you."

A fat young woman flops onto a cot on her back, and bops her feet up and down to unheard beats. "Elvis Presley, Elvis Presley, Elvis Presley . . ." she chants.

"Can you afford to make me teeth?" another woman asks me.

I let myself get lost in the flow of free associations and interruptions, slipping further and further off the axis. It feels good.

A woman is singing opera. "I'm Armenian," she informs me, spreading her robed self like a proud butterfly showing off its wings. "I am an opera singer."

At her back, not to be outdone, the Elvis fan begins to sing, too.

"Let's twist again," she belts at the ceiling, "like we did last summer . . ."

The song follows me out of the ward as I walk away from the delirium, back to the war and the madness that lurks outside the gate.

The war was over a few days later. Israel agreed to a ceasefire and, as a last gesture, dropped more than a million cluster bombs over southern Lebanon. It was a dirty end to a dirty war. Cluster bombs are nasty and deadly, lying in the grass like innocent plastic things, tempting children and still killing them months later, when the winter settled over the earth and Ramadan came to wrecked towns. Long after the world had relegated the war to history and the madness of summer, kids and poor farmers with their rough hands tripped over them in their olive groves, and died.

When peace came I drove out of Lebanon the same way I'd come, crawling along that bomb-wrecked road to the Syrian border, past the burned-out cars and craters of a blasted landscape. The refugees poured in the other way, rumbling homeward again. They grinned and hung from their cars, flashing victory signs, waving Hezbollah flags and pictures of Nasrallah. The scorched road was a party of honking and kissing and blaring stereos. They believed they had won; they believed that Israel had lost. And I was limping away, scattered and shaking.

It was a festival night in Amman. Fireworks exploded into the sky because the war in Lebanon had ended, because it was summer, because there were weddings. My boyfriend, Tom, came from Iraq and met me there, in the city destined to be passed through on the way to someplace else. We went to a cigar lounge and sat out on a limestone terrace in the summer night. Jordan spread out like a jewelry box laid open, its velvet darkness studded with dusky lights. We smoked and watched the night. The heat pressed our skin. I smelled like a shower, like soaps and creams. Clean clothes lay soft as flower petals on hardened skin. I felt like a reptile, dressed up. Underneath the cleanness of the non-war, I was still not there. I had survived, I was alive. The shadow of death had passed over my body. But I had left myself there, in the salt and blood and crazy sunlight. I was stuck there and I didn't know what to make of pasteurized Jordan, dark and lush and humane, the whisper and tinkle of a summer terrace. Sparks and blasts burst up from the horizon, fireworks set off by laughing men on dark hilltops, fading even as they bloomed, their crashes ringing in the valleys, up to the stars. Each explosion shook my heart like a bomb, every crash brought the war back around me, and then I felt tears on my face. Tom looked at me and I sat there crying. "Let's get the check. Please." We crossed Jordan in a taxi and I locked myself back into the sterilized womb of a hotel, with smooth sheets and satellite television and thick robes, with the heavy door that kept the world away. Clean and removed, like a little piece of America. I stayed there all night, until morning came.

This is the first thing I learned about war. Remember?

You can survive and not survive, both at the same time.

# EPILOGUE

I don't want to write this last part with any decorations or adornment. I don't really want to write it all. By now I have given up on pulling poetry out of war.

Raheem's son got killed. U.S. soldiers shot him in the chest.

His name was Mohammed, and he was twenty years old. It happened on a Tuesday at noon, April 2007, out on his block in Baghdad.

The soldiers were rumbling in a convoy on an overpass leading to the Green Zone. The overpass ran alongside Raheem's street. One of the armored vehicles hit a homemade bomb. The soldiers shot into the streets below.

Mohammed had gone to the neighborhood store to buy ice cream for his younger brother. The store was six doors down. He was on the street at the wrong time. They shot him in the chest.

He crawled over to a door and banged on it. He was bleeding badly. At first the people hiding inside didn't move. The soldiers were still shooting in the street; they were too scared. Mohammed lay there bleeding until the shooting stopped. When quiet came the neighbors dragged him inside the shop and called his mother. She appeared and washed his face and sat with him. She tried to talk with him, but he couldn't speak.

It took Mohammed two hours to die. The soldiers had sealed off the neighborhood and closed all the roads. Nobody could take him to the hospital. They said later that if he'd gotten to the hospital, they could have saved him. But movement was impossible, and so he bled to death in a convenience shop.

Two more months, and he would have finished high school. He wanted to study physical education. He wasn't much of a student, but he was a good athlete. He lifted weights, swam, and played soccer.

The grocery store is called Hathal's Shop. That is the name of the man who owns it. Now Raheem turns his eyes away because he can't stand to look at it.

Raheem was reporting in the southern port city of Basra when his son died. Basra was under the control of Shiite militias at that time, and it was a lethal assignment. He had called home and chatted with Mohammed half an hour before what Raheem now refers to as "the incident."

Raheem asked his son how he slept. Mohammed said that he had slept well, and that he had seen a television program about Iraqi poetry. They both loved poetry. Raheem reminded him to study, not to waste too much time watching TV. Then they said good-bye.

When they phoned Raheem from the hospital, he was working on a computer in the hotel. A relative of his, a young woman who worked at the Yarmouk Hospital in Baghdad, was on the phone. Her father had driven Mohammed to the hospital when the roads opened.

"Mohammed was shot by the soldiers," she said. "He is injured."

This happens a lot in Arab countries. People lie to soften the blow. It's considered socially acceptable; it's considered necessary. Doctors don't tell terminal patients they are dying. But Raheem is a good reporter. He could smell the lie.

"Please tell me the truth," he said.

So she did.

Raheem yelled at the driver to pay for the rooms, and ran to collect his things. They reached Baghdad at nine that night. The next day they buried Mohammed in Najaf, and soon Raheem was back at work.

Raheem was supposed to be the one in danger, working as a journalist. Mohammed didn't like it. He had pestered his brothers, reminding them not to mention their father's job outside the house. Sometimes he asked Raheem to cancel his reporting trips out into the provinces. Raheem never did.

As for Mohammed, he was as safe as anybody in Baghdad. He rarely left the neighborhood. His school was a stone's throw from the house.

Nobody in the family goes into Mohammed's bedroom anymore. They gave his clothes to the poor. Raheem guesses the rest of his things are still in the room, but he doesn't know because he can't stand to look. Only Bashar, the younger brother, is able to cross the threshold. The only time Raheem dreamed about Mohammed, it was about the room. It was a simple dream. Mohammed was looking out of his room, smiling at his father.

More than a year later, I asked Raheem if he thought he was beginning to heal.

"Whenever I am alone, I can't control my tears," he said. "Even when I am walking in the street. Alone in the house, and even when I am sitting on my computer during the working hours. But I am always trying to be strong in front of my family."

Raheem's wife can't stand the house anymore.

"Everything in it reminds her," he says.

I was in Cairo when I heard about Raheem's son. By then, I had already packed up my apartment. I was staying in a hotel, waiting for a Russian visa. I had asked for another job, and I was going to Moscow, in large measure because I didn't expect to find any war there. When I got the note about Raheem's son I was sitting among boxes and dust-streaked notebooks in the *Los Angeles Times* bureau, packing up all the things I'd written down during six years of chasing war. When I read the news I dropped my head into my hands and cried for a while, sitting there at the computer. I thought about quiet Raheem and the careful, proud way he spoke of his children. Then I wrote him a note. There is nothing you can say. Even if I were there I wouldn't hug him. We have never touched. And he wrote back, sounding hollow and gracious, saying thank you. And then I cried some more, even though if there's one thing I learned at Raheem's side, it's that crying doesn't do any good at all.

For a while Raheem was trying to get a visa to live in the United States. He worked with an immigration lawyer. He fretted over how he would find a job. What kind of job do you want? I asked him. Anything, he said, so that I can offer something to my family. He was fifty-five years old, ready to pick up and start from scratch all over again.

Ten years in the Iraqi army, eight years in the hell of the Iran–Iraq war, nine years living alone in foreign countries, missing his children's childhood so that he could buy them a house. Six years and counting of this latest war. Quiet all the way. Courteous and dignified and careful. Laughing despite it all, listening, offering friendship. All of that and he was still chasing this meager dream: to live in peace and earn enough money to support his family.

I was a little surprised when he told me he was hoping for a U.S. visa. Didn't he resent the land whose soldiers killed his son? I asked him. Wouldn't it be hard to live in the United States after what happened to Mohammed?

"Do you mean because he was killed by U.S. soldiers?" he said. "Of course I don't have such feelings against the Americans."

"So you don't blame the Americans for what happened?"

"Not in general. As you know, in each society there are good and bad people. I blame those who have a quick decision of shooting at civilians."

"For the war itself, for invading Iraq?"

"I don't blame them for that," he said. "I was one of those supporting such a step."

It was true. I remembered our trip into the south. Raheem had been happy. He had been optimistic. I remembered the small smile on his face when he watched the Shiites march in public for the first time. The ice-cream parlor in Nasiriyah that we'd visit at dusk, when the white owls rose out of the swamps and little boys scampered barefooted after a soccer ball in the darkening streets. His morning strolls to the market, the chats he had with strangers. The wonder in his eyes as he savored the days, as we wandered through Iraq together, watching history happen. Back then the future looked clean and good, and Raheem was full of simple hope—that he and his sons would find stable jobs because Saddam was gone. I've never seen him so happy again. Every time I made it back to Baghdad in the subsequent years, at some point one of us would say to the other, "Remember that first trip down south?" We'd talk about the people we met, about the amazing things they'd said, about the stories we found, and we'd smile. Iraq had never been that good again.

In the end, the American visa came through. But Raheem balked.

Financial crisis had gripped the United States. The Iraqis who'd crossed the Atlantic before him sent back dire reports—they lived in empty apartments; they couldn't earn enough money to support their families; they couldn't find work. The surge brought American soldiers pouring in to police the streets, and for the time being Baghdad had grown quieter, life more livable. And so he waits. Raheem is an Iraqi; his country and mine are tangled together and so our lives meet, pause, and part. All those hard years he would have snatched at a chance to start life anew in the United States. The invasion of his country brought that opportunity at last, but it also weakened the U.S. economy and helped turn the promised land of the past two centuries into a place that suddenly looked to Raheem like a dubious proposition. War is a total change, unleashing all things light and all things dark; we are pushed forward and our lives are invented by the history we live through.

These days, I watch "the region"—we used to call it that, as if it were the only one—from a distance. People are still being tortured, and demonstrations disrupted, in Egypt. In Afghanistan, they throw acid into the faces of girls who try to go to school. As for the U.S.-backed warlords of 2001, Haji Zaman has been driven back out of the country; Hazrat Ali has emerged as a notoriously corrupt security official in the U.S.-backed government; and Abdul Qadir was assassinated—there is a story among old sources from those times that Zaman may have been involved; that it was a clash over drug smuggling. Saudi women still can't drive, mingle with men who are not blood relatives, or leave the country without permission from a male guardian. Qaddafi is still lording it over Libya. Hezbollah still holds its guns, and people in Lebanon whisper that another civil war will come one day—that it's a question not of whether, but of when. Iraq Body Count says that around 100,000 Iraqi civilians have been killed since the invasion. There is a graph with red spikes, like a picture of shattered windows and broken bones. Nobody knows how many Afghans have been killed; it is thousands and thousands of people; by some estimates, tens of thousands. In Iraq, 4,349 U.S. soldiers have died, and 873 in Afghanistan, and more all the time. That is not counting the deaths of local people who are tallied as combatants, or wading into the question of whether they were or weren't. Either way, that's six digits of people, dead for a cause I cannot articulate except in the most abstract terms.

But we lived through it, and we are living still. And in the end, survival is not a meager redemption; it is substantial and it will not last forever, either. Maybe there is greater redemption still to come, an understanding or clarity of vision. I am waiting for it.

# ACKNOWLEDGMENTS

When you ask strangers to tell their stories, you ask for blind trust. The surprising thing is not that people sometimes say no; it's that, usually, they say yes. I am deeply thankful for the many people who paused long enough to relate their stories; without them, there would be no book. They often spoke at considerable risk, perhaps with the implicit hope that violence can be eroded by talking, over cultural and political and religious divides, across oceans, in spite of everything. Many of them never made it into the newspaper or this book, but I remember them all, and they have permanently informed my work. I thank them.

These pages contain the invisible work of scores of translators, local reporters, and drivers who risked their lives and labored long hours to transmit the plights and graces of their home countries to a foreign audience. The ebullient Majeed Babar lightened my first days at war in Afghanistan and permanently impressed upon me the need to look for society's most vulnerable victims, even or especially in the midst of conflict. Naseer Ahmed, without a day's training in journalism, plunged fearlessly into Tora Bora to translate. Batsheva Sobelman and Efrat Shvily patiently demystified Israel, while Maher Abukhater showed me the ropes of Palestinian politics in the West Bank and Fayed abu Shammalah guided me through Gaza. In Baghdad, I am deeply grateful for the friendship and patience of the Sphinx-like Salar Jaff and, of course, Raheem Salman. Suheil Ahmed, Mohammed Arrawi, Caesar Ahmed, Said Rifai, Saif Shakir Humood, and Zeinab Hussein were also instrumental and inspirational colleagues. In Cairo, Hossam

Hamalawy was a gifted colleague and dear friend. Sayed Bedoui and Jailan Zayan also played key roles in my understanding of Egypt and, by extension, the collective Arab experience. In Beirut, the wise and patient Raed Rafei helped deepen my understanding of Lebanon. In Amman, Ranya Kadri was a steady source of insight and gossip, as was Leena Saidi in Beirut.

From those first days in Afghanistan, Tim Weiner imparted the lasting sense that the best journalism is informed by deep appreciation of places and people. It was Tim, too, who years later convinced me that there was a book, and that I could write it. Lisa Junghahn talked me through the formation of the narrative, and pointed me to other books that would help the ideas take shape. My agent, Kathy Robbins, was an early believer in this book and lent badly needed moral support during a cold, dark Russian winter of writing. At Doubleday, Bill Thomas shepherded the book from proposal to print. Kris Puopolo was a dedicated, enthusiastic editor who exercised great patience throughout the process. An old friend from Texas, Brad Tyer, gave me an incisive, illuminating read of an early version of the manuscript. Ted Anthony offered valuable suggestions early on.

At the *Los Angeles Times*, I was privileged to work for John Carroll, Dean Baquet, Simon Li, and Doug Frantz—dynamic, intellectually curious journalists who would go to any length to foster and defend a good piece of reporting. Scott Kraft lobbied, defended, and advised me through the years. Marjorie Miller was a tough, honest, inspirational boss and an insightful editor. David Lauter, Mary Braswell, Mark Porubcansky, Roger Ainsley, Kari Howard, Geoffrey Mohan, Davan Maharaj, and Paul Feldman were patient, gifted editors and, along with Mike Faneuff, became members of an extended foreign-desk family that kept me grounded through the years. Finally, Rick Meyer taught me about narrative writing and story structure, and remains, in my mind, one of the truly great people.

I am also grateful to Rana Sweis, Jehad Nga, Rone Tempest, John Kifner, and Mark MacKinnon, each of whom did something wise, kind, or illuminating at a critical moment.

My husband, Tom Lasseter, lived through much of this book with me, from the places and events of the news to the slow limp of the writing process. He was my first and best reader, and I have relied on him for advice, insight, and support. Inevitably, my lasting impressions of these conflicts were shaped by our ongoing conversations and pooled experiences. In a sense, this is his book, too.

Finally, my family—especially my mother Kathleen Stack, sister Martha Stack, and brother Greg Stack—were patient, loving, and supportive throughout extended absences and frightening days. I am grateful for them, and for the memory of my father.

# ABOUT THE AUTHOR

Megan Stack has reported on war, terrorism, and political Islam from twenty-three countries since 2001. She was awarded the 2007 Overseas Press Club's Hal Boyle Award for best newspaper reporting from abroad and was a finalist for the 2007 Pulitzer Prize in international reporting. She is currently the *L.A. Times*'s Moscow bureau chief.